PENGUIN BOOKS

EXILE

Taslima Nasrin was born in the city of Mymensingh, Bangladesh. After graduating from Mymensingh Medical College, she worked as a government doctor in public hospitals until 1993. When ordered by the government to choose between her job and writing, she chose to resign from public service to continue her literary pursuits.

Nasrin is one of the most uncompromising feminist writers of the Indian subcontinent. Her writing has earned her immense popularity, but also controversy. In advocating for women's rights, she has not only faced attacks from religious fundamentalists but also encountered opposition from the state and patriarchal society at large. Fundamentalist groups demanded her execution and even placed a bounty on her head. As a result, she was exiled from her beloved homeland in 1994. Fatwas and numerous lawsuits against her freedom of expression still hang over her in Bangladesh. After years of exile in Europe, she settled in West Bengal, India—but was later expelled from that state as well. This Bengali writer has found no refuge in either part of Bengal.

Several of Nasrin's books have been banned by the Bangladesh government, including *Lajja* (a fact-based novel in defence of humanity), *Amar Meyebela* (a memoir of her childhood), *Utal Hawa* (about her teenage and early adult years), and the third and fourth parts of her autobiography, *Ka* (translated as *Split: A Life*) and *Sei Sob Andhokar*. West Bengal's government also banned *Ka*, although the Kolkata High Court overturned the ban two years later.

Taslima Nasrin has received numerous awards and honours. In India, she won the Ananda Purashkar twice for *Nirbachito Kolam* and *Amar Meyebela*. She received the Sakharov Prize for Freedom of Thought from the European Parliament, the UNESCO Prize for promoting tolerance and peace, the French government's Human Rights Prize, the Simone de Beauvoir Prize and the Edit de Nantes Prize from France for her fight against religious extremism. Other honours include the academy award from the Royal Academy of Arts, Sciences and Literature of Belgium, and the Kurt Tucholsky Prize from PEN Sweden. She has also received honorary doctorates from Ghent University and the University of Leuven in Belgium, the American University of Paris and Paris Diderot University. She has held fellowships at Harvard and New York University.

Taslima has authored more than fifty books across poetry, short stories, novels, essays and autobiographies. Her works have been translated into twenty-five languages, including English, French, German, Italian, Spanish,

Swedish, Norwegian, Icelandic, Finnish, Dutch, Arabic and Turkish. A vocal advocate for humanism, human rights, women's liberation and free thought, she has delivered speeches around the world—including at prestigious institutions like Harvard, Yale, Oxford, Edinburgh and the Sorbonne. Globally, she has become a symbol of the fight for freedom of expression.

Maharghya Chakraborty is a research scholar, an avid cinephile and a translator.

EXILE

a memoir

TASLIMA NASRIN

translated by
MAHARGHYA CHAKRABORTY

PENGUIN BOOKS
An imprint of Penguin Random House

PENGUIN BOOKS

Penguin Books is an imprint of the Penguin Random House group of companies
whose addresses can be found at global.penguinrandomhouse.com

Published by Penguin Random House India Pvt. Ltd
4th Floor, Capital Tower 1, MG Road,
Gurugram 122 002, Haryana, India

Penguin
Random House
India

First published in Hamish Hamilton by Penguin Random House India 2016
Published in Penguin Books in 2018
This edition published in 2025

ISBN 9780143429135

Typeset in Adobe Caslon Pro by Manipal Digital Systems, Manipal
Printed at Gopsons Papers Pvt. Ltd., Noida

www.penguin.co.in

MIX
Paper | Supporting
responsible forestry
FSC® C191020

Contents

Contents

Exile in Two Homelands

A Writer's Testament

In the cultural tapestry of Bengal, a writer's voice should transcend borders—yet I, a Bengali writer devoted to the propagation of truth and the bestowal of human rights, have found myself cast out by both East and West Bengal. Despite never engaging in any violence or crime, my words—my truths—have been deemed too dangerous. My crime, if one could call it that, lies in my unwavering commitment to equality, secularism and human rights.

Throughout my life, I never considered East and West Bengal as separate entities. I belong to both, and yet, both have rejected me. East Bengal rendered me an outcast; West Bengal followed suit. In both lands, there seems to be no room for a writer who speaks difficult truths. My books cannot be published, my works cannot be launched, printed, staged or adapted. No films can be made based on my stories. Every possible effort has been made to erase me from cultural memory.

Drawn by love for my language and heritage, I left behind a comfortable life in Europe and America to settle in Kolkata. There, I built a quiet home on Rawdon Street. Yet after three years of peaceful living, the West Bengal government placed me under house arrest on 9 August 2007. I had committed no crime, but my confinement was indefinite. The police forbade me from stepping outside; the chief minister sent the police commissioner to threaten me with expulsion—from the city, the state, even the country. Still, I refused to leave, standing firm in my innocence and in my belief that I had done nothing wrong.

My advocacy for women's rights, secularism and equality was never a threat. Rather, it was a call for justice. Yet, a manufactured riot in November 2007, involving fringe elements claiming to represent Muslim sentiments, was used to justify my final expulsion. These individuals did not know me or my work; their real grievances lay with a government that had failed them. Nevertheless, I became the scapegoat.

On 22 November, I was forcibly removed from my home and flown out of the city with no belongings but the clothes I wore. I have been in exile ever since—unwelcome in both Bangladesh and West Bengal, regardless of change in political leaders or parties. Unlike other exiled writers who could return home when regimes fell, I remain excluded.

The pain of being a refugee cannot be easily explained to those who have never been one. I hope that no one—friend or foe—suffers such punishment without cause. My only transgression was to speak the truth, and for that, I have paid with silence, exile and erasure.

Preface

I wrote *Exile* nearly five years ago. The book was to be launched at the Kolkata Book Fair in 2011 and my publishers had even organized an event to inaugurate it. However, Chief Minister Mamata Bandyopadhyay had taken a less-than-kind view of the entire thing and had made sure the evening never took off. My name had been prohibited in West Bengal, much like how it had been prohibited in Bangladesh so long ago.

In *Exile*, I wrote about the series of events leading to my ouster from West Bengal, then Rajasthan and eventually India, my house arrest, and the anxious days I had had to spend in the government safe house, beset by a scheming array of bureaucrats and ministers desperate to see me gone. Without a single political party, social organization or renowned personality by my side, I had been a lone, exiled, dissenting voice up against the entire state machinery with only my wits and determination at my disposal. But there was one thing I was sure of—I hadn't done anything wrong, so why should I be punished unfairly? Why wouldn't I, a citizen of the world, be allowed to live in a country I love? Why would a nation that prides itself on being a secular democracy bow down to the diktats of a section of dishonest, misogynist, intolerant zealots, and banish an honest, secular writer?

Despite being forced to leave, I have eventually cocked a snook at all the prohibitions and bans and threats, and come back to India. I have come because I have nothing else but India, and because I hope India will one day truly encourage free thought. I wish to live in this country and be allowed the freedom to express my opinions even if they are contrary to others'. I wish for neighbouring nations to learn from India's example and be inspired, they who yet do not know the meaning of the freedom of speech. Not that I have a completely stress-free life in India either; the old threats have continued and taken on new forms. Nearly twelve years ago, an imam from Kolkata had set a price of 20,000 rupees for my head, a sum that had soon increased to 50,000 and eventually to an unlimited sum. A director of the Muslim Law Board from Uttar Pradesh had also declared a reward of 500,000 rupees, while an ISIS offshoot from Kerala had put up a post on Facebook calling for my assassination. A leading politician had expressed his ire over whatever I had allegedly written against Islam years ago and declared that I should not be allowed any access to the media to express any views whatsoever on Islam. Everything that I was made to go through—the ban on my book, my exile from West Bengal, stopping my articles from being published in newspapers and journals, stopping the telecast and production of the TV series written by me—was a result of the government's vote bank politics and blatant appeasement of the fundamentalist elements. A politics built on sycophancy is the first sign of a rotting democracy. Aren't our political mavericks aware that fanatics seek to plunge society into darkness, that they are against human rights and women's rights, and that they consider any opinion contrary to theirs a sort of violation?

Writers across the world are being persecuted, whipped, tortured, incarcerated and exiled. But, leave alone dictatorships, even democratic governments are no longer interested in safeguarding the freedom of speech and expression. Whenever I try to point out the significance of such a fundamental right, I am informed that even the freedom of speech must have its limitations and that it cannot be used to hurt someone's sentiments. Wouldn't it be extremely difficult to ensure that you never hurt someone's sentiments? People keep hurting us, intentionally or not, by words or deeds. Our world is populated by a multitude of opposing mindsets. They clash and hurt each other constantly but they also have an inbuilt mechanism to manage hurt. Unfortunately, a few bigots within Islam use the excuse of injured sentiments to cause further mischief, refusing to listen or be placated.

It is a moment of crisis for democracy when a citizen is robbed of their right to speak and express their opinions. Social change makes it necessary that a few feathers will be ruffled and a few egos will be wounded. It hurts people's sentiments when you try to separate religion and the State, when you attempt to abolish misogynist laws; good things cannot be achieved without hurting religious sentiments. A lot of people had been outraged when the Crown and the State were being forcibly separated in the Continent. Galileo's and Darwin's views had upset many pious people of their times. The superstitious are routinely offended by the evolution and advancement of science. If we stop expressing our opinions because someone will be hurt by them, if we curb the growth and development of scientific knowledge, if we forcibly try to stall the march of civilization, we will end up inhabiting a stagnant quagmire, bereft of knowledge and growth. If the objective is to say exactly what everyone would love to listen to, then we would have no need for the freedom of speech and expression. Such rights are important primarily for those whose opinions usually don't follow the status quo. Freedom of speech is the freedom to say something you might not like to hear. Those who never hurt other's sentiments do not need the freedom of speech. A State that chooses to side with those who seek to oppose such freedoms, instead of ensuring that they are brought to book, will be responsible for its own eventual annihilation.

Some time back one such draconian law against freedom of speech was abolished by the Government of India. I was among those who had worked towards this goal and our success was a significant acknowledgement of the systematic persecution many have had to go through because of such laws. I have had to face it too, which is why I am glad to have been part of such a reform initiative, despite not being a pure-born citizen of India. The world is constantly vigilant that no one hurts the sentiments of those who are opposed to human rights and women's rights. When will the world learn to see all as equal? When will it learn to stop pleasing extremists and begin according respect to reason and humanism instead?

This crisis is not India's alone; it is being felt across the world. It's not so much a battle between two faiths but a war between two opposing world views—the secular and the fundamentalist, the progressive and the prejudiced, the rational and the superstitious, between awareness and ignorance, freedom and enslavement. In this fight I know whose side I am on; I am forever in favour of my opponents' freedom of opinion even if I do not wish to support or respect it. My lack of support does not mean that I will attack my opponent during their morning jog, or shoot them in public, or hack them to death. I will neither kiss nor wound my opponent; I will instead express my opinions through my writings. If someone does not like what I have to say, they have the right to respond to my opinions in kind—in words. They do not have the right to kill me. This is a basic condition for the freedom of speech which many fanatics wilfully choose to ignore.

Can faith be sustained thus? There were once so many religions and yet so few exist to this day. Where are the imperious gods of the Greeks and where is their Olympus? Where are the powerful deities of the Romans or the exotic divinities of the Egyptian pharaohs? They have been cast into history, just like Hinduism, Islam, Christianity, Judaism and Buddhism too will be forgotten one day, to be replaced by an epoch-appropriate new faith or a rationalist and scientistic outlook.

The terrorists at the Dhaka café were around twenty years old. They were not poor, not illiterate. Heavily indoctrinated in Islam, they shouted 'Allahu Akbar' while slaughtering people. Those who could recite a verse from the Quran were spared while others were tortured and hacked to death with machetes. Those terrorists had nothing but religion as their guide. Young men have been brainwashed with Islam, at home, madrasas and mosques. They have been fed the belief that non-believers, non-Muslims and critics of Islam should be exterminated. By killing them, they have been convinced, they will go to heaven. They have also been taught that jihad is mandatory for every Muslim and Muslims should strive to turn Dar-ul-Harb (the Land of the Enemy) into Dar-ul-Islam (the Land of Islam).

There is no point trying to confuse the issue by saying that poverty, frustration, lack of jobs and the absence of hope force people to become terrorists. It is, in fact, the other way around. The new terrorists are often rich and literate, highly qualified professionals, who have been seduced by fanaticism. They join ISIS because they know they will be at liberty to do whatever they wish to, and be given the sanction to rape, kill and torture at will. Many organizations and institutions in Bangladesh have been funded by Islamic fundamentalists from rich Arab countries for decades. Madrasas and mosques have long been breeding grounds for Islamic fundamentalists. Islamization in Bangladesh started not long after its creation in 1971. It is tragic that Bangladesh, whose very birth was premised on secularism and a rejection of the two-nation theory, has degenerated into an Islamic fundamentalist country. The government must own up to an administrative failure to foresee and contain the rise of fanaticism.

In the early 1990s, when I was attacked by Islamic fundamentalists, a fatwa was issued against me, a price set on my head, and hundreds of thousands of Muslim fundamentalists took to the streets demanding my execution; meanwhile, the intellectuals remained silent. The government, instead of cracking down on the fundamentalists, filed a case against me on charges of hurting the religious sentiments of people. I was forced to leave the country and that was the beginning of what today's Bangladesh is—a medieval and intolerant nation of bigots, extremists and fanatics. Without allowing criticism of Islam, it will be difficult for Muslim countries to separate the State and religion, to make personal laws based on equality, or to have a secular education system. If this does not happen, Muslim countries will forever remain in darkness, breeding and training people indoctrinated by religion to not tolerate any differences, and where women will never enjoy the right to live as complete human beings. People like to believe that Islam is a religion of peace. I, however, have witnessed the opposite since my childhood. The time has come for people to unequivocally tell the truth and be willing to listen to it too. Islam and Islamic fundamentalism don't have too many differences; Islam isn't compatible with democracy, human rights, women's rights, freedom of expression. You will not be able to kill terrorism by killing terrorists. You have to kill its root cause. You have to stop brainwashing children with religion. In the present scenario, a call for sanity and introspection is as good as a cry in the wilderness. This must end. The good and the sensible must break their silence; the inaction of the good is the asset of the malevolent.

This is how the world will continue to endure—ignorance, stupidity and bigotry walking hand in hand with awareness and intelligence. The narrow-minded and the political will forever seek to plunge society into darkness and chaos, while a handful of others will always strive for the betterment of society and to have good sense prevail. It's always a few special people who seek to bring about change; that is how it has always been.

I hope no one else is exiled for being different ever again. I hope no one ever has to suffer the ignominy I went through. To all the dissidents of the world, my warmest regards.

Taslima Nasrin
October 2016

Forbidden

I have lived in Harvard for almost a year—a rather plaintive, uneventful year, not too terrible but nothing extravagant either. I had, rather impulsively, rented the third floor of the three-storey white house at number 50, Langdon Street, right opposite the Harvard Law School. One could walk from there to the John F. Kennedy School of Government, one of the most renowned schools in Harvard. Or so I had heard, since fame and wealth has seldom attracted me. For me, what has been of the utmost importance are the people—whether they are honest, whether they are good, whether they keep their promises or not.

My office had been set up at the Carr Center for Human Rights Policy of the Kennedy School—a small world populated by the computer, the desk, the Internet, the printer, paper, sundry stationery, the sideboard laden with tea, coffee or biscuits, the delicious spread at the cafeteria downstairs, and me with the Harvard identity card hanging around my neck. I used to believe the card held magical qualities. It could open all the hidden doorways and portals of Harvard, allowing me free access to all its nooks and crannies and the secrets they held. It would allow me to get my hands on the rarest of books in the library, stay late into the night in my

office, open a bank account in two minutes, or find a magical
cure for the most persistent of ailments!

So, I would spend most of the day in my office,
occasionally venturing outside to a nearby restaurant for
lunch—Indian, American or, if the mood struck, seafood! In
the afternoon I would go swimming, or on a walk, strolling
past the myriad lives, some neat and some in disarray, laid
out around me across the neighbourhood. I fancy that I
used to cut an odd adolescent figure as I walked aimlessly in
jeans and tops, all fifty kilos of me. I remember Greg Carr,
the handsome Harvard fellow who took me to the stadium
and explained to me the intricate details of a Harvard versus
Brown football match, who wrote so many sweet emails to
me, came to see me in my house in a Ferrari and invited me
over to his penthouse. Then one fine day, who knows why,
all of it had abruptly stopped. Perhaps because I had argued
with him over America's war on Iraq or something like that.
I remember how that budding feeling of love had suddenly
vanished; the mails and personal calls had abruptly stopped.
I have never been good at figuring out the motivations of
the rich, but I must confess I will always respect Greg Carr.
He had been the one to open the Human Rights Center
at Harvard, serving as a perennial reminder that though
so many people have the necessary means, few manage to
contribute to the service of human rights and dignity.

I would spend my time talking and arguing about a
hundred things with the fellows and professors of Harvard,
writing my autobiography or essays, composing love letters
to lovers I was yet to meet, or writing long research papers,
like the one on secularism written while at Harvard. At times
I would travel, within the country or elsewhere, Europe
sometimes, for a seminar or to collect a prize, or simply to read

poetry somewhere; seminars at Tufts and Boston, a speech at the General Assembly of Amnesty International with Mary Robinson, the UN High Commissioner for Human Rights, poetry-reading sessions at the Harvard Center in Boston with Eve Ensler of *The Vagina Monologues* fame, helping with the fundraiser of the Women's Studies Department of Harvard, attending classes by Michael Ignatieff, Samuel Huntington and other renowned visiting academics, discussing the Iraq war with Noam Chomsky in his room in MIT or over email, writing against war, watching the Red Sox at Fenway Park, visiting my friend Steve Lacy who had been battling cancer, debating humanism at the Harvard Chaplaincy, going for soirées at Swanee Hunt's, or setting off to New York, or to Kolkata for the book fair, before dashing back to Harvard again.

In the meantime, the BBC would, at intervals, keep me updated on the rising tensions in Bangladesh. The third part of my autobiography, *Dwikhandito* (Split), had been published in Bangladesh as *Ko*.[1] That had been the original name but the publishers in Kolkata had put their foot down, making me change it. From the moment of publication in Bangladesh, the book had caused an unprecedented furore. I was being abused with the choicest of monikers by the print media—authors and academics had joined ranks in a relentless crusade against my moral character, or lack thereof. I was being called a 'shameless slut' because I had named the series of men I had slept with; the pages concerned were being photocopied and handed around as proof of my degeneration. Syed Shamsul Haque[2] had once taken me on a trip during which I had developed a rather nuanced understanding of his character; which I had then written about in the book. As far as I was concerned, I

saw no reason for him to get upset over this. And yet he
was upset and seething like a hyena, primarily because, as
the publisher Mesbahuddin informed me, I had written
about his secret relationship with his sister-in-law. The big
reveal had perhaps been only a sentence long in the entire
narrative and yet he was driven to such anger that he filed a
defamation suit against me worth ten crore takas. He even
gave a series of interviews lamenting how I had ruined his
life and reputation, sullied the glorious name he had earned
as an author over nearly half a century. He insinuated
that there must be a larger reason behind my shameless
behaviour, or why else would I dare to write as I had about
respected members of the civil society. Inspired to protest,
he filed the suit and stated that he hoped others like him,
similarly violated by my viciousness, would follow suit and
take necessary action against me.

They called me from the BBC to ask for my reaction,
and make me aware of the many nasty things Syed Haque
and Sunil Gangopadhyay had said about me. How their
voices were laced with a scathing melange of anger, disgust,
sarcasm and ridicule when speaking about me! I could
understand why Shamsul Haque, his secret exposed, might
say vicious things about me, scream, spit, swear and cry in
anger, and why he might threaten to drag me to the courts in
an effort to prove my words to be untrue. However, I could
not understand why Sunil Gangopadhyay[3] had reacted so
violently. There had hardly been anything against him in
the book and neither had he ever been a firebrand member
of any men's rights group. In fact, he had maintained time
and again that whatever happens between two consenting
individuals behind closed doors should never be made
public. Isn't it criminals who cannot reveal their actions to

the public? Why should the burden of harbouring criminals always be placed on women!

The news spread like wildfire. It spread to a section of the civil society in Kolkata, carefully nurtured, some alleged, by Sunil himself. Not because I had written anything against him in this book but in apprehension of what I might in the next. If I could be banned and prohibited, I could subsequently be discredited as an unworthy, irresponsible, unbalanced writer. I could easily be branded as a liar. No one would listen to me; no one would want to read what I write. Before the storm could die down, news arrived that the CPI(M)-led Left Front Government of West Bengal had decided to ban *Dwikhandito*. Apparently, twenty-five renowned literary figures had petitioned the chief minister, Buddhadeb Bhattacharya, against my book, and the latter had read the book himself before deciding on bringing the axe down on it. The reason cited, however, was that I had hurt the religious sentiments of a certain section of people. The book had already been banned in Bangladesh. Syed Shamsul Haque had moved the court with his defamation lawsuit and had passionately pleaded against the book, resulting in the high court banning it before the government ever could. Perhaps emboldened by these events, an almost unknown poet from West Bengal filed another lawsuit against me— this one worth eleven crore rupees. Authors prohibiting authors, filing lawsuits against authors—these things are perhaps unheard of anywhere else in the world. One would assume writers would stand behind writers and speak out against the injustice of banning a literary work. The more I see the scholars of West Bengal and Bangladesh, the more it amazes me to realize how selfish and opportunistic most of them are, how dependent on being in the government's good graces. All assertions of ethics or morality remain strictly confined to the printed page or the podium—no trace of it stains their beliefs, behaviours or lives.

So, eminent literary figures from West Bengal and Bangladesh dedicated themselves to my downfall. One only had to listen to them, or read what they had to say about me to understand how horrific and cruel slander can be. Humayun Azad[4] wrote, 'I did not even deem the book fit to be read. Even I have been abused in various ways in it; she has produced a litany of lies. However, she could at least not accuse me of anything sexual because I have never taken up on her advances. After having read about the recently published *Ko* in various journals and newspapers, it has seemed to me as nothing but a prostitute's naked confessions, a sordid account of her wretched existence.'

Humayun Azad used to write critiques of religion. He started on a book on women's rights after coming to know that I was writing one. Strangely enough, I do not recall sensing in him any respect for women. In fact, there was a time when he used to compose misogynistic tracts. He may have taken to writing the book *Naari* (Woman) after witnessing the popularity of my *Nirbachito Kolam* (Selected Columns), perhaps realizing how writing about women would garner him more popularity, but the innate tendency to regard women only as sexual objects is a difficult mindset to change. Thus, he could lie glibly; being a tenured university professor, he could claim to have never taken me up on my 'advances'. As if I had ever made any in the first place! He could so easily describe the autobiography of a strong woman—a doctor, a celebrated author, winner of numerous literary and human rights accolades—as 'a prostitute's naked confessions, a sordid account of her wretched existence'.

Even the worst misogynist would not be able to accuse a woman of something like this without knowing a single thing about her. I feel perturbed thinking about the sort of future we are nurturing if a jealous, lying cad like Humayun Azad is a university professor. In a patriarchal society, there is no dearth of equally misogynistic fools to feed and foment people like him.

Nima Haque[5] commented, 'There are limits to independence. Taslima has overstepped these limits. Not only does she deserve rebuke for this travesty in the name of literature, she deserves punishment too.' I used to know Asad Chowdhury[6] fairly well; in fact, he used to be very appreciative of my writing. He commented, 'Literature is an amalgamation of the personal, the social and the communal. Shameless descriptions of debauchery can never be passed off as literature.'[7]

In West Bengal too, the vultures had begun to gather. Samaresh Majumdar[8] wrote, 'Nearly ninety years ago there lived a famous prostitute in Sonagachi[9] called Nandarani. Nearly all of Kolkata's high and mighty had been her regular clients. If she had wanted to write a novel about them, she could have done so a long time ago. However, in her personal life, she had known how to live in society with quiet dignity and civility. Taslima Nasrin, unfortunately, has been unable to partake of Nandarani's sense of self-respect. She has changed her men like women change clothes, valorized sex over a more mental connection. Other women have thus far been unaware of her duplicity. Everyone is entitled to freedom of speech; she has fairly utilized it and we have had to hear her. It is, however, our responsibility to judge its merits the best way we can. It is fine to swear like a sailor in front of one's friends, the same is termed obscenity when done in public. Whatever she is confessing publicly now, she had been equally complicit in letting them come to pass. In fact, her only goal had been to sell her books and garner cheap publicity.' The poet Subodh Sarkar[10] wrote, 'She has sent a sexual bomb called *Ko* from Sweden which has exploded in Dhaka. The book is apparently about society, family and religion but what has grabbed the most eyeballs in this are the titillating passages on sex and the fact that sex can even trump issues like Iraq and America in this wretched world. Alas! Is she so sexually depraved that she cannot leave even her father or those like him alone! They are saying there will be more such lists of your sexual conquests; people in Kolkata have begun to grow anxious already. I am sure you have Italians and French on your list too. In fact, quiet soon you might even be counted one of the foremost prostitutes of the world. A handful of Bengali scholars would even write about you, about how a writer was forced by socio-economic circumstances into such a lifestyle. People from the seamier districts will soon inquire about which currency you get paid in. Is it in US dollars? Swedish krona? Rupee or taka? You had wished to give a voice to women who have never had a voice of their own. So what went wrong with that righteous image? Now those very women will disinfect their hands if they even accidentally happen to touch you. Even all the perfumes of Arabia will not sweeten your little hands ever again.'

Shirshendu Mukhopadhyay,[11] when asked about me, commented: 'From what I have heard she has described her sexual relationships with a number of intellectuals. While I find nothing wrong with that per se, especially if she has been true to her own self, what I do find appalling is that she has done so simply to create a stir. This I cannot condone. A part of an author's responsibility is to recognize the fine line between literature and obscenity.'

Even Nabanita Dev Sen[12] did not have anything nice to say about the book. Bani Basu[13] remarked, 'If an autobiography reads like a publicity gimmick then one has to question its authenticity. This curiosity is temporary since the writing itself hardly has any merit. It simply has no literary value.' Strangely enough, Bani Basu later read my column in *Dainik Statesman* (the Bengali edition of the *Statesman*) and called me up to tell me how much she likes my writing. I am not entirely sure, however, if she has confessed to this appreciation to anyone else.

Mallika Sengupta[14], an up-and-coming feminist poet, commented: 'This is simply sex for the sake of sex. It is a laundry-list, not an autobiography. I am especially unsure about its credibility, much as I have been unsure of her before. I am not sure I believe her as an author and a feminist. Most of the relationships have been made up by her, and the list of people she has slept with is obviously meant to create a stir. This is hardly a unique ploy and it also explains why she has lost public support. Not many wish to write salacious tales of the bedroom like her, and thankfully, these are the people who keep literature safe. This is also why feminism is alive and fighting out there, where it makes a difference, rather than simply languishing in Taslima's bedroom.'

I had always considered poet Gautam Ghosh Dastidar[15] a friend. Responding to *Dwikhandito*, he wrote: 'These contradictions, this conscious use of unreason, half-truths, bitterness and brazenness—these are the trademarks of Taslima's character. I doubt she understands the meaning of ethics, fame being her singular obsession. This leads her to treat notoriety as fame, compelling her to shamelessly bare herself and her partner under the guise of writing an autobiography. It highlights a complete dissociation from any ethical responsibilities on her part. Even if we were to believe these accounts as truth, one still wonders whether she has the right to reveal such personal encounters—whether she can so glibly disregard certain promises made in relationships, irrespective of how fragile they are. However, it is foolish to expect her to adhere to ethical concerns which have not developed in her in the first place.'

The Naxalite writer Azizul Haque[16] wrote, 'A physically and morally bankrupt author has finally renounced her shame and come down to the streets. She still wears clothes, perhaps out of sheer force of habit. Is this freedom of speech? What next? A rabid dog barks to protest against human fascism and that is its fundamental right? By this logic, if someone claims complete freedom of speech, another can claim the freedom to use force. So why can't a crime of passion be a fundamental right? What can anyone say when a woman is hell-bent upon turning her own body into a public urinal? If someone puts a urinal to its proper use, what is the point of raising a hue and cry? My advice is: Don't ban them, simply cast them aside. If you see garbage on the road, you either step around it or you get it cleaned up. Let the protest gather at the printing press, where it rightly should. Where are the sentinels of culture, the workers who will picket the publishers, the typesetters, and the binders, and give rise to a movement calling for a complete rejection of this rubbish that is masquerading as a book?'

Ashok Dasgupta, the editor of the Bengali daily *Aajkal*, wrote, 'There are two reasons why one must summarily reject Taslima's *Dwikhandito*. It is tasteless, obscene and is nothing but an attempt to malign someone's character. There have been cases filed in Kolkata and Dhaka already. Though these are not the reasons behind the ban, let us take a closer look at the first set of accusations vis-à-vis taste and obscenity. Firstly, Sunil Gangopadhyay had commented that when two consenting individuals form a relationship, it is a sort of a contract which should not be broken by either party at their own convenience. Secondly, the dusty yellow-jacketed booklets sold by the wayside are perhaps replete with a thousand equally lurid sexual encounters. Nevertheless, they do not drag living or actual people into the quagmire. Thirdly, why do we even have to believe that what an author writes about someone they know is the unembellished truth? Fourthly, perhaps Taslima herself has no family, and no social responsibilities, but the people she has maligned have certain social roles, families, and children. Even if one can tolerate the other 393 pages of filth, why should we have to condone the two pages of incendiary vulgarity? Even people like Shankha Ghosh[17] and Sunil Gangopadhyay, never in favour of banning a book, have considered this to be an exceptional situation.'

While such cruel assumptions and accusations were being levelled against me by intellectuals and writers from West Bengal and Bangladesh, I received a request from the Bengali magazine *Desh* to write a rejoinder. Written one midnight in New York, the article began with these famous lines by Rosa Luxemburg: 'Freedom is always and exclusively freedom for the one who thinks differently.'

After all these years, when I look back at the hazy grey road I have walked down, when sudden flashes of memories, tiny fragments of forgotten dreams, shake me to my core, I cannot help but stumble helplessly and sift through cold, forgotten things lost in time. What use are these reminiscences? Those dreams were cast aside a long time back, so much so that they are barely recognizable now. To dredge them back up again, to clear the clutter and the cobwebs off places long abandoned, is an entirely futile exercise. Yet, my exile has forced me to turn to my past again and again, made me spend long, terrible nights in a sort of dazed stupor, immersed in the darkest despair. And on such nights, I have written about that girl.

I have written about the timid, bashful and self-effacing girl who, brought up within the strictest confines of a traditional family and its everyday rules and petty injustices, got used to her dreams and desires being tossed aside without a word, while struggling to keep the preying hands of male relatives at bay. I have written about that rather plain little girl who grew up with long-nurtured dreams of a love that she finally found in her youth, who secretly got married and wanted to spend her life just like any other woman. I have written about the girl who, betrayed by her husband, the love of her life, had been compelled—by grief, regret, pain, despair—to contemplate suicide as her fragile world came crashing down around her. I have written about the girl who painfully gathered her shattered dreams in an effort to go on living, who wanted a place of her own in this cruel, unforgiving society, and who was forced to submit repeatedly to the guardianship of men in accordance with social mores. Yet she was hit by an onslaught of such cruelty, spite and viciousness that it destroyed her unborn child and made her bleed every night. I have written the tale of how she gathered what little strength she had left to stand up on her feet again, not once leaning on someone else this time, fighting and living alone and only for her own self. I have recollected how she became her own refuge, how she learnt to snub social censure and archaic customs, and how every mistake she made, every stumble, every fall, only made her stronger. She gradually learnt to consider life, with all its wretchedness, as her own, and not be beholden to someone else—this is the tale I have written, of evolution, of her creation, as she was burnt to steel by the fires of patriarchy.

Did I do anything wrong? I don't believe I did but many people around me felt that I committed a grave offence, a heinous crime, by writing such a tale. And so, I was put to a public trial. It would have perhaps not been such a big deal if I had not revealed that the girl was me, Taslima, and not an imaginary woman whose tale I had concocted. In fiction, I am allowed to fabricate a life story, celebrate a woman's difference, and her journey of self-discovery. However, the moment there is a whiff of truth in the tale, the moment I have asserted that this is me, this is my tale of overcoming what life has put in front of me, of becoming my own person, of living life on my own terms, it is not surprising that I have offended so many people. Indeed, how can a woman speak like this! I am truly a sore misfit in this patriarchal environment.

I am a forbidden name in my country now, as well as in my beloved West Bengal, a prohibited person, a banned book. My name cannot be uttered lest the tongue catch fire, I must not be touched as I might pollute, and I should definitely not be read lest it spark rage and unrest. This is me; thus I have always been.

Even if *Dwikhandito* leaves me shattered into a thousand fragments, I will never admit that I have done anything wrong. It is not wrong to write one's autobiography, to want to share one's deepest and darkest secrets. The first condition of writing an autobiography is the complete transparency regarding the facts of life, and not sly compromises to avoid uncomfortable truths and proverbial skeletons. With my last ounce of integrity, I have tried to adhere to this principle and not hidden anything. While the first two volumes, *Aamar Meyebela* (My Girlhood) and *Utol Hawa* (Restless Wind), did not cause any dispute, the third created a furore in Bengal. I did not engineer this controversy, others did. People have accused me of deliberately choosing controversial material, which is simply not true—especially in the case of a memoir. I have only been candid regarding the significant events and people that have contributed to my life and my growth. I have spoken frankly about my world view and my blind spots, my dreams and my despair, my joy, my tears, my love, my hatred, the beauty and the ugliness that surrounds it all. I have not chosen a sensitive or controversial issue to write about, I have chosen my life. If that life has been sensitive and controversial, then how do I possibly make it staid and uncomplicated while writing? I have been accused of having written the book as a gimmick, primarily to cause trouble—as if the sole reason for wanting to write must be something nefarious, as if honesty and truth cannot be sufficient incentives, as if courage, the same quality that people apparently used to appreciate in me once upon a time, cannot be a reason either. I am used to debates over my writing; that is how it has been for me since the very beginning. Is my disinterest in making compromises with patriarchy not sufficient reason for controversy?

Different people have different ways of defining an autobiography. Most love to read about lives which are replete with lovely words and thoughts, culminating in a plethora of stunning didactic aphorisms. Hence, great individuals have usually written their life stories to have these serve as beacons for someone else, to show them the path to the truth. Sadly, I am not such a person; neither am I wise, nor a saint— when I write I don't do so out of a selfless desire to illumine someone's way. I write to lay bare the wounds and grievances of an otherwise insignificant person.

Despite not being a great author or a renowned personality, I cannot deny that a series of remarkable incidents have come to pass in my life. If millions of people take to the streets demanding my head because of my beliefs and convictions, if my books are banned because I disagree with the status quo, if the State feels threatened enough by what I say to take my home and my country away from me, how can I say that I have lived an ordinary life? Since this story, and various coloured and ornate versions of it, is already being told and shared, why should I not take up the job myself? In fact, who would know more about my life than me? If I cannot lay myself bare, if I cannot reveal my darkest secrets, the incidents which have left their indelible trace on me, if I cannot confess to what is good in me or what is bad, to my faults, my mistakes, my joys and my sorrows, if I cannot own up to my acts of kindness or those of cruelty, no matter what I write, it will definitely never become an autobiography. I cannot write just for the sake of good literature. I value honesty too much to do so.

Whatever life I might have lived, howsoever wretched or sordid, I can at least attest to the fact that I have not been unfaithful to myself. Even if my readers feel repulsed by me, I would take comfort in the fact that I have not cheated them either, that I have not fed them a pack of pretty lies in the guise of my life's story. I have told them the truth even when that truth has been unpalatable, knowing fully well that I can neither alter nor deny whatever has happened in my life—I can acknowledge the unpleasant as much as I can appreciate the beautiful.

The attack and the insults that I have faced from all quarters stem from one simple fact—I have spoken the truth. Not many can handle the truth. While the truth of *Aamar Meyebela* or *Utol Hawa* was easy to accept, the truth in *Dwikhandito* has been simply too much for most people. So, the people who made suitably remorseful noises of pity when reading about the insults I was subjected to in *Aamar Meyebela*, who sympathized with me after I was betrayed by my husband in *Utol Hawa*, the same people took to shaming me after reading about my affairs with multiple men in *Dwikhandito*. This can, of course, mean only one thing. As long as a woman is oppressed and helpless, as long as she is weak and in despair, one can take pity on her or even like her. However, the moment she realizes that she is no longer weak, the day she grows a spine and demands that her voice be heard, the instant she breaks nonsensical taboos to claim responsibility of her own mind and body, she becomes an outcast and an object of loathing. I have always been aware of this duplicitous nature of society, and yet I have never been afraid to be myself.

One of the most important reasons behind the controversy over *Dwikhandito* is the notion of sexual independence. Since most people in society are firmly rooted in patriarchy, they cannot come to terms with a woman's declaration of her right to her own body and sexuality. The sexual independence I have staked my claim to is not simply at the level of discourse; it is something I have practised in my life. That does not imply in any way whatsoever that I will be accessible to any and every man who might desire me. Our society is not yet equipped to either acknowledge a woman's sexual rights or to understand that a woman can be sexually chaste and yet be intimate with any man she desires.

Prominent male authors were having a field day calling me a whore, all the while reaffirming how deeply implicated they were within this self-serving patriarchal set-up. They can shamelessly exploit a prostitute for sex and still use the word as a slur whenever it suits them. The use of women as sex slaves is yet another fact of centuries of oppression. In *Dwikhandito* I have written about my fight against patriarchy and the oppression of women and religious minorities. Yet, the only thing everyone seems to be talking about is my sexuality. They haven't noticed my pain, my tears—the only thing they have noticed is the number of men I have been with, and my audacity in having spoken about something as dark, hideous and primal as sex. In the history of the world, whenever a woman has dared to stand up to patriarchy, whenever she has tried to stake a claim to her own freedom, she has been labelled a whore. Years back, in the introduction to the book *Noshto Meyer Noshto Godyo* (Profane Writings of a Fallen Woman), I had written: 'I adore the mantle of the fallen woman that has been ascribed to me by society. It is an undeniable truth that when a woman wishes to rise above her conditions, when she stands up against the repressive forces of society, State or religion, when she becomes aware of her rights and rebels against the forces seeking to push her back, civilized society invariably shuns her as fallen. The first condition of a woman's emancipation is that she must transgress, without which it will be impossible for her to extricate herself from the grasp of social conventions. The truly emancipated woman is one who everyone rebukes as fallen.' I believe in this adage to this day that a woman must be willing to 'fall', defying social conventions, if she truly desires to win her independence. It is no small reward for a woman to be called a whore by our slowly decaying society. Till date, of all the awards that I have won, it is this epithet, that of the 'whore' or the 'prostitute' that I cherish the most. I have earned this award because I have truly been successful in delivering a crippling blow to the filthy body of patriarchal power. This is the true measure of success of my lifelong battle, my career as a writer, and my journey as a woman.

Two writers, one from Bangladesh and another from India, filed cases against me because of the book. They did not just desire compensation; they wished to have the book banned. I have never managed to understand why a writer would call for the prohibition of a fellow writer's work. How do these people, the guardians of free speech and free thought, behave like fundamentalists? There has been so much fiction, so many lies that have been written about me but I have never run to the courts demanding something be banned. Like Evelyn Beatrice Hall, I have always maintained: 'I disapprove of what you say, but I will defend to the death your right to say it.' Why do our celebrated writers keep trying to disavow this cardinal truth regarding the freedom of speech?

So many writers the world over have left written accounts of their lives. These accounts are never simply a patchwork of the most favourable aspects of their life, but are candid appraisals of human foibles, their mistakes, indiscretions and sins. Human life, regardless of the greatness of the individual, is incomplete without the occasional moments of darkness. St Augustine's (354–430) frank accounts of his antisocial and dissolute lifestyle in Algeria in the seminal *Confessions*— with his admission of sexual excesses, licentiousness, and even becoming the father of an illegitimate child—are never burdened by the need to conceal and excise. Even Mahatma Gandhi was known to have slept with women in his bed in order to test the limits of his vow of abstinence. Jean-Jacques Rousseau (1712–78), in his autobiographical writings—also titled *Confessions*—has been startlingly frank about his misdeeds despite being fully aware that very few of his contemporaries had the acumen to appreciate his needs for complete honesty. The results are frank confessions of his sexual pursuit of a number of women, including Mademoiselle de Warens, whom he was known to have considered a maternal figure. Benjamin Franklin's (1709–90) autobiography is replete with anecdotes of his wild, misspent youth, and goes on to recount how he had adopted his illegitimate son William into the family. Bertrand Russell (1872–1970) in his autobiography has confessed to his many illicit love affairs with a number of women, including Lady Ottoline Morrell and Vivienne Eliot, the first wife of the iconic British poet T.S. Eliot. Leo Tolstoy's memoirs are marked by his unabashed admissions of visiting brothels at the age of fourteen, his sexual affairs with lower-class and married women, and his battles with venereal disease.

One can always wonder why these people felt compelled to reveal to the readers such stories that society might not be willing to condone. They did so simply because they did not wish to hide their true selves by denying events that were so significant to their lives. Have they been attacked because of such a stance? On the contrary, they have been applauded for their efforts, for having had the courage to reveal the truth. In the West, the relationship between a man and a woman has long since come out of the closet. Many writers have begun to frankly explore their lives and relationships through literature, like Catherine Millet in her book *La Vie Sexuelle de*

Catherine M. (The Sexual Life of Catherine M. [2001]) which is a thrilling tale of her sexual exploits with numerous men during the age of free love in the swinging sixties. The fact that the book is full of stunning descriptions of intercourse has in no way affected its standing as literature. In *Living to Tell the Tale* (2002), the first volume of his autobiography, Gabriel García Márquez has left no tale of his sexual affairs with various women untold. Does that mean they will call Márquez names for his lifestyle and move the courts to demand that his book be banned?

Biographies of famous personalities have been published in every civilized country in the world—produced through years of diligent research into private archives. For instance, uncomfortable questions regarding Tagore himself have begun to be asked, especially about his marrying off his young daughter despite being such a vocal advocate against child marriage. One can always ask if the readers need to know these previously unknown pieces of information at all. The simplest rejoinder would be to remind oneself that if these were indeed spurious information, then writers from the world over would not go through months and years of back-breaking research before embarking on narrating the story of someone's life. Through the discovery of previously unknown incidents, the life of a renowned personality and their work too can be studied vis-à-vis a fresh perspective that had hitherto been unavailable.

The average Bengali male writer has never shied away from playing sexual games with numerous women, albeit in secret. In real life, though they might conveniently excise these stories from their memoirs, they are perfectly willing to let these characters populate the fiction they write. No one, however, questions this duplicity. All questions arise when a woman dares to write about sexuality, be it in fiction or otherwise. Sexuality, in such a milieu, is the fiefdom of the male author and woe befall any woman who dares encroach upon it. As a woman, I must be demure and guarded. I must not dare to write like a man because they have the exclusive rights to a woman's body, her breasts, her arse, her vagina— be it in literature or in real life. Women do not possess these rights because patriarchy has not deemed her fit to possess them. The source of all the unrest lies in the fact that I have not cared about these restrictions, and written about things which I was not allowed to write about, irrespective of how tragic or heart-rending my story actually is.

Men have always taken pride in the number of women they have been with. This is entirely different for women, however, especially if they wish to write frankly about love and sex. It earns them epithets like traitor and whore. I have spoken the unspeakable in my recollections, transgressed boundaries and uttered obscenities, revealed intimate compromises made behind closed doors, inconsequential and irrelevant things. But I have never believed that these events have been inconsequential! In fact, these incidents have been foundational in the making of the woman I am today, my beliefs, my ideologies. They reveal how I have grown, bit by bit, constructed by constant clashes with society at large, a real woman who is anything but an archetype. I believe, at least in order to understand myself, this self-explanation is critical.

It has been pointed out that though I was perfectly within my rights to harm my own reputation, I had no right to toy with someone else's. Some have even alleged that I have tried to socially or personally defame them despite the fact that the book is my autobiography and not someone else's. There is one thing that I simply do not understand: why do people who are so sensitive regarding their reputation do things that they know will harm it? Have I broken someone's trust? I do not remember ever making promises that I will never speak about these incidents to anyone! Apparently, there are unspoken contracts! The fact of the matter remains that the men who were accusing me of breach of personal contract were the ones who were anxious about their quasi-divine reputations being irrevocably tarnished if their dirty secrets were to tumble out. And so they raged, their eyes as red as blood, threatening brutal punishment for my transgressions!

What if I truly believe that these incidents should be revealed? Who decides between what should be done and what shouldn't? What if I don't believe that what I have said is obscene? Who draws the lines and who takes the call on what is obscene and what is not? Only I alone have the final say in what I wish to include in my autobiography and not any random person who has arbitrarily assumed the guardianship of good taste! Critics have described my independence as hedonism. The fact remains that our definitions of ideas of taste, sin and beauty have traditionally been formulated according to the pedagogy of patriarchy. Consequently, a woman's demure nature, chastity, beauty, resilience, fidelity and assorted qualities have come to be codified as the essential features of the ideal feminine. Thus carefully structured, our consciousness remains in perennial fear of facing harsh, unforeseen truths. It makes us cover our ears and tremble in disgust, symptoms visible among many critics these days. They have asked if I can be called a writer at all, and have even wondered whether my autobiography is worth being serialized and published. Truly everyone, including the smug journalist who believed that a pen in my hand was a bad omen, has the right to recollect their life's journey. Even if I have been utterly irresponsible and unreasonable, as has been alleged, the right is still irrevocably mine to exercise. George Bernard Shaw had noted: 'A reasonable man adapts himself to the world. An unreasonable man persists in trying to adapt the world to himself. Therefore, all progress depends upon the unreasonable man.' I, Taslima, have always been of the unreasonable kind. I am too simple a writer to claim that the progress of the world is dependent on me in any way whatsoever. However, to the erudite and the cultured, I would gladly be unreasonable or stupid. It is this stupidity that has forever assisted me in standing firm even under the crushing blows of patriarchal retribution; my stupidity and irrationality have been my most prized possessions.

The other accusation has been that I have deliberately hurt religious sentiments. Those who know me are aware of how vocal I have always been against religious tyranny. Since organized religion is almost entirely patriarchal, the agents of patriarchy would obviously not take kindly to insults against their religious texts and ideologues. These custodians have driven me out of my country, yet another price that I have had to pay for speaking the truth.

This was not the first time that fear and paranoia regarding a communal riot had been carefully channelled to prohibit my writing—it had happened before in Bangladesh. The repeated incidents of communal violence that have come to define the political atmosphere of the Indian subcontinent are, however, not caused by my writings. They are caused by systematic oppression of Hindu and other minorities in Bangladesh, the persecution of Muslim minorities in Gujarat, repeated incidents of violence on Biharis and Christians in Assam, clashes between the Shia and the Sunni

in Pakistan, and countless other such incidents. I may not be
an author of great consequence, but whatever I have written
thus far has been in the service of humanity, to foreground
that everyone, irrespective of faith, race, gender, has an
equal right to live with dignity. No, my writings have never
caused riots; whatever catastrophe they have caused has been
limited only to my life. I remain the only person who suffers
the consequence, the only person whose life is thrown into
turmoil, and the only person who has to lose her home.

The Bengali daily *Anandabazar Patrika* stood firmly by
my side against the wave of slander and criticism that had
ensued, bringing out a special issue of their journal *Desh*
with contributions by a number of figures, including me and
Shibnarayan Ray.[18] Their editorial, especially, was fantastic,
and one cannot help but recall it:

> In those days, the city at midnight used to be ruled by
> four young men—it was a time of poetry and a realm of
> imagination. However, times have changed. Now about a
> dozen intellectuals, in broad daylight and in their complete
> prosaic senses, lord over Kolkata and the rest of Bengal.
> This is Buddhadeb Bhattacharya's Bengal where the
> esteemed Chief Minister, playwright, translator, cultured
> and a patron of the arts, has ruled in favour of banning
> the third volume of Taslima Nasrin's autobiography
> *Dwikhandito*. Why has the book been banned? The official
> reason cited is that it might incite communal tensions. In
> the meanwhile, a few thousand copies have already been
> sold, and like her earlier writings, there have been tense
> arguments, heated debates and even legal suits. Despite
> this, there have been no reported instances of communal
> unrest yet. This, perhaps, is the biggest symbol of social

evolution that one could have expected. It begs the question as to why the socially evolved Left Front Government of West Bengal, which has always prided itself in being a champion for democracy, went so far as to order a ban. The Chief Minister has stated that he chose about twenty-five eminent people whom he asked to read the book before ruling in favour of the ban. This would imply that the three-decade-old Left Front Government took the entire decision based upon the opinions of a handful of intellectuals, opinions that have resulted in restrictions on an author's right to express her opinions freely. During the high noon of colonialism the imperial powers would often resort to banning books they deemed dangerous; the difference lies in the fact that they would also take full responsibility for their actions. Similarly, during the Emergency, Indira Gandhi or Siddhartha Shankar Ray[19] never had to resort to using the intelligentsia as a shield for their repressive measures. The progressive Left Front Government of West Bengal has indeed established a new model in this regard; a model that clearly spells out that the State will issue directives but not take the ensuing responsibility. Not that the State has to take responsibility at all, especially if it has such a ready supply of renowned intellectuals who would stay up late into the night to read Taslima Nasrin's autobiography at the Chief Minister's behest and give such informed opinions! Why should the powers that be give up such a golden opportunity of being able to use the cultural elite to rule culture and taste itself, and still protect their reputation of being evolved and liberal?

Have the Chief Minister and his cohorts considered what their joint efforts have done to the state of democracy

in West Bengal? The entire world is now aware of the
Stalinist regime that is in power, where the State can
quash dissenting voices at will and create support for its
actions by the help of a certain section of the cultural elite.
If this is not an instance of cultural fascism, then would the
esteemed Chief Minister be gracious enough to explain to
us what is? Perhaps, there are other deeper reasons behind
this virulent opposition of Taslima Nasrin's book. Possibly
it has been too dangerous to allow someone to talk whose
revelations about her own life threaten to expose hitherto
unknown secrets about someone else's. Otherwise, what
can justify a reason as preposterous as stating that the
book has been banned because twenty-five people have
said so!

Shibnarayan Ray, one of the most erudite men on either side
of the border, wrote:

I can claim with certainty that the exiled Taslima
Nasrin is the rightful successor to the discursive legacy
of Mary Wollstonecraft, among any other in either
Bengal. I considered *Dwikhandito*, the third volume
of her autobiography that was recently banned by both
Bangladesh and West Bengal, an exceptional literary work.
In the mother's womb our appearances undergo a series of
mutations to finally arrive at the human form. However,
since the moment of birth there begins a focused attempt
to shape the child according to certain socially acceptable
prototypes. Over the centuries, in various societies, the
prototypes may have undergone radical transformations,
but the intent behind them has remained unchanged—
to construct citizens according to certain pre-set types

and eradicate any possibility of independent or original thought. The ruling oligarchy initiates this production of citizens using convenient tools like religion, traditions, customs and pedagogy. Every child, though, possesses an innate ability to forge their unique self-identity, provided the process is aided by efforts, determination, honesty, reason, and intense dedication. Most do not succeed. However, those who do manage to come up trumps against every hurdle placed before them, emerge as the rare individuals whose sense of self is always reflected in their actions, their lifestyle, their ways of thinking, and their creations. We have known many such individuals—from Socrates to Vidyasagar, Giordano Bruno to Manabendra Nath Roy—but very rarely do we get a chance to read about their amazing journeys in any detail. In this regard I must say that I consider Taslima, much like French philosopher Simone de Beauvoir, an exception. The greatest contribution of her autobiography, especially *Dwikhandito*, is the fact that it provides us a glimpse of the path traversed by a young Muslim middle-class girl, against all odds, in her journey towards becoming the woman named Taslima Nasrin—the narrative that was laid out in the first two volumes finds completion in the third. Consequently, the book is of immense literary as well as historical value and anyone who ventures to read it, despite the bans imposed by the governments on both sides of the border, would undoubtedly find this unadorned honesty extremely refreshing. Similarly, many will perhaps find the book inspirational especially with regards to coming to terms with one's true self. The kind of books that find favour with the reading public these days are primarily tales of social attrition and decadence,

or satirical sketches. Despite her hardships, Taslima
has never bowed down to forces of oppression and has
been a tireless advocate for a more humanist outlook
in life. In the first two volumes she had written candid
accounts of her childhood and adolescent years which
had deeply perturbed the elite civil society of both West
Bengal and Bangladesh who consider the concealing of all
uncomfortable truths as the primary condition of being
called civilized.

Nearly a hundred years ago, Begum Rokeya Sakhawat
Hossain[20] had written, 'We have never been able to rise
up against any form of social oppression mainly because
whenever any of our sisters has tried to stand up for her
rights, religion and traditions have been used as convenient
excuses to mercilessly crush and silence her. Men have used
our religious texts as God's will in order to forever keep
us in the dark. Begum Rokeya had had to suffer untold
persecution for her brave admissions, and the essay was
heavily edited when it was first anthologized and published.
A hundred years later, it has yet again been proposed that
Taslima's book will be cleared for publication if certain
sections from it can be expunged. In the course of a hundred
years, have we made any progress at all?

Many daily newspapers in West Bengal too wrote against
the ban, lengthy editorials and op-ed pieces were dedicated
to the issue, despite some renowned authors and artists
coming out in support of the decision. On the other hand,
no newspaper in Dhaka wrote anything against the ban and
the entire decision was more or less accepted. Nothing is as
contagious as hatred; once let loose, it uses lies and subterfuge
to spread, sometimes even faster than light!

So much happened because of *Dwikhandito*! It prohibited a way of thinking, divided the readers for or against the ban and fuelled anxiety regarding the consequences of criticizing religious dogma. It also played upon the fear and paranoia about communal unrest, and raised suspicions about the government's attempts to appease the Muslim vote bank, since many had alleged how the ban was justified because the book had insulted the Prophet. However, I have always been vocal about the freedom of expression, regardless of whose rights we are considering or how contrary those views may be to my own. In the aftermath of the controversy, like me, my faith too has remained unbroken. Five of my books have been prohibited in Bangladesh thus far, unlike just the one in West Bengal. However, the reasons behind the prohibitions have been identical: I have hurt the religious sentiments of a community. Since the Dark Ages, when the Crown and the Faith had been coterminous, ruling powers have silenced voices of dissent citing the protection of religious sentiments.

The first person who attempted to challenge the ban was Sujato Bhadra.[21] He moved the court, demanding to know whether, as a free citizen of the nation, his right to read a published book could be curbed and by whom. In his defence, renowned lawyer Joymalya Bagchi made a series of very powerful arguments in court in support of the freedom of speech and expression. I have never managed to personally thank Mr Bhadra and Mr Bagchi; neither have I managed to thank the judges who finally overruled the ban. I couldn't thank them simply because I had not for a moment believed that the battle was mine alone. Almost always after a ban, the writer recedes into the background as questions regarding free speech and freedom of an author automatically assume centre stage—rights that are due not simply to an author but to the entire body social. There are always a handful of men who fight for the perpetuation of other's rights, men who, unknown to others, end up creating history. Sujato Bhadra is one such person.

Two years after it was banned, *Dwikhandito* was finally freed for publication. The victory was not simply a personal one; it was a triumph of free thought, freedom of speech and the freedom to express one's opinions without fear of retribution. There had been many fighters along the way—writers, publishers, those in favour of the ban and those against—who were present in court that day. No matter how dark the circumstances, it provided a glimmer of hope that personal opinions notwithstanding, no one really wants a book to be banned. Yet, a lingering sense of disquiet remains—that people almost always choose to remain silent.

And Then One Day . . .

My Harvard stint came to an end, plunging me into a familiar quandary. A new city, a new country—these had been recurrent concerns over the past years in a never-ending quest to find a land where I could finally and firmly plant my feet. I had tried time and again to shed the mantle of the wanderer, the forlorn traveller, but always in vain. This time, I was resolved—I wanted to come back to Bengal. The dream had been a long-cherished one, a constant companion in all my lonely travels abroad. So much had happened in Bengal in the meanwhile—the ban, the outrage, the relentless slander! Yet, leaving behind the glitz of the western metropolis, its fresh air and clean water, and its bright shiny lights, I returned to Kolkata. I had already made arrangements to lease out a fully furnished house in Triangular Park for a month, tired as I was of an endless array of hotel rooms. I spent a month in that house—a month full of people, commotion, friendship, work, surprises and curiosity—while searching for a new place in the city where I would be able to live out the end of my days. My long-nurtured dreams began to take flight, their enormous wings spreading and shielding me from sight.

I had met a kind man in the Indian embassy in Sweden who had confessed, much to my surprise, to being an admirer of my work. When approached for a visa, he had issued an Entry (X) visa for me which, I later came to know, could be renewed every six months to allow me to stay indefinitely in India. I was now no longer a tourist; I could be a citizen! All of a sudden, my desires were no longer old secrets tucked away safely in some corner of my soul—perhaps even without me being aware, they had started becoming tangible.

So, one fine morning, I found myself at the Kolkata airport, talking to a hitherto unknown voice, demanding that the absolutely startled man find me a house immediately. It became apparent that he had never come across someone keen on renting a house without even having seen the place once! Everything had to be arranged that very morning— the dusty empty house, new bedding, some stray pieces of furniture, utensils and the like. Not that there was anyone at hand to tell me about these things—how to find the house, where to buy furniture, what to do about food and other such chores. They who usually surround me—because of my name or perhaps because of me—were embarrassed to reveal that they had no answers whatsoever—at least not the correct ones. My life in Kolkata thus began with many small mistakes.

Within a couple of days, the house began to appear lived-in. In six months, it seemed like I had been there for nearly three decades. I planted a lot of flowers on the terrace, the ones I remembered from childhood. The smell of the flowers would permeate the house, becoming particularly heady in the dead of night. I would move the pot of *hasnuhana*, in full bloom, near my bed, the smell lulling me to sleep like it used to when I was a child. It was a safe house, in the heart of the city, but not too accessible—there were two immense iron gates and a guard at the entrance between me and the world. The smell of spices in the open terrace, the clothes left to dry flapping in the wind—incredible scenes that kept evoking memories of my childhood, long lost along the way. Awash with light and air, the house on 7, Rawdon Street soon became my home.

Kolkata remained the same except for one huge difference. Nikhil Sarkar,[22] a true friend for all seasons, the person with whom I could always speak my mind, a truly erudite, well-read and talented individual, was not in the city. I could sense that, perhaps unknown even to me, my world had gradually begun to feel empty. My parents, Nikhil, none of them were there, and the less said about my relatives the better. There were only a handful of acquaintances who I could call friends, besides some of my admirers who would frequently visit. Sometimes I would wonder if I had been fooling myself with this house of cards, especially when everything increasingly seemed so transient—as if life itself had become an enormously puerile joke.

The doors of 7, Rawdon Street, however, remained forever open to everyone, including strangers. I have always been innately hospitable. So many people, right, wrong, cunning, naïve, have passed through my doors but I have never felt like judging any of them. Stupid and harmless, that is how I have always been.

I could simply walk out in my house clothes, just a pair of flimsy slippers on my feet, and shop off the pavement, buying things cheap at a bargain. I could pick up a stray kitten from Gariahat and bring it home with me. It was a simple, unadorned life which could, however, instantly transform into a glamorous one—the crowds would spill over outside the stall at the book fair and the police would have to be deployed to manage the admirers. Despite all this, I could still connect to my readers, even without socializing with the literary circuit of the city. That was just as well because I have never been comfortable with uninterrupted devotion or admiration, and as far as I knew, the elite of the city did not take kindly to blunt talk and the harsh truth. So I spent my life on my own, in solitude, content with my frequent travels and my life abroad when something or the other would call me away—to read my poetry somewhere or collect a prize somewhere else.

That is not to say some good things were not happening for me in Kolkata. BAG Films approached me for the rights to my short story 'Frasi Premik' (The French Lover) to adapt it into a feature film, and paid me for the copyright. A book of short stories from the last 100 years of *Anandabazar Patrika*, with a preface written by me, was published amidst much pomp by *Anandabazar*. They even approached me for publication rights to my complete works. A month-long miniseries based on my novel *Shodh* (Vengeance) was telecast, and became more popular than many other daily shows. It even led to offers of writing for television, which I graciously took up. At the same time, a theatrical adaptation of my short story '*Phera*' (The Return) was being performed at theatres like Girish Mancha, Madhusudhan Mancha and Rabindra Sadan. I would regularly attend the shows and this, in turn, introduced me to many other splendid plays being performed by independent theatre groups. I was even invited on stage by Rudraprasad Sengupta[23] to felicitate award winners at the end of a week-long theatre festival organized by his group, Nandikar.

Many of these instances helped me feel secure about being a part of the cultural and artistic community of Kolkata;

gradually, I began to feel as if I belonged in this city, that I was not from a different land. My bond with Kolkata, in fact, dated right back to my adolescence. One day I resolved to invite for dinner all the old acquaintances I could locate from that time—the many whose poems I remember publishing or little magazine publishers who had published my work. Some of them were still writers but had not exactly progressed over the years; others had given it all up to become business owners or even witch doctors! Despite that, every bit of all this made it clearer how much I craved the past. So when any of my relatives visited me from Bangladesh—my brother, his son Subho, Aunt Jhunu—I used to almost smother them with love.

Kolkata too had resolved to draw me in with open arms. Gradually, hitherto impossible things—a Bengali newspaper in the morning, a Bengali magazine or a book in the afternoon, the evening adda in Bengali or a boisterous and noisy Bengali dinner at night—began to feel commonplace. Invites started pouring in for various talk shows on television, gallery inaugurations, book launches or simply poetry-reading sessions. Simultaneously, despite my own Bengali Muslim upbringing, I was working towards realizing a long-cherished dream of founding a humanist organization—the Secular Humanist Collective—bringing together people from various backgrounds with a common goal of extricating oneself from dogma. Keeping myself deliberately in the shadows, I, instead, concentrated on the primary objectives of the collective: the formation of a truly secular state, society, pedagogy and law, the education and development of women, and working to curb the tyrannical tendencies of the madrasas. Steadily, interested people from across the state began to come to us, joining forces

in their own way to help us work for the deeply oppressed
Muslim society of Bengal. Our collective may not have been
adequately large, our scope and abilities limited—organizing
events and performances, holding meetings and processions,
and distributing leaflets—but our dreams made up for the
lack. The light was strong, the effect too was startling, but
we also had to accept that it might not immediately breach
all the way through the shadows.

At the same time, I was writing a series of articles for
Dainik Statesman, aimed at undermining the inequities
between men and women prevalent and naturalized over a
thousand years and finding possible ways ahead towards a
goal of restoring social justice. Enriching and engrossing
debates, be they literary, political or cultural, continued
with eminent people like Shibnarayan Ray, Amlan Dutta[24]
and Prasanta Roy[25], despite the vacuum created by Nikhil
Sarkar's absence. One fine day, I decided to donate my body
to the cause of medical science after my death, registering
myself at the Kolkata Medical College. The eyes and the
kidneys would be preserved for donation, it was agreed.

Invitations also began to arrive from other states, for
seminars and literary events, letting me travel across the
country—Kerala, Madhya Pradesh, Bihar, Orissa, Assam,
Maharashtra and Delhi. I was somehow convinced that I
would spend the rest of my life in Kolkata, leading me to
even impulsively buy an entire house, a beautiful two-storey
one and that too on a day's notice. Meanwhile, I had formed
a deep attachment to an up-and-coming young poet. With a
certain doctor too, there was a strange, unresolved connection.

That dark, terrifying day came quite unexpectedly.

Though I usually prefer being homebound, around
that time I had begun to feel a tad restless. Dr Inayya had

been inviting me to Hyderabad for a while to attend the launch of the Telugu translation of *Shodh*, which had been translated by his wife. Despite having refused twice, I agreed on his third attempt, perhaps because I was looking forward to a change in scenery too. It would be a one-day trip, so no toothbrushes, no suitcases and no luggage. I selected a simple blue chiffon sari for the day, convenient because it can do without ironing. Not that it has ever mattered to me, that sort of thing. I have always been a little uninvolved about clothes, or looking pretty, and had stopped putting lipstick on too at one point of time. At least now I run a comb through my hair and put a light colour on my lips, more so to protect them from becoming dry than anything else.

I confess to have been surprised as soon as I stepped into the airport at Hyderabad. Dr Inayya was there, waiting to greet me, but he was quite alone—there wasn't a single security officer in sight. Assuming that there would be police at the venue, I readily accompanied Dr Inayya to the hotel I was to stay in. They had booked a room in a five-star hotel for me to use before the event, and I spent the rest of the time there, watching television and making tea for myself as I waited. Soon, there was a call from the reception telling me that it was time for me to leave for the book launch. I must admit that I was not entirely sure what the event was all about, and asking Dr Inayya yielded very little because I could not entirely comprehend what he explained to me, or tried to, in his strong Telugu accent. So when I asked him if he had made arrangements for police protection, I could not understand what he said in response.

I pressed on. 'Wherever I go, they make separate security arrangements for me. Haven't you done so too?' This time,

however, with a lot of effort, I could catch a stray bit of
what he was trying to tell me—'Not really! It's a small event,
you see. And there hasn't been much publicity. There's no
point getting into trouble with the police unnecessarily, you
see!' Trying to comprehend what he was saying, I replied,
'Rather than getting into trouble with the police, they are
necessary to make sure there is no trouble.' He simply
laughed in response.

I do not know why I didn't correct Dr Inayya that day,
why I didn't remind him that I had refused his invitations
twice because I had not felt safe travelling to Hyderabad. The
radical Islamic activists of Hyderabad had previously created
quite a racket, vandalizing bookshops that had been selling
Lajja (Shame). I have always been absent-minded. I had
simply forgotten about the considerable Muslim population
of Hyderabad, a sure signal that the fundamentalist
elements too would be of a considerable number. Islamic
fundamentalists have always accused me of being anti-
Islamic; it is a title that becomes impossible to erase once it
has been awarded. Neither a life built on atheism, secularism,
humanism, and a keen scientific outlook, nor my sensitivity
and humanity—nothing can expunge the stubborn stain of
my alleged anti-Islamic tendencies from the minds of the
people.

The event was scheduled to be held at the Hyderabad
Press Club. Two books were to be released, one of them
being the translation of *Shodh*. My talk, scheduled after the
launch, was preceded by a Telugu writer and a translator who
spoke about their work and their experiences with translation.
I chose to speak instead on human rights, especially because
of the feminist underpinnings in the book and its protagonist
Jhumur who refused to be treated as mere property and stood

up for her rights. As always, in my usual mild-mannered voice, I tried to explain how a woman could not be treated as personal or social property. My voice, unfortunately, has never quite gotten tuned to the vitriolic one required at a protest meet. No matter how angry I get, how upset, no matter what harsh things I say, the timbre and pitch remain as polite, calm and sedate as always.

It happened just as we were about to leave for lunch. Suddenly, a group of men, chanting and shouting in Telugu, barged in through the front door and started advancing towards me. Neither could I understand what they were shouting, nor could I wrap my head around why they would want to attack me. All of a sudden, they began to pick up whatever they could lay their hands on—bouquets, books, bags, chairs—and threw them at me. A few bystanders, attempting to shield me, only ended up getting hurt while I stood cowering behind the journalists who were busy clicking photographs. I was not worried about what might hit me; I was preoccupied with what I felt sure was impending death. Someone, I don't know who, grabbed me by the arm and pushed me towards the rear entrance hoping to get me out to the car through the back. By then, a mob had gathered at the back entrance too and it became instantly clear that there was no way we were going to get to that car. I attempted shutting the back door only to have the glass kicked in by one of the assailants. My mind had already blanked out every other thought except for the need to find a way to save myself. I ran to the front door to find the entire club surrounded by these men. In desperation, we shut the front door from the inside—I and a group of defenceless women in the room, and a few men too—piling chairs for a makeshift blockade.

I was told to hide behind the pillars or under the table, but I knew no matter where I hid in the room, if the mob broke in through the barricade, there was nothing to stop them from getting to me. By then, the raucous sloganeering outside had become plainly audible—'Taslima Nasrin Murdabad'— along with a myriad of other kinds of screams and yells. All of a sudden, we heard a commotion behind the stage, to realize to our horror that some men were trying to break in through the hidden door behind the curtains. I realized all too well what that would mean. The first thing they would see on entering the hall would be me cowering behind the pillars, and there would be nothing to save me from their clutches. The journalists, even at the risk of getting severely injured, were trying to stop the men from breaking the front door open; many had abandoned their cameras in trying to save me, holding the makeshift barricade with all their might. On my part, as I stole from one corner to the next, it seemed like a long and terrifying wait, as if I had been asked to count down to the last remaining seconds of life, waiting for the final bell to ring! The *mangalsutra* that I had worn out of sheer whimsy had long since snapped; the end seemed nigh. The people in the room were frightened out of their wits by the screams and clamour coming from the outside, their anxiety and fear spiking with the steadily soaring din of the mob. I kept imploring for someone to inform the police, but the people there, having never come across a situation like this, were clueless and clearly out of their depth.

I remember that I kept wondering whether the people in the room were worried—whether they were anxious that somehow the knife or the bullet meant for me would end up hurting one of them. While stunned at first, many of the organizers as well as the audience had regained their senses and, sensing further violence, they had already begun a steady exodus, leaving me behind. Petrified, I remember shrinking further against the wall while trying to fathom just how many more blows would be required to break down either of the doors—a few more kicks, a couple of strong blows, and the barricade would topple over. I could almost sense death as I prayed feverishly for the police, aware that not many knew the event was being held at the press club. I couldn't cry, nor could I faint as I kept thinking of how they would kill me—would it be the knife or the bullet? Perhaps they would beat me to death or crush me under their boots? Faced with a riotous mob, their clamour reaching a terrifying crescendo, I was beginning to feel even more alone as the room began to thin out. These were the people who issued fatwas against me, who announced rewards for anyone willing to bring them my head, who took to the streets calling for retribution against me, who regularly burnt my effigies and my books in public. Hitherto they had never managed to get close enough to cause actual damage. Faced with terrible odds, I could almost see my end—what was death like? Would it hurt? Would they shoot me through the heart or through the head, or would they dismember me? Or perhaps they would rape me, repeatedly, and crush the life out of me.

The police arrived just as suddenly. They broke through the barricade before the mob could and enveloped me in an impenetrable blanket of security. Gradually, my frozen body seemed to sense freedom again, my fists unclenched as I heard the fundamentalists being herded into the police van. Eventually, amidst a tight ring of security, I was taken to a police car and my well-wishers could finally sigh in relief.

I have stared death in the face; I have seen how they kill, how they destroy and pillage in plain sight without any fear of repercussions in the name of the Prophet. It was indeed miraculous how I survived. I have long suspected that that is how death would find me, just as suddenly, while reading poetry somewhere or talking about human rights. What have I done to deserve this? Is it a grievous sin to speak out against religious dogma, superstitions and oppression? Is it a crime to take the side of humanity and basic rights? For all my purported faults, they are determined to burn me at the stake of hatred and intolerance!

I have been nurtured by love, love of countless readers from India and the rest of the world, love of many rational, liberal and tolerant individuals. I have shed tears not at the hatred and violence I have witnessed but at the voices of care and concern that have inquired about my well-being, who have assured me their unyielding support. I do not feel alone any more because I have come to realize that all of us who believe in the ideals of a just democracy and freedom of expression are larger in number while the intolerant, violent radicals who seek to undermine freedom of speech and human rights are far fewer. This is not my fight alone! Anyone who has a stake in a just society, a beautiful, caring State, and a safe world, must necessarily take up the fight against this small but destructive force.

Bringing this train of thought to a screeching halt, the car reached the police headquarters. I began to pray earnestly: let there be only Hindu policemen, let there be no Muslim policemen around! Religion is a truly dangerous thing! As they began to introduce me to the high-ranking officials in the department, the only thing I could do was to surreptitiously check their name tags to ascertain their faith. Most of them, however, were unfailingly kind and polite, and they seemed to know of the radicals who had attacked the press club.

The footage of the attack was being replayed on a television, interspersed by comments from the police officer-in-charge. Eventually, he made me sign two complaint letters against the men, assuring me that they would be brought to justice. Not that I was actually worried since I knew I would soon leave the city and never come back.

The flight had been scheduled for the evening but the police managed to call the airport and convince them to bring the time of departure forward. I was escorted to the airport directly from the police station, and even though journalists were not meant to know about my departure, there was a huge crowd of them waiting for me there already. Perhaps, they had been waiting there for hours! Regardless, I refused to give any interviews, though that did not deter them in the least from thronging the airport. It was the same as I stepped into the airport in Kolkata. There was a sea of reporters waiting for me, none of whom were supposed to know my itinerary. A similar scene awaited me at home, the courtyard buzzing with journalists and camera crews, though I refused to entertain even a single one. I was determined that I would not personally protest against what had happened; the protest had to emerge from the people. I have fought for the freedom of speech and expression all my life, so why should I have to make a display out of my shock and terror to reiterate the importance of these rights? Everyone had seen what had happened and was that not enough? Did I become a writer only to have to fight for the freedom to write? How much longer would I have to bear torture, and then describe the same for the benefit of others? Did I not have a right to be angry? Would I have to spend the rest of my life being beaten and broken, pleading to be understood, in tears, being pursued and hunted?

My friends were anxiously waiting for me at home. As for me, I was numb inside, alternating between burning rage and cold, unfeeling ice. Everyone wanted to know what had happened, the why and the how and everything in between, but I did not wish to say a single word to anyone—the only one I wanted to see was my cat. The phone was ringing incessantly but I had no desire to answer it. I wanted my friends to leave, wanted to cuddle with my cat, lick my wounds in solitude, and fall asleep. It seemed I had gone a thousand years without sleep, but the moment I would try to sleep, the images of the attack would reanimate in front of my eyes, and the cruel, vicious, angry faces of the attackers would taunt me again. Perhaps they had not meant to kill me. However, while it was happening I had not been aware that the goons had been sent by the local MLA in a bid to boost the sagging popularity of his party. I had assumed them to be a group of fundamentalist zealots, who had found me within their grasp at long last and who would never waste such a golden opportunity to ascend to Paradise by murdering a defenceless and unarmed woman. I have had close escapes before, but this time I had given up all hope of escaping from their clutches. They did not kill me, because they did not wish to and not because they could not. Anger has been known to drive people to the worst of crimes, least of all murder.

I have risen from the dead. I am resurrected.

House Arrest

I was attacked in Hyderabad even though I had not uttered a single word against Islam. From what I later learnt, the attack had been a ploy to generate popular support for the Hyderabad-based political party All India Majlis-e-Ittehadul Muslimeen (AIMIM). In fact, an AIMIM leader declared at the Andhra Pradesh state assembly, 'People who spread anti-religious messages must be summarily executed.' Coming out in full support of the incident at the press club he went on, 'The Muslims are proud of what our local leaders have done. We will not tolerate any disrespect to the Prophet.' The president of the party, an ex-member of Parliament, supported the former, 'Our party workers deserve praise for what they have done.'

Another Islamic group, Majlis Bachao Tehreek, claimed that the original plan had been to kill me, but the AIMIM had instead let me live. The three MLAs who had been arrested were soon released on bail, and the AIMIM clearly spelt it out that if I ever went back to Hyderabad, I would not be spared: they would kill me—yes, that is how explicit the message was. Various people informed me that the AIMIM was trying to muster local support and increase their influence before the imminent municipal elections. Those who would be able to cause me harm would be considered saviours of Islam and they would consequently command the support of the larger Muslim community. A woman called Taslima was out to destroy Islam and the only way to stop her and save the faith was to kill her. Killing her would earn a hefty reward off the fatwa and would also ensure Paradise in the afterlife. It is a very convenient equation which the Islamic fundamentalists use to agitate the poor, uneducated and backward Muslims of secular India. It is also the perfect way to ensure the support of the entire minority vote bank, considering that such radicals are representatives of the significantly large Muslim population of India, nearly a fourth of the entire demographic. There is perhaps nothing sadder than the fact that more educated and civilized representatives are not chosen.

The incident came up in discussion in Parliament and was strongly condemned. News channels conducted a series of panel discussions on issues surrounding freedom of speech, and the radicals from Hyderabad joined these debates to vociferously argue their case. The crux of the matter remained that I had said anti-Islamic things, insulted the Prophet Muhammad and hurt religious sentiments. Consequently, I had been attacked, but it had not been enough and I deserved more. It did not seem to occur to anyone to point out that I had not uttered the word 'Islam' even once in my entire speech that day. My deportation from the country remained the primary demand—I was an outsider, I had no right to hurt the sentiments of the Muslims of India. I could not ask them if that meant Indians had the right to hurt those sentiments or whether that meant no one in the world had the right to hurt Muslim sentiments. It would have been just as well if they had told me to my face that they did not believe in petty concerns like the freedom of speech and expression.

I have had to face many difficult situations and withstand a lot of pain in life. However, sometimes a few words of kindness have gone a long way in alleviating some of the torment. An editorial in *Anandabazar Patrika* managed to do something similar, one fine morning:

> The recent attack on Taslima Nasrin, that too on the eve of the diamond jubilee celebrations of India's independence, has only served to reveal the feeble and unstable nature of the nation's socio-cultural milieu. The attempt to physically and mentally harm the renowned and much-debated author can only be described as barbaric. The three local leaders at the forefront of the attack have served to foreground the uncomfortable truth that cultural intolerance in this country is not a stray, disconnected set of incidents. It is well-organized and carefully orchestrated, a menace that has afflicted everyday politics in an enormous way. Taslima Nasrin may have come under the wrath of Islamic fundamentalists in her own country and abroad, but her experience of the same must be radically different in the context of the supposedly secular, pluralist ideals of one of the biggest democracies in the world. We are sure she will now have to reconsider travelling freely within the country. She might even choose to surround herself with increased security, removing herself from the ambit of democratic rights altogether. It is a shame for our nation too—sixty years of independence has clearly been unable to teach us about the fine line that runs through personal viewpoints and tolerance.
>
> It is here perhaps that the root of the problem lies. Intense criticism of this incident has already poured in from everywhere, even from the political parties. Every

person has to be made aware of this basic difference; there is no going ahead without that valuable lesson. In the march from prehistory to modernity, it has become amply evident that the cornerstone of human civilization is the need to be able to accept a contrary viewpoint or ideology, even if one cannot respect it. This is not simply desirable; it is necessary. We require exemplary punishment for offences arising out of intolerance, for people who dare to assault a painter for putting the erotic games of the gods on canvas or who try to attack an author for perceived slights to their ideologues. If society is unable to foster civil liberties and cultural acceptance, if it cannot teach the message of tolerance, then it is the State that must take the initiative.

Though many such protests emerged, the perpetrators of the Hyderabad incident were never punished. They were arrested, taken to the police station, perhaps treated to tea and biscuits, and then let go. AIMIM was a part of the ruling coalition of the state; it was evident there would never be any actual punishment for their crimes.

I can never understand why people are so cruel and so stupid; there is an inextricable link between cruelty, stupidity and religious fundamentalism. Besides, cruelty by itself is devastatingly contagious. The radical elements of Kolkata soon took to the streets in protest. There had already been murmurs as to why the local pro-Islamic groups had so far been quiet when their brethren in Hyderabad had done so well. So, one fine day, they shook off their despair and began clamouring for my head, burning effigies and all. Students from madrasas, young boys barely in their teens who had never even heard my name, were deployed for the task. None of them had ever read a word of my writing, but they were protesting against my actions as their leaders had instructed them to—they were the soldiers who would save Islam from my noxious influence. This active institution of brainwashing has a long legacy within the madrasa and the masjid. My only concern is that even when they have no idea about me as a person, if they are going to organize meetings and processions in the name of Islam, should it not be necessary for them to have some basic knowledge of Islam in the first place!

The AIMIM leaders from Hyderabad were specially invited for a public meeting at Esplanade in Kolkata. There, in broad daylight, they decided upon the price on my head. When the public demanded to know how much the prize money should be, a leader from the pulpit declared it would be five lakh rupees. Immediately, one of the delegates from Hyderabad corrected him: 'Unlimited!' The leaders on stage cheered along with the jubilant cries of the hundreds of people who had gathered, and passed the fatwa unanimously. This entire scene transpired right in front of many senior police officers who were present at the meeting. The radicals came, declared their verdict with complete impunity, and left. Not a single ripple appeared anywhere. Isn't it a truly charmed life they live in India?

There were two things I especially noticed after returning from Hyderabad. Stringent security measures had been adopted for me, including more policemen at the front gate. Anyone wishing to see me was asked to leave their details behind with the security before being granted access. The other thing that became increasingly clear was that they had strict orders not to allow me to go out of the house. If I wanted to go anywhere, I would be told that it required permission from their senior officer. Then this senior officer would be called, but the permission would never arrive. After this had gone on for a few days, it became clear that I had been placed under house arrest. Friends were allowed to visit me but I was not allowed to go out—not to the market, to see a friend or even visit an ailing well-wisher. This was, of course, all new for me and I simply assumed that it would return to normal in a few days. But as days passed, that possibility seemed to diminish. Meanwhile, I had been invited to Taiwan for a poetry festival and I needed to go to the travel agency to make arrangements for my trip. Not that I really had to go to the agency myself, it could easily have been solved over email. However, just to see the city, to breathe in the outside air, to taste freedom again, I wanted to go out. I know how precious freedom is; I know its taste, its fragrance and its touch well. It has a primal call, one that makes the blood boil over; much like the raging untameable sea. However, I also realized another simple thing. Letting me go to the travel agency was a clear indication that while I was free to fly off to wherever I wished, my movements at home would never be free.

The police who were on guard were regularly given tea and food from the house. I would get biscuits for them, *mishti doi* and other sweets from Mithai, various snacks and munchies, home-made noodles, mango or orange shakes, and tea. I made sure they were well-tended to and treated like guests; I left books and magazines for them to read, bought two fans for the summer, besides chairs and myriad other things. Sometimes, they would come into the living room to watch cricket matches on TV; one of them even began taking his afternoon siesta on the sofa after lunch. Two of the men, Sankar and Tapan, had become like family I suppose. The posting at my house was supposedly regarded as a lucrative one among the policemen, many of them furiously competing for it. They would be devastated when transferred and requests would pour in for glowing letters of recommendation.

Just to understand whether the government had altered its stance on the matter, I began making requests for permission to go out, every week and a half or so. On one such forlorn afternoon, I informed Sankar I wanted to go out. 'Where do you want to go?' It struck me how much things had changed all of a sudden. They never used to be so blunt; I would usually get into the car and tell them where I wanted to go.

Surprised, I composed myself and calmly replied: 'Behala. I wish to visit Dipankar da.' Sankar and Tapan had somehow integrated themselves into my life. They had welcomed me into their home too, had invited me to dinner, and had even begun treating my home as their own. I realized that all of these comfortable certainties had been upturned, all relationships, codes, faith had been compromised irrevocably. All that remained was an enormous question mark that lay hanging over me like a pall, growing and becoming more sinister every day. Sankar left the room silently, leaving me to wait and wonder. After about half an hour or so, he came back only to inform me rather robotically:

Sankar (S): You don't have permission to go there.
Taslima Nasrin (TN) : And why not?
S: I don't know.
TN: But you should! Why will I not be permitted to go to Behala today?
S: I told the officer-in-charge. He informed our senior officer. The senior officer called back after a while to say it can't be allowed.

TN: Why? Why can't it be allowed?

S: He did not tell us why.

TN: Why didn't he? Please ask him. Tell him I am very
    curious to know the reason why it can't be allowed.

Yet again, Sankar left the room silently, this time not returning
either as a man or as a robot to inform me about the reason.

A few days later, I had to urgently go to Salt Lake to
visit Shibnarayan Ray who was unwell. The senior officer's
decree, however, arrived soon enough:

Senior Officer (SO): No, that's not possible.

TN: Why not?

SO: Because Salt Lake is outside our jurisdiction.

TN: But I have visited Salt Lake before! Jurisdiction has
    never been an issue!

The men remained silent, a peculiar mix of expressions on
their faces—fear, anxiety and a certain amount of uncertainty.

I had not visited Birati in sometime, it was imperative that
I go. Yet again, the same order: 'Not Possible.' One senior
officer informs his senior who passes the request on to yet
another senior; and thus the wheels of judgement keep turning.
Next, I informed them that I wanted to go to Howrah:

SO: No, not possible.

TN: This is within Kolkata, isn't it? So, what is the problem
    now?

SO: We haven't been informed.

TN: Who will go to the market? Should I starve?

SO: We don't know. All we know is that we can't let you
    go out.

TN: I can't even go to the market by myself any more?
SO: We have orders; it can't be allowed.
TN: Why?
SO: We don't know why.
TN: It is your senior officer's decision?
SO: Yes.

It seemed to me the decision had, in fact, come from higher up.

These changes were visible elsewhere too. Some professors of Allahabad University had invited me to a seminar. They had been trying for quite a few years and I had only just accepted, much to their elation. As soon as the news of the Hyderabad incident broke, they wrote a letter informing me that the event had been cancelled. Of course, the letter did not bother to mention a reason—I guess they assumed I would understand why. What they were perhaps unaware of is that although I understood rather well the real reasons behind the tantrums thrown by the fundamentalists, I have never managed to understand why academics, authors, cultural luminaries, the government and its politicians, all cower and bow in response. Rather, perhaps I do understand but have never managed to accept it.

As if one fatwa had not been enough for life to become unbearable, another was issued by popular singer Kabir Suman, the erstwhile Suman Chattopadhyay. He appeared on television with a copy of my book and read out all the damaging things I had written against the Prophet. He did not stop there but went on to read out the relevant page numbers, ending with a fervent endorsement of the new fatwa. Truth be told, Suman has perhaps become so zealously Islamic only after having converted to Islam. As the saying goes, neo-Muslims are nearly always a tad more radicalized than the most ardent fundamentalist. If I am to be absolutely honest, I did not fear the threats made against me by the Islamic radicals as much as the fatwa issued by Kabir Suman. He repeatedly claimed that I had written heinous things against his Prophet—this was the same angry, fearsome Suman who had always been known to be an atheist, who had written songs insulting God. I do not believe Suman has any faith whatsoever in Islam or the Prophet. His politics has always been communal.

I remember how I spent that night—the first time I felt such fear that I bolted all the doors and windows shut, but still failed to get any sleep. The only true fatwa that had been issued against me had been by Suman and not the radicalized Islamic groups of Kolkata. The latter could never prove their allegations, could never clearly state where and how I had insulted Islam. Suman, on the other hand, had faced the camera armed with my book, read sections out to the audience, explained to them the insulting things I had written in the pages of *Dwikhandito*. That night, any radical pro-Islamic activist could have resolved to kill me for my crimes, even at the cost of their own lives. Who had been responsible for that? It had not been a zealot. Instead, it had been a renowned artist with a reputation for being progressive and liberal.

These memories seem too fantastic at times, almost suffocating, making me crave for a breath of free air. The people I had expected to find beside me when I was under fire were the ones who turned against me. In fact, they stunned me with further attacks, leaving me completely and utterly alone. I could feel the ground slip from beneath me; people who had found nothing wrong with my writing or my ideology had become my biggest critics. Even those who were known to be stringent detractors of religion seemed to have a problem with my point of view.

I could feel invisible shackles on my feet as I walked— the imaginary sounds were a constant reminder of where and how far I was allowed to go. I was never someone who could turn a blind eye to a wrong, and here I was under house arrest without having committed a crime! A hundred nerve endings were screaming for rebellion, not letting me rest, making me pace to and fro in the beloved house which had begun to resemble a beautiful prison. Those who came to visit would hear about my predicament, make all the appropriate sounds of pity, and then be on their way. Perhaps there was truly nothing they could have done; and if they could have, they were not sure if they should.

One day, wishing to test how far the restrictions had been extended, I informed the police that I wished to meet Jyoti Basu. The request was immediately conveyed to the higher authorities. For all intents and purposes, there had been no real need for me to meet Jyoti Basu; he had simply been the only person in the city who I could wish to visit and perhaps not have the request turned down. The former chief minister of West Bengal was also one of the founding members of the CPI(M) and had been with the party since its inception, besides having served a nearly twenty-three-year term as chief minister. A remarkable individual, he agreed immediately when I requested the meeting. The thought never occurred to him that he should refuse, given that his party had orchestrated the ban of my book, and then had placed me under house arrest instead of being on my side after I was attacked in Hyderabad. Nor did he inquire why I wanted to meet him or what I wished to speak about.

I did not have to wait long for the incumbent CM's approval either. The news arrived soon enough, bringing a smiling Sankar in its stride. They were all fond of me, these men; my incarceration a difficult situation for them too. Regular government employees, none of them had any stake in the government's decrees, nor any clout to alter them.

I bought a huge bouquet of flowers, a lot of sweets and mishti doi from Mithai, and set off for Indira Bhavan. Having repeatedly fallen prey to enforced captivity, these small spells of freedom had become a source of exhilaration. On reaching Indira Bhavan, we were informed by Jaikrishna, Basu's closest aide, that the latter would not eat any of the sweets, so it would be unnecessary to unload them from the car. They could have been given away to guests I suppose, but faced with Jaikrishna's stern cautiousness I did not wish to argue. I was taken inside and asked to wait. Soon enough he arrived, wearing a green lungi and a white kurta, the familiar mysterious and inscrutable smile on his lips. Despite my awe, our conversation went smoothly, almost lulling me into believing for a moment that I could speak so easily to someone of his stature. As it is, I have never been particularly adept at conversing with politicians, because I understand so little of politics. I have never consciously tried to chat up a renowned public personality, only sharing information or satisfying curiosities when someone has voluntarily expressed interest in me. This is not because of any arrogance on my part, but simply reticence. I have always felt it best to express one's admiration from afar rather than insinuate oneself into someone's busy life. At the same time, there have been instances when, despite my reservations, I have had to break my self-imposed rules—when figures like François Mitterrand, Jacques Chirac, Lionel Jospin or Simone Veil have wished to meet me, or when I have been summoned by the greats, Günter Grass and Allen Ginsberg.

Not that a relationship of any sort has ever developed with any of them! I have met them, had sterling conversations, and received much warmth and welcome. The farewell, however, has usually been a permanent one. I have always been rather tardy when it comes to keeping in touch with people. The important people too, quite expectedly, don't come around the second time. Seven years earlier, that was exactly how I had met Jyoti Basu. I had never expressed any interest to anyone about it, but all of a sudden I had been informed that he wished to meet me—in fact, even the date had been set! Undoubtedly a well-wisher, perhaps having thought excessively highly of me, had arranged for it. Nonetheless, I had been beset with worry about what to say to such a great personality; I was unsure of my worth, completely ignorant about anything political. Despite all my apprehensions, Jyoti Basu had visited me with his wife, and had spoken to me as if I had been known to them for a lifetime. Only a truly great man could have spoken to a complete stranger with such warmth and openness, and I remember thinking he was someone I could meet again. Not that we had spoken about ethics or politics! Instead, he had regaled me with these amazing stories, fragments of joy and sorrow, episodes from his childhood and teenage years.

After my book was banned by the Government of West Bengal, an undemocratic act violating the freedom of speech and expression, I had assumed Jyoti Basu would be in favour of the ban, in solidarity with his political party. However, much to my surprise, he had spoken out against the ban. I have never felt the need to touch someone's feet to show respect, and neither had I done so with him. However, every time I had met him, I had tried to express my immense admiration and respect for him in my own faltering way. He had perhaps never been aware of how great a gesture it had been on his part to have gone against his party's dictates—it gave us, those of us who had been fighting for the right to speak and express ourselves freely, immense courage and fortitude. He had many detractors, there were many who called him arrogant. Perhaps he had been truly so. Nevertheless, when I heard his comments against the ban, I do not remember thinking him to be arrogant. Instead, I remember finding him intelligent and wise. No other communist leader had spoken even a word against the decisions of the party, regardless of their personal viewpoint or the fairness of the decree. That perhaps had been the saddest thing of all, to have to renounce one's agency and common sense in order to be part of a mindless political organization. Despite there being no place for organized religion within the ranks of communism, the powerful Marxists ruling West Bengal banned my book because I had hurt religious sentiments, thereby firmly planting the flag of divisive communal politics on the pyre of democratic rights. The victory had been so definitive for the fundamentalists that it had enabled them to march in violent protest and set prices on my head in public.

At a time when I had been a pariah for the communist leaders of West Bengal, when I had just become a banned name, a problem that could unsettle the Muslim vote bank, Jyoti Basu had met me. In turn, I had never complained about anyone to him. We had simply sat and talked, him narrating tales of his village in Bangladesh, family and friends, and his childhood and adolescent years. He had told me stories about the Partition, the ensuing communal violence, the

Bangladesh Liberation War, and finally Independence. He had talked to me about my writing and its historical relevance.

Except Jyoti Basu though, as the days passed, I was not allowed to meet anyone else in India. They let me go abroad however, first to the poetry festival in Taipei and then to Paris. I could also feel, each time, that my return was less than welcome. In Kolkata there was no change in my solitary, confined life, making me wish I could demand to know how much longer they were planning to keep me in captivity. There was no one to answer my questions though, leaving me to writhe in the dark, invisible shackles on my feet. There is this curious thing about shackles—the only people who know their story are the ones wearing them or the ones who put them on.

Conversations

He came to meet me one sudden September evening when, trapped in my own home and forbidden from looking at the world outside, it felt as if moss was about to cover my skin, and my soul seemed like the desolate, overgrown yard of a haunted house. Prasun Mukherjee, the commissioner of Kolkata Police (shortened to CP just as Buddhadeb Bhattacharya was the CM). I had been warned in advance by Vineet Goel, director general of special branch of Kolkata Police, that the CP wished to see me, and he arrived within ten minutes of the call. I was obviously taken aback that such an important man was visiting me, and try as I might I could not figure out a satisfactory reason for the visit. So, I assumed it was a routine one since I was so important to them and they were giving me such fantastic round-the-clock security. Two other senior police officials had previously visited me to make sure I was not worried and to assure me of the security arrangements. One of them, the rather handsome Shamim Ahmed, had told me in passing, 'The people who attacked you in Hyderabad are not the sort one should trifle with. All of them are highly educated people with degrees from foreign universities; they speak such fluent English that you would often think they are not Indian.' His reverence and admiration for them had been quite palpable; apparently the men had been from the famed Owaisi family of Hyderabad.

I greeted Mr Mukherjee with tea and refreshments. We had previously mostly spoken over the phone; the few times we had met, the conversation had involved nothing but cursory social pleasantries. This time it went on for nearly two hours, mostly on the following lines:

CP: Things are not looking good.

TN: Why not?

CP: A group of non-Bengali Muslims has chalked up a plan to assassinate you.

TN: Is that so?

CP: Yes. But I am making all arrangements for your security. My boys are all here and the security has been beefed up. I hope you've noticed.

TN: Yes, of course. Thank you. I feel quite safe now.

CP: But you shouldn't have gone to Hyderabad. That was a mistake.

TN: They have been insisting for a few years. I have always refused but this time they were so earnest in their request for me to be present at the launch of my book that I changed my mind. And I had never been to the city either.

CP: You shouldn't have gone.

TN: I didn't know they had not made security arrangements. The organizers did not take it into account that something of this sort could happen.

CP: Hmm. It was a mistake.

TN: Why was it a mistake? It's not as if I knew from before that something like this would happen!

CP: Why did you go to Hyderabad?

TN: My book has been published in Telugu and the publishers invited me to be part of the launch.

CP: Your book was published in Hyderabad? Why? Why have they published it in Telugu?

TN: Because I write in Bangla.

CP: I know that.

TN: Bengali books are usually translated into many languages, just like mine was translated into Telugu.

CP: Really?

TN: Yes. My books have been translated into other languages too.

CP: Are you telling the truth?

TN: Why should I lie?

CP: Which other languages?

TN: Marathi, Hindi, Oriya, Assamese, Panjabi, Malayalam . . .

CP: Really? Why? Why have your books been translated?

TN: Because people who speak these languages have shown interest in reading what I write. So, publishers have gotten these books translated.

CP: Whatever it is, you shouldn't have gone to Hyderabad.

TN: I have visited other states before this, to places where I have been felicitated, though I like interacting in such cultural gatherings too. And it is always a pleasure to interact with the readers.

CP: You have gone to other states as well?

TN: Of course. I get invitations from many states.

CP: Who invites you? Why do they invite you?

TN: Publishers invite me, or sometimes literary societies do. I don't always go to all these places. But nothing unpleasant has ever happened anywhere, and there are ample security arrangements. I have been to Delhi twice, once on an invitation by *Women's World* and once for the Radical Humanists. The second time there was no security at all but nothing happened.

CP: Really? Why had they invited you?

TN: Usually, I am invited to speak on human rights or women's rights, or to read from my own writing.

CP: Who comes to listen?

TN: People do.

CP: Hmm.

TN: (*sighs*)

CP: What were you speaking on in Hyderabad? Why did they attack you?

TN: The book they were publishing is *Shodh,* the life story of a woman. In my speech I spoke only about a woman's right to live with dignity and respect.

CP: Did you say anything about religion?

TN: I did not even utter the word, not even once. Neither did I mention Islam.

CP: Then why did they get so angry?

TN: There has been a rumour going around about me that I am anti-Islamic. That is why I was attacked. Though, I have subsequently learnt that the entire thing had been orchestrated to draw the Muslim votes by claiming they were saving Islam from my evil.

CP: There is a fatwa against you in this city too.

TN: There are so many fatwas against me. Now that bit seems to have calmed down. And perhaps you can step in and have a word with the imam of the Tipu Sultan Masjid. The last time he had issued a fatwa, you had called him to your room to talk and he had later denied ever having issued any decree in the first place. Why don't you do something similar again?

CP: Forget about the imam, he is not an important factor here. The ones who are coming forward, issuing fatwas, they are not dangerous. They are the good guys. The bad guys are dangerous; they are scheming in the shadows, and getting ready. I have information that they have finalized a plan to murder you.

TN: Do you know who they are?

CP: Yes, I do.

TN: If you have all the information, then why don't you arrest them?

CP: That is not possible.

TN: I don't think anything will happen. Besides, the security people are here. I don't think they will dare try and kill someone in Kolkata.

CP: How can you say that? Do you think I am saying this without concrete information?

TN: But nothing has happened! Siddiqullah Chowdhury and his cronies had claimed they would picket the Writers' Building. Even that did not happen.

CP: (*Loudly, in reproach*) Will you be giving me information or should it be the other way round?

TN: I read it in the papers.

CP: (*Disapprovingly again*) The papers know nothing. We know everything. How will journalists know what is brewing in secret within the city?

TN: That is true. But these people, why can't they be arrested? Conspiracy to commit murder is an offence punishable by law, isn't it?

CP: No, they can't be arrested, especially because this is a minority issue.

TN: How can that be an excuse? Isn't the law the same for everyone?

CP: Religious sentiment is an entity in its own right.

TN: That is true. But these terrorists, the ones you are talking about, have they ever read any of my books? I don't think they have.

CP: I don't know all that. All I know is that they are ready, they have a plan in place, and they are just waiting for the right opportunity. Besides, there's going to be a huge strike sometime around the middle of November, to protest against your actions; it's going to be an ugly thing.

TN: How?

CP: What if there is an angry mob that descends here?

TN: Really? Won't they be stopped before they can reach the house?

CP: Of course, I will provide you with every bit of protection. You must have already noticed how I have beefed up the security. However, if a mob does turn up here and one of our boys shoots one of them, there is going to be a riot.

TN: What are you saying?

CP: I am telling you the truth.

TN: But why will there be a riot?

CP: Yes, that is what will happen. Do you want shots to be fired? Do you really want someone to get shot because of you?

TN: No, I don't want that.

CP: If even one of them gets shot, a riot will be inevitable. The news will spread to the Muslim areas and that will be enough.

TN: But why a riot? This is not a communal issue! It's a question of the law. Does the law discriminate between the Hindu and the Muslim?

CP: It has to! Before you say anything about the law, consider yourself! Have you found support from any quarters?

Even after Hyderabad? Has any political party taken a stand on your behalf? Everyone needs the Muslim votes. You have to try and understand these things, that you will find no support from society at large.

TN: But I get the support of the common people.

CP: Who has told you that?

TN: I am telling you. People are calling me, writing to me, telling me how much they love my writing.

CP: All that will amount to nothing. What matters is that you don't have the support of a single political party. You are in a very bad spot.

Helping himself to the tea and refreshments offered, Prasun Mukherjee continued.

CP: The leaders of the minority communities wish to meet the CM. They are pushing for your deportation and they want to block the CM's convoy in protest. If that happens, we might have to beat them back. Do you know what that means? It will be the next big news. A riot is a foregone conclusion.

TN: That is unbelievable!

CP: No, it's not. There will be a riot in Kolkata because of you, if you continue to stay here.

TN: There will be a riot in Kolkata if I stay here? I have lived here for so many years, but nothing has ever happened. And now I am meant to believe that there will suddenly be a riot?

CP: If you don't wish to believe, that is entirely your problem. But that is what will happen. Now the decision rests on you.

TN: Which decision?

CP: I suggest you go away for a while.

TN: What do you mean?

CP: I mean you have to leave Kolkata, at least for a few days.

TN: Where do I go?

CP: Go to Europe.

TN: Europe? But it's not as if I have a house there somewhere!

CP: Then make some arrangements.

TN: When do I return?

CP: Once everything has calmed down.

TN: (*With a laugh*) I remember when they put me on a plane from Bangladesh in '94. Back then too they had told me, come back once everything has calmed down. It has been thirteen years, and things still haven't.

CP: If you want to come back, then of course you can.

TN: But I cannot go to Europe. I closed that chapter entirely when I came back. Now if I go back, I would have to stay in a hotel and that is not possible for me. Besides, my sister is arriving in a couple of days. She plans to stay for a while.

CP: Take her with you.

TN: But where?

CP: Go to America.

TN: She is coming from America. Why should I take her back there?

CP: Then go somewhere else.

TN: I have already explained it to you; I can't go to Europe or America. I don't have that kind of money.

CP: Then go to a place within the country.

TN: Where in the country?

CP: That you have to decide. You don't have acquaintances in any of the other states in India?

TN: I have many. I have my publishers in Kerala, Maharashtra and Orissa. In fact, the Government of Kerala has been very gracious towards me. The minister for education, M.A. Baby, had invited me over for dinner, and the minister for forests too had sent an invitation for breakfast.

CP: Then go to Kerala. Ask your publishers to make arrangements for your stay.

TN: But then people will get to know about it. The last time, a group of Islamic radicals had staged a protest against me.

CP: Inform the Kerala government about your visit. They will make arrangements for your protection, so don't worry about that. Where else did you say? Maharashtra, was it?

TN: My Marathi publisher, Anil Mehta, is there. He is a wonderful person.

CP: Why don't you go to Madhya Pradesh? They have such vast forests there.

TN: You want me to go away to the forest?

CP: (*Laughing in embarrassment*) No, it's just that I love the forest. That's why I said it.

TN: I don't like the forest.

CP: Then what do you like?

TN: I love the sea, the mountains.

CP: Then go to Kerala. Go and enjoy the surf there.

TN: And when should I return?

CP: Not before three to four months at least. Come back after the fires have died down.

TN: But I don't see any fires.

CP: You might not, but we do.

TN: Oh!

CP: Once you come back, please move from this house. Move to the south of the city, preferably near Ballygunge. This place is too close to the Muslim-dominated areas.

TN: It is so difficult to get an apartment! I have seen so many but I still haven't managed to find one in a good locality. I had taken this one on rent rather hurriedly because I had no other options. The rent is quite steep, so I would ideally like a slightly cheaper place.

CP: Don't worry! We will find you one!

TN: But how do I simply up and leave this house? I have so many important things here, so many books, certificates and documents. How can I just leave everything behind?

CP: Is there anything expensive?

TN: There are a few gold medals, etc.

CP: Take your valuables along with you.

TN: With me? As in, I should just wander about with all my valuable things with me? And what would happen to my house? What about my cat?

CP: Don't worry. My boys will watch over your house and your cat.

TN: You are asking me to go away for a while, but for how long? Why are you not telling me clearly when I would be able to return?

CP: Come back after a few months.

TN: And you are sure everything will be fine after a few months?

CP: Yes. How long can it last? It will all calm down after a few months, at the most within a few years.

TN: I don't believe things are so bad. You are telling me there will be unrest if I stay in Kolkata; but wouldn't things go back to being bad once I decide to come back? Will they let me be once I come back after some time?

CP: Don't worry about that now. We will cross that bridge when we come to it.

TN: Then we must cross this one now. I do not believe anything can be solved by running away. If they realize I have fled because I am afraid, then it will be a huge victory for them.

CP: When did you rent this apartment?

TN: About three years back.

CP: This is not a good locality. This is too close to the Muslim areas. An attack can happen any moment. How big is the flat? How many square feet?

TN: I am not entirely sure, perhaps around 1700 or 2000. Different people have told me different things.

CP: (*Looking around the place*) We will find you one just like this. Is the bathroom that way?

TN: Yes.

CP: (*Entering the study*) Is this the study?

TN: Yes, this is where I spend most of my time.

CP: Why? What do you do here?

TN: I study.

CP: (*Approaching the computer*) You write on this?

TN: Yes.

CP: In Bangla?

TN: Yes.

CP: So strange!

TN: Why should that be strange?

CP: Will you show me how you write on this?

TN: (*I write 'It is not possible for me to go anywhere. No, not possible at all' in Bangla*) That is how.

CP: (*Smiling*) How do you know which key is which Bangla alphabet?

TN: I have been using the computer for years now. It's become a thing of habit to relate the Roman alphabets to the Bangla ones.

CP: (*Moving towards the door, on his way out*) When will your sister be here?

TN: In a couple of days. She is unwell, wants to consult a few doctors.

CP: Listen to me. Try and leave as soon as possible. And let me know quickly once you have decided.

TN: I need some time to think.

CP: There is nothing to think of. You have to leave as soon as possible!

As Prasun Mukherjee left, the police officers stationed outside the door shot up from their chairs with salutes, their deference to their senior officer fairly evident. I remember closing the door, walking to the study and sitting down. Numbed by the encounter, grief seemed to clog my throat. After Usri had gone home, leaving me in complete solitude, with the earth still trembling beneath my feet, I could think of only person who I could talk to just then—Manas Ghosh, in whose newspaper[26] I used to write a column every Wednesday. Having heard everything, he immediately assured me that he would talk to Trinamool Congress leader Saugata Roy. Within my own limited circle of acquaintances, there have never been many people who I could approach for advice in times of need, or people who understand the language of politics. Most have been people like me, completely ignorant of the workings of the political machinery. Soon enough, Manas Ghosh and Saugata Roy arrived at my place. Hearing of Prasun Mukherjee's visit and our conversation, all Manas Ghosh could do was to shake his head frequently and mutter, 'That's very bad.' However, no matter how hard I try I have never managed to understand whether he had meant to say anything else after that. Saugata Roy, much more forthright, admitted,

'This city seemed so much better with you living here. I will miss you.'

Shocked, with a shaky voice I inquired, 'What do you mean you will miss me? Do you truly believe I will have to leave?'

'The government has told you to leave; they must have done so keeping your security in mind. Where will you go now? To Europe?'

'No. I am not going anywhere.'

Saugata Roy called Priya Ranjan Dasmunsi, who was then the minister of parliamentary affairs and information and broadcasting in the Congress-led UPA government, and we got to know that he had spoken to the papers in my support after the incident at Hyderabad and had demanded the perpetrators be punished. Subsequently, he had had to suffer for his views. When asked what those consequences had been, I was greeted with silence—evidence enough that opposition from fellow party members, especially the Muslims, had forced him to change his stance.

Since Prasun Mukherjee himself had come to warn me, both the men were convinced that there were tensions simmering in the city, even if the city itself seemed totally at peace. To everyone what had been evident was that the commissioner of police had come to me, and that was no small thing. They were sure that my security situation was too dire and the entire urban police force would be unable to protect a single individual; so it was perfectly justified to ask me to leave. Thus convinced, the only help the two felt they could offer me was their sympathies. Perhaps just to that end, they admitted that it was too late to debate over this and that we should continue the conversation the next day. It was mutually decided that we would reconvene in my study to figure out if there was any way to save me. I spent the entire night in distress. As planned, the two of them came the next day but we still could not find a possible way out of my predicament. Finally, I took a firm stand on my own—I was not going to go anywhere.

Meanwhile, another incident had taken Kolkata by storm. A poor Muslim boy named Rizwanur had fallen in love with Priyanka, a rich Hindu girl, and the couple eloped and got married under the Special Marriage Act. Soon enough, the girl went back home to her family and Rizwanur was found dead. The incident had created an uproar in the city, with some calling the death a suicide and some alleging murder. Senior police officials had apparently interfered in the personal lives of two consenting adults, and had even called the couple to the police headquarters at Lalbazar for interrogation. The media reported relentlessly on the scandal, with all accusing fingers pointed firmly at the police, especially the commissioner and two senior officers. Despite the trouble in his own life, Prasun Mukherjee still found the time to call me to remind me that I had to leave soon. The conversation, this time telephonic, went thus:

CP: Hello!

TN: Hello! I trust everything is well.

CP: Is that possible any longer? You must have seen it on TV, all that is happening. Rubbish! Anyway, why are you not leaving?

TN: Where should I go?

CP: Wherever you can. How many times do I have to tell you that staying here will only serve to invite trouble and probably incite a riot! The Muslim organizations are planning something big. You don't understand . . .

TN: I don't have anywhere I can go.

CP: But you have to go somewhere!

TN: If I don't have anywhere I can go, what am I supposed to do?

CP: Why are you not going to Kerala?

TN: The same thing will happen there. Why should the Government of Kerala want to bear my burden? Wouldn't they be afraid too, like you, that something might happen? You can't give me adequate security, so how can we assume they can? The government there knows I live in West Bengal. I go there for a couple of days for events and such; why should they take responsibility for me?

CP: Hmm. Then you will have to keep the visit a secret.

TN: How do I do that! They won't let me keep it a secret! Someone will get to know.

CP: Why can't it be kept a secret? Just don't tell anyone!

TN: I don't go around telling people things. These things cannot be kept hidden. I don't think we can do something so big like moving to another state in secret. The Government of Kerala will not be fine with this and I cannot go anywhere without being sure that I will get proper security. Taking such a risk is out of the question.

CP: Can't you go somewhere like Thailand or Singapore?

TN: How? I don't know anyone there. And where would I stay; it's not as if I have tonnes of money that I can spend on hotels.

CP: You don't understand! They are calling for strikes!

TN: I don't think they are that big an organization.

CP: At least can't you go to Santiniketan?

TN: Santiniketan?

CP: Don't you have anyone you know there?

TN: No, I don't.

CP: You have so many friends. None of them has a house there?

TN: Some of them do. But how can I just ask them? Why don't you ask someone? Sunilda has a house there too! If arrangements can be made, I can go there.

CP: You will have to leave Kolkata. Think about it, where you can go. Let me know at the earliest, we must not delay any further.

TN: I will try.

Bewildered, I tried to wrack my brains, to come up with a place I could go. I still could not shake the feeling that nothing bad would happen. I had spent years walking the streets of Kolkata without any security guards; that would not have been possible if there indeed had been so many enemies. At any rate, there would at least have been attacks if that were true. I was confused but there was no one at hand who I could seek out for advice or support. The few I did speak to could not understand my predicament or, if they did, did not know how to respond. A few days later, Prasun Mukherjee called again, this time coming right to the point:

CP: The CM has ordered you to go to Kerala as soon as possible. Leave today, if you can.

TN: Kerala?

CP: Yes. He has had a word with the Government of Kerala and all arrangements have been made for your security. You have to go.

TN: And what happens when the people there get to know? There are Islamic fundamentalists in Kerala too, you know. Do you expect them to just sit quietly and watch?

Do you expect the people threatening me in Kolkata to be quiet too? Won't they pursue me to Kerala for vengeance?

CP: You have to go, it doesn't matter how. The CM has ordered it.

TN: I understand that. But I have to think about my life first. I can't wander off to die just because all of you have asked me to! You have to officially inform me that I have to leave Kolkata. Otherwise, if I die in Kerala, as in if I am murdered there, everyone will blame me. They will say I had lost my mind to have left Kolkata and gone off to Kerala! Without knowing the reason behind my decision, everyone will make me responsible for what happens. If I have to go I will tell everyone that I am going; I will not run away and hide.

CP: No! The entire thing has to be kept confidential. No one must know!

TN: That's not as easy as it might seem. People know me, they will recognize me. I cannot hide myself anywhere, and neither do I wish to. I never lie and even if I stay silent, they will guess the reason. Why should I leave the state in secret, not tell anyone why I am going, and go to die in Kerala? They will think I chose to die! Instead, let me tell everyone everything.

CP: No! It must be kept a secret!

TN: But I don't want to keep it a secret! I want to tell everyone. So, either you will do it or I will. Either you tell everyone that the police cannot guarantee my security and hence you have asked me to leave the city, or I will.

CP: Fine, I will do it.

As he hung up in anger, I was filled with a strange sense of contentment because I had been able to say what had to be said. Having already lost everything in life, I had nothing to lose. I had done nothing that could require me to leave one city in secret to hide myself in a deep hole in another.

A few days later I got a call from Sunil Gangopadhyay, who had always had the best of relations with the Left. We had been friends for a long time too.

SG: Taslima? This is Sunilda.

TN: How are you, Sunilda? It has been so long. I hope you are well.

SG: Yes, I am doing well. How are you?

TN: I am not doing so well, Sunilda, they are not letting me leave the house.

SG: Hmm . . .

TN: Whenever I ask to be let out, they inform me that it's not possible. How can someone live like this? I hope you can understand how suffocated I feel.

SG: That is why I have called. I have received news that the police have chanced upon a tip about a group of non-Bengali Muslims who have made plans to assassinate you. The best course of action for you, right now, would be to go somewhere abroad.

TN: I know. I have had a conversation about this with Mr Mukherjee. He has advised me to do the same. But Sunilda, aren't there Islamic radicals everywhere in the world? Aren't there zealots in Europe and America? There will be a risk irrespective of where I go. And why should I leave? If it had been possible for me to go back to Bangladesh, I would have done so a long time ago. I wouldn't have stayed on here despite the attacks and the insults. I don't have a place where I can go! I had cut off all my ties with Europe thinking that I would live in

Kolkata. I have lived abroad for a long time and I don't wish to do so again. If someone wishes to murder me in Kolkata, then let them go ahead. I won't leave.

SG: I feel you should reconsider.

TN: I already have Sunilda. I don't have anywhere to go. If I have to die, I will die in this city.

SG: Fine. There's hardly anything else I can say to that. Take care.

TN: Yes. You too.

His call shook me right down to my core. I realized that the chief minister was using Prasun Mukherjee, Sunil Gangopadhyay and others like them to convince me to leave Kolkata.

A few days later an even more renowned figure called—Buddhadeb Basu.[27] Unfortunately, he had nothing new to tell me except to ask me to leave like the others had done. Basu even confessed that he had had a word with the chief minister and the latter was firmly of the opinion that I should leave.

The next call, a while later, came from the landlord's wife. Though Dr Debal Sen had been the landlord on paper, it had been his wife Sharmila Sen who had always been my point of contact. She had always been warm and cordial. After a couple of months of my stay, she had increased the rent from 18,000 rupees to 20,000, having already informed me that the initial price was a little lower than the market rate for the house. I had immediately consented to the increase. Besides, there had been a maintenance fee of around 2500 rupees. All in all, for 22,500 rupees per month, I had a fantastic little house to myself and it had served me quite well. But I must admit that the facilities a tenant usually enjoys were mostly not available for me. The intercom had worked only for a few days before breaking down and no amount of complaints had succeeded in getting someone to fix it. I had had to maintain some old termite-infested pieces of furniture left behind by the owners and, under the guise of a prayer room, a storage space stuffed with the owner's personal papers, etc. I had never made a fuss about these things; Mrs Sen had told me she had no space back home and I had complied. In order to make the house habitable, I had had to get a bunch of old broken things repaired with my own money, and I had never mentioned those either. Debal Sen was a respected cardiologist and photographer. He had gifted me a copy of his book of wildlife photography and I must confess that I had found it to be the work of a skilled professional and not an amateur effort. I remember seeing this genial, considerate man change over the course of three years.

Every six months I used to have to renew my residence permit in order to be able to stay on in the city. This required something called a 'proof of address' to certify that I was not a terrorist, that I had an 'address' in Kolkata. The electricity bill of the rented house had been in Dr Sen's name, so he had always signed my 'proof of address' on my behalf. As the pressure to leave gradually grew, one fine morning he refused to sign the document certifying my address—in fact, it seemed he had seen the piece of paper for the first time, an unrecognizable foreign object. Soon after, Sharmila Sen, who had always been effusive in her praise of how carefully and beautifully I had maintained the house, called to inform me that I would have to leave the house. Her voice, over the telephone line, had sounded a little odd:

Sharmila Sen (SS): You will have to leave my house.
TN: What! What does that mean?

SS: Please try to understand . . . I have found a tenant who
is willing to pay more for the house. I want to accept the
offer. He wants to take possession next month.

TN: But you cannot do this! I have to find another place
first! Otherwise, where will I go?

SS: It would be best if you can vacate the house by the end of
this month. You have a lot of friends, why don't you ask
some of them to find you a house?

TN: Fine, let me look for a house. I will leave as soon as I
find one.

SS: The thing is, the rent that you are paying is too low for
a place like this.

TN: How much rent are you expecting? If I pay you that
amount, I'm assuming you won't ask me to leave.

SS: It's 50,000; you can have it for 45.

I was stunned. I had never heard of house rent increasing
from 20,000 to 45,000 rupees in one such leap.

TN: As far as I knew, rent can be increased by a couple of
thousand rupees. How can you ask for more than double
the present sum?

SS: I have to, I can't help it. If someone is willing to pay me
so much money, why should I not take it? He wants to
see the house tomorrow.

TN: Let him. But you have to give me time until I find a
new place.

SS: Please hurry then!

She called again, a few days later, to repeat the same thing:
'Please leave the house.' Gradually, the frequency of the
calls increased, till they almost became a daily affair. The

conversation, however, remained the same: 'Please leave the house.' I began to wonder if Buddhadeb Bhattacharya had deployed them too to convince me to leave. In fact, someone had mentioned Dr Sen's close ties with the government!

DGP Vineet Goel had always been pretty respectful. Eventually, as he began to call me up, I could sense his voice gradually changing—the language, the tone, and the intent, all quite different from before.

Vineet Goel (VG): You have to go away somewhere.

TN: What do you mean?

VG: The city is in a bad state. Go away for some time.

TN: But the city seems like it always does! I don't see anything wrong!

VG: There is going to be a large protest march against you.

TN: I have to leave the city because of that? There are so many protest marches in the city every day, against so many people! Do they all leave the city?

VG: I am telling you this for your own good. Do you not want the security we are providing you? If there is unrest, we will have to remove all the security arrangements in place. How do you plan to live in this city then?

The growing darkness began to swell, threatening to devour me.

Death Waits Past the Window

The senior officials of the police were determined to instil in me a paralysing fear of death—that it surrounded me, hounding my every move, and waiting to pounce upon me. They left death behind for me, as a constant, unyielding companion. It had been injected into my veins, a horrifying image stealthily planted in my head—a horde of Islamic radicals storming into my house, pelting me with bullets, ripping my flesh open with a thousand cuts, decapitating me, dismembering me, dancing and celebrating in glee over the pieces of my body. Day in and day out, this macabre scene would keep replaying in my head; looking out of the window, instead of the sky, I would see haunting visions of my lifeless body. Standing near the hasnuhana in the balcony, I would only see the plant wet with blood, the red staining everything around it. Sitting in that lonely room, forced into house arrest, I wrote about death.

Death

1.

Death waits past the window.
As soon as I open the door

We will come face to face,
Unfazed, it might even come and sit beside me,
Perhaps even hold my hand.
Just so, the very next moment
It can drag me off to nothingness.
Every waking moment it seems to be laughing at me
From the shadows,
I hear it in the water splashing in the shower
Or on lonely afternoons,
When it comes and whispers in my ear.
At night I stay awake,
In the din made by its absolute stillness.

It follows me as I walk out of my room,
Follows me wherever I go, the palace or the slum,
Turning as I turn, seeing what I see,
Sticking so close that when I open my mouth
I breathe it in a little every time.
Can someone live with so much death?
It seems, to get away from death
I must take refuge in death.
What choice do I have otherwise!

2.

Let me live a few more days, a few more months,
Or a few more years, my love.
Let me live at least for two more,
Let me finish all my work,
And I will never turn you down again.

It will be best if you give me five—

Would you be so kind?
After all, what have I ever done to you?
I have never spoken against death,
Never written a contrary word either.
How much can I finish in five?
Now, if I had gotten eight or nine,
I wouldn't make excuses any longer—
After all, we all have to make do with what we have.

Ten would be best, but would you even consider it?
Even you have a life,
Why should you linger and wait for me?
But if you do, if you do agree,
Then hear me one last time.
Just two more years, for a round twelve;
I know that too will be gone in a flash.
Though we had met about twelve years ago,
It seems just the other day,
And I haven't blinked once, haven't looked away.
Do you see how swiftly the years have passed?
Oh lovely death, give me fifteen more years,
And those too shall pass just as fast.

I can no longer tell what is in store,
As you surround me from all sides
Would I have begged if I had been free?
No, I would have lived as I pleased.
They do not wish for me to live any more,
And as you loom over me, poised to strike,
I am reminded of how things have changed.
Even you wish to live; even Death wishes for life.

As for me, I count my days and years by your grace,
My debts not to life, but to your kind mercy.
So let me live a while longer, my love,
That I may write to my heart's content, all that I wish against
you.

3.

They have brought out the spears and pitchforks,
Swords and poisonous snakes,
Hatred and religion,
And myriad other weapons—
To kill me and save their faith.
For a thousand years, men have killed for their faith,
They have spread their faith across continents,
By missives composed in blood.
For a thousand years, men have placed their faith above
humanity.
Men have written the sacred books,
Given these lifeless tomes life
So they may devour people in turn.
If faith, bound and gagged, had been free,
It would have railed and cursed, and killed itself in shame.
Two thousand years ago, before it all began,
Faith would have died to save humanity.

4.

There is nothing on the other side, no one—
In fact, there is no other side.
Death will not take me to the hereafter,

Or to some seat of judgement, or a door,
Beyond which lies eternal flames and pestilence
Or the eternal blessing of Paradise.

Once I leave this world
My body will lie in the morgue for a while,
They will cut it open,
And then my bones would be sold,
Cheaper by the dozen
Till, one fine day
That too has crumbled to dust, and ceased to be.

Those who believe in the hereafter,
Let them go and embrace death,
And knock on the bejewelled door;
Infinite wealth, wine and women, await them inside.
Let me be in this world, in the forest,
The mountains, and the fuming sea,
Let me sleep on the grass, wake by the songs of the birds
And wrap the sunlight around me like a quilt.
Let me laugh, let me love under the moon,
Let me walk in the crowd, in the sun and the rain,
Let me live.

Those who are happy with the other side, let them be happy.
If I have to, let me bear my burdens on this earth,
My here and my hereafter.

5.

I have cried for life simply because you stand waiting past
my door.

Our eyes meet, every now and then, you smile shyly,
And I know you love me; that you want me.

If you hadn't wanted to kiss me,
Would I have begged to love?
If you hadn't been waiting,
Would I have dug my heels into the earth?
Would I have backed up to the wall? Tried to grab and hold
on?
If you hadn't reached out for me
Would I have run amok, in search of life?

If death had not stood waiting at my door,
I would never have pushed it away, would never have run.
Rather, I would have searched the world, and brought it back
home.

Exiled

In a daze, I have begun speaking to myself. I have begun to remind myself that I was not born in India, though there is no way, be it in my education, my tastes or my cultural heritage, that anyone can justifiably say I am not Indian. If I had been born a few years earlier, I could have been a citizen of India; my father had been born before the Partition. India's political history forced my father to live through three changes in his citizenship status, and it has forced me to do the same twice.

Once upon a time, there lived a Hindu farmer called Haradhan Sarkar in a remote village in erstwhile East Bengal. One of his sons had converted to Islam for some unknown reason. I don't remember his name. Perhaps it had been Jatindra, which became Jamir, or Kamal, which became Kamaal. I have descended from that line of the Sarkars, going back nearly six generations to Haradhan. The latter's children must have migrated to India after the Partition, becoming citizens of independent India, while my grandfather, Jamir or Kamaal Sarkar, had stayed back because of his Muslim first name.

When I was a child, I had been told that it was impossible for Muslims to ever be united—they have always fought among each other, like the Muslims of East Pakistan had fought their counterparts in West Pakistan over secularism and the Bengali national identity. Though I was born after the Partition, I had always nursed a strong attraction for the idea of an undivided India and Bengal, having even written poems and stories about it in my youth, much before my first visit to India. I have never given credence to the idea of a barbed frontier between people of similar languages and cultures, between families.

In fact, right from my childhood, I have never been religious—this has led me to consciously invest in ideals of humanism and feminism. My father had not been religious either, perhaps one of the things that unconsciously fed into my world view. That is how I grew up, overcoming superstitions, customs and institutions steeped in misogyny. When I first came to India in 1989, it never felt to me that West Bengal, or any other part of India for that matter, were places in a foreign land. The day I first stepped on this soil, from that day onwards, I have believed that I belong to an undivided nation, where it is impossible to distinguish between India and Bangladesh. Not because of my Hindu ancestors, or the similarities in culture, or because I look Indian and speak one of the many languages spoken in India—it's because the very essence of being Indian is deeply entrenched within me. Similarly entrenched is an awareness of Indian history, be it as a victim of history or as someone who has been enriched by it to whatever insignificant degree. I have been a victim of poverty, colonialism, religious diversity, intolerance, greed, communal hostility between the Hindu majority and the Muslim minority, violence, the Partition, the mass exodus thereafter, the Two Nation Theory, the gradual breakdown of democracy, the ever-prevalent caste system, riots, pogroms

and wars—it is these events which have given shape to
what it means for me to be Indian. In addition to this, the
fundamentalism, the terrorism, the corruption, the poverty
and the perpetual deprivation that constitute the state of
Bangladesh has further added to my experience.

I was exiled from Bangladesh, once a fragment of India's
history, by the blindness, lack of knowledge and intolerance
of the Islamic radicals. The doors of my country having closed
for me, I had knocked on India's gates. The day those gates
opened to let me in, it did not feel even for a moment that
I was migrating to a foreign land. Why is it that even today
I consider other Asian countries or Europe and America to
be foreign lands, but never so with India? Even after having
lived almost a dozen years in Europe, I was never able to
fully accept it as home; in India, it did not even take a year
for me to get so deeply attached. This could only have
happened because of the shared sense of history that I have
always felt with the people here; after all, the forefathers of
Bangladesh were originally people from India who had been
converted to Islam on Indian soil. If forces of intolerance and
fundamentalism are ascendant in Bangladesh because of the
pervasive corruption and cowardice of its political leaders, if
ideals of democracy, freedom of speech and free thought are
being summarily ignored, if a lynch mob is demanding the
head of a writer who has been advocating human rights, then
who must accept the responsibility of coming to her aid—
should it be Europe and America, or should it be secular
India?

At such a time of need, India had barred its gates to me,
and Europe had welcomed me with open arms. However,
in European society I had always felt like an outsider—so
much so that after coming back to India, it had felt as if a

twelve-year-long deathly spell had broken. The peace and content had perhaps been due to the fact that the social milieu had appeared familiar, much like the one I had grown up in. I was writing like before, was trying to contribute to society in my own way, and working towards helping women become educated, self-sufficient and aware of their rights and freedom and the ways to fight for the same. I was trying to inspire through my writing a spark of bravado and rebellion that would help women in achieving these goals and end centuries of oppression, torture and fear.

So, it is deeply sad and ironic that whatever had happened to me in Bangladesh is about to happen yet again, in progressive India, that too in the highly progressive state of West Bengal. I have been put under house arrest in this country, and have been repeatedly told that public places are no longer safe for me, and neither are friends' houses. Effectively, I had been hidden away in the dark, while the people who had issued the public threats were allowed to walk, all sins forgiven, with their head held high. They had all the rights—the right to call strikes and disrupt daily life, the right to destroy someone's life in the name of religion, the right to spread terror. On the other hand, those who raised their voices against terrorism, communal hatred, lies and injustice were to be forced into silence. Time and again, I have been warned about radicals marching in protest against me, advised to leave and go somewhere safe and come back only after things calm down. Do things really go back to how they were? I had been told the same thing before being put on that flight out of Bangladesh, and in the next thirteen years nothing had changed. My leaving will be a huge victory for the fundamentalists and a huge setback for supporters of free thought, free speech, democracy and secularism.

This cannot be allowed to happen since the ensuing damage would be more devastating for India than it would be for me. Once such a demand is met, there is no telling what new ones would come up soon—undemocratic assertions would gain ground along with fresh lists of people to exile, arrest, prohibit, burn or kill. The devotees of secularism would gladly accept each and every decree issued by the fundamentalists, not realizing that such acts of capitulation only serve to whet the appetite of fanatic elements for more preposterous claims and dangerous requests.

Never in my dreams did I ever imagine that I would suffer in India as I had suffered in Bangladesh. Unlike Bangladesh, Muslims are a minority here, but certain circumstances remain the same—the fanaticism, the intolerance, the violence, the public executions, the murderous violence and the tendency to rubbish science and development, just to name a few. I often feel the need to ask what purpose would my death serve them; irrespective of their personal gains, even the leaders know that my death would help Islam in no way. Islam would remain the same it has always been, beyond reproach. The faces of extremism, their language, cruelty and aspirations are the same everywhere in the world—they simply desire to push society back by thousands of years, and revel in that power.

Gradually, my world has begun to shrink. Someone like me who used to love to roam around the city has been put in chains; my garrulous mouth has been sewed shut. I am not allowed to go out and join the protest marches, or attend the film, theatre and music festivals. I have been warned to not so much as step out of my dank, suffocating house. No, I do not accept this as my fate. I still believe I can live a normal life. I still believe India will not punish me in a manner reminiscent of communal Bangladesh. I have faith that this country and the love of its people will provide me security, that I will be able to spend the rest of my days here. I love this country, I think of it as my own. If this nation were to disavow me and quash my last bit of hope, it would be akin to death.

I have nowhere else to go, no other country, and no new home. India is my country and my home. I have spoken the truth and consequently I have had to face the wrath of zealots and the shrewd politicians who wish to use them to garner votes. How long will this ordeal last? Despite all the rebukes and insults, I have not been able to fully give up on my dreams yet. I keep dreaming that for an honest, secular writer, India is still the safest nation in the subcontinent.

Farewell, 22 November 2007

A small protest march had been organized in Park Circus the day before—something about the government's actions in Nandigram, the Rizwanur murder, and demands for Taslima Nasrin's exile. About fifty clerics had taken to the streets, none of them with even the slightest intention of calling for a revolution. Perhaps they had been peacefully asleep in their beds when they had been dragged out to the street to march, ending with the police herding the entire lot, along with the leader, into their vans. The leader was previously known to have tried to cause trouble under the guise of 'The All-India Minority Forum'.

Immediately after, however, a group of youths emerged from one of the by-lanes of Park Circus, and amidst raucous laughter began pelting the police with stones and empty Coke bottles. The police just stood there for a while, getting hit, before shooting a few rounds of tear gas to bring the situation under control. The group of lungi-clad boys set fire to a few cars, buses and trucks, attacked a few journalists and broke their cameras—a familiar sequence of events that is more contagious than having any particular reason or motivation behind it, much like beating up a pickpocket. Traffic was diverted from the Park Circus area, causing massive jams throughout the city. A few of the boys were caught on camera holding placards that read: 'Taslima Go Back!' I called up a few friends to inquire who the boys were and almost everyone told me that these boys probably had no clue who I was, nor had they ever heard my name before. Primarily Urdu-speaking uneducated boys from the Bihari community, they were usually petty thieves or pickpockets or daily wage labourers who were doing exactly what they had been told to do, and my friends assured me that I had nothing to worry about. In stunned disbelief, I saw paramilitary forces and the army being deployed to handle the situation, and a citywide curfew was soon declared. At night, CPI(M) State Convener Biman Basu declared to the media: 'If there is unrest because of Taslima Nasrin, she should leave the city immediately.'

The security chief of the police, Vineet Goel, called me the next day to inform me that all plans for my assassination were in place; the radicals would march to my house after the prayers next Friday. Like before, I asked him again, 'Why aren't you arresting them?'

VG: There are reasons.
TN: What reasons? With all of you here, surely they will not
    dare come!
VG: We cannot touch them.
TN: Why?
VG: We can't touch the Muslims. There'll be a riot.
TN: But this is not a Hindu–Muslim issue, it's a terrorism
    issue. If someone's done something wrong, shouldn't
    they be punished? How can the fear of a riot be reason
    enough not to do anything?
VG: No, we can't risk a riot.
TN: Then what do I have to do?

VG: You have to go to Jaipur for two days.

TN: Two days?

VG: Yes, just two days.

TN: Everything will be fine after that?

VG: Sure.

TN: Why Jaipur?

VG: We have a luxury resort there. Go and relax there. We will bring you back after two days.

TN: I will not go to Jaipur. If you cannot give me security in this house, then let me go somewhere else on Friday.

VG: Where?

TN: Behala.

VG: No, we cannot give you any security in Behala. Wherever else you go, it will solely be your responsibility.

TN: Salt Lake?

VG: We cannot give you any security in Salt Lake either. It will be your responsibility.

TN: Then let me go to Belgharia. It's just for a day. My publisher lives there.

VG: No, that's not possible.

TN: Durgapur? Bolpur?

VG: Wherever you go, you will alone be responsible.

TN: You are telling me they have made plans to kill me but you cannot give me any security. Then why was I given protection all this while? Only so that you could cut it off at my time of need? I had no clue about any threats! You informed me that I was in danger! And now you are telling it will be solely my responsibility. I don't know what I am supposed to do here.

VG: Listen to us. Go to Jaipur, it will be for your own good.

TN: What is most surprising is that such a huge police force does not know how to combat the plans made by a handful of men. If it had been sudden, I would have understood. But you are completely aware of everything in this case. And yet you cannot save me?

VG: Sorry, we can't.

The West Bengal Police informed me quite irrevocably that they would not be able to protect me from an attack by the Islamic fundamentalists. Astounded, I tried to make sense of what was happening. I had never asked the government for security but ever since my first visit in 1993, I had always been provided with adequate protection. But this time the same people were informing me that they were not responsible for my security and the only way they would help me was if I consented to leaving West Bengal. Never before had I heard something like that, or faced such behaviour either. I had always considered myself to be an ordinary citizen, never demanding stringent security arrangements or wanting the government to spend its money on me. Like an ordinary citizen, I had only ever craved freedom and a normal life. In the beginning, there used to be quite a few sentries at the door, but eventually the number had dwindled to two. If I had to go out somewhere, a single officer in plain clothes would usually accompany me, but he too would go home at night after bringing me back. The decrease of security personnel from 200 to two had reassured me that I was safe in Kolkata, that the love of the people would keep me secure, and that the number would soon come down to zero. It was a strange turn of events that the administration was threatening to cut off all protective measures after informing me of an impending attack. Why did they do that? They might as well have removed all security arrangements without telling me anything; at least that way, I would have had fewer things to be anxious about.

Around noon, a car came to pick me up for the airport. My brother was with me and we were handed two one-way tickets to Jaipur. A throng of policemen was there to see me off as I boarded the flight. They stood there perhaps till the plane vanished from the Kolkata sky, their way of bidding me a silent farewell. Neither was I aware that the conspiracy to drive me out of Bengal had finally succeeded that day.

There was a sea of policemen at the Jaipur airport. Apparently, they had received the news about my arrival only a short while back; the Kolkata Police had simply told them that I was going to attend a literary event. They took me to a cheap hotel which they said had been booked from Kolkata. It definitely was not the luxury resort that I had been promised; rather, it quite resembled the inexpensive, run-down, riverside shanty hotels of Mymensingh in Bangladesh. Considering I had never been fortunate enough to have stayed in such a hotel, one could chalk it down as an experience. The police began asking me questions about when my event was going to be.

TN: But I don't have an event to attend.
Police (P): Then why have you come here?
TN: They have sent me here from Kolkata.
P: Who has sent you?
TN: Kolkata Police.
P: Why have they sent you?
TN: I don't know. They told me I had to go away to Jaipur for two days.
P: They have informed our CM that you have an event to attend here.
TN: There is no event.

They continued talking among themselves in Rajasthani. Time and again, one of them would come up and ask me about the event details only for me to repeat that there was no event. Each time it agitated them and they would ask me the same questions all over again. The crowd of journalists and cameras outside only added to the growing anxiety among the officers. I would not have known about the cameras had I not switched on the television in the hotel room. The news channels were all talking about me—everything from the hotel I was in to the room number; the latter bit of information even I had not been privy to. I parted the curtains to be met with the sight of a mass of cameras, all relentlessly trained towards my window. I began to tremble. Even after knowing that the fanatics were baying for my blood, how could the media reveal my location on national television? Was the point then to invite the extremists to hunt me down and tear me to pieces on live television? A grand adventure they would be able to telecast throughout the day to soaring ratings and viewership?

Restless, I began to call various people but not a single officer of the Kolkata Police picked up my calls. The police officers in Jaipur could not understand English or Hindi. Confounded, I began to think of ways I could convince the media outside to stop the live updates of my impending doom. Unable to sleep, my thoughts were interrupted by loud banging on the door at about one at night. Calling out, I realized it was the police.

P: Open the door!
TN: No, I won't. Who are you?
P: I am a senior police officer. You have to leave our state immediately.

TN: I can't understand what you are saying.

P: Open the door!

TN: I am sorry. But it's too late and I won't open the door. Come and speak to me in the morning.

P: It can't be said in the morning. You have to leave right now. It's the CM's orders.

TN: Please call me from the reception and we can talk.

The senior officer called me from the reception.

P: You have to check out of the hotel right now.

TN: Where will I go so late at night?

P: That is entirely your problem.

TN: There is no flight to Kolkata now.

P: We don't know anything about all that. We just know that you cannot stay in Rajasthan.

TN: Why not?

P: It might agitate the Muslims in this state. It might escalate to a law-and-order situation. So the CM has ordered you to leave Rajasthan.

TN: Have there been problems already?

P: No, but there might be. It's just a matter of time.

TN: So, you are asking me to leave based on something that 'might be'?

P: Yes.

TN: Fine, I will leave the hotel. But not before it's morning. I will go straight to the airport to catch a flight to Kolkata.

P: We can't let this go on till morning. You have to leave before that, before sunrise.

TN: How long before the sunrise?

P: You have to leave before five.

TN: Fine, I will.

P: Come down to the reception at around five minutes to five. A car will be waiting to take you to the airport.

Hanging up, I felt relief wash over me. It was best that I left such a much-publicized address as soon as possible. Besides, the incident gave me a perfect reason to fly straight back to Kolkata. I tried sleeping for a while but my brother spent the night awake, sitting on the bed. He has always been a lot like our father; if Dad had to go anywhere in the morning, he always used to stay up and wait for the dawn.

Walking down to the desk at five in the morning, I was met by a throng of policemen and journalists. Pushing through the jostling crowd, the police managed to get me into the car, and the convoy set off—our car, flanked by a row of police cars, and the media bringing up the rear. After a while, when the car showed no signs of stopping or slowing, it began to seem to me that something was not quite right. The airport was not supposed to be so far away! I tried asking: 'Why is it taking us so long to reach the airport?'

The police in the car were large, thug-like men with thick moustaches, some in the front seat and some in the rear, with me and my brother in the middle. Getting no answer to my question, I tried again and again, but each time in vain:

TN: Why is it taking us so long to reach the airport? The airport isn't so far away!

P: We are not going to the airport.

TN: Then where are we going?

P: To Delhi.

TN: But why?

They remained quiet.

TN: Why am I being taken to Delhi instead of Kolkata? I want to return to Kolkata. Take me to the airport.

They still remained quiet.

Assuming they did not speak English I asked my brother, who spoke the language far better than me, to repeat the questions in Hindi. That didn't yield a different result however: the men began to speak among themselves in Rajasthani, seemingly having forgotten or resolved to ignore our existence in the car.

The day had begun to break and the car was speeding down the highway, cutting through the sleepy landscape. The police were occasionally looking back to check if we were being followed. All of a sudden one of the men turned around and spoke in Hindi:

P: We are going to Delhi because those are our orders.
TN: Whose orders?

He fell quiet again.

TN: I am supposed to go back to Kolkata. Why am I being taken to Delhi?
P: We don't know anything.
TN: Why am I being taken to Kolkata?

The police remained quiet.

TN: If we are going to Delhi, then why are we going by car? Why not take a flight?

After repeating the question nearly five times, we were finally given a monosyllabic answer: 'Security'.

Meanwhile, I received a call from Kolkata letting me know that a team of representatives from the Delhi bureau of Star Ananda was in pursuit of our car and my ordeal was being telecast live on their channel. We were sure the car had already left Jaipur—we had been told we were headed to Delhi—but we couldn't figure out where exactly we were going. Soon I received an agitated phone call from one of the journalists following our car:

Journalist (J): 'Didi, where are they taking you?'
TN: I don't know! They have told me we are headed towards Delhi but I don't know why.
J: This is my phone number, didi. Please keep me updated. We are with you every step of the way, please don't worry.
TN: I will take the morning flight to Kolkata. That is what I had discussed with the Rajasthan Police. I am confused as to why they are taking me to Delhi now.
J: We are here; let's see where things are headed. Don't worry, have faith in us. Not just me but thousands of people like me deeply respect you, didi!

The term of endearment he used and the Bengali language served to calm me down a little. The fact that I was not alone in this ordeal, that there was someone with me every step of the way, went a long way in lessening my anxieties for a while.

After travelling a fair bit, the car suddenly came to a halt at a desolate parking lot behind a motel. Barring one single officer, the rest of them got out and left, without so much as a word, leaving us to wait. None of them came back, however, and half an hour later a new group of officers came and took their place and we set out on our journey again. A while later, I received another call from the journalist I had spoken to earlier:

J: 'Didi, the police have dragged us out of our cars and beaten us up. They have herded all of us inside a motel room and locked us in.'

TN: What are you saying! This is terrible!

J: They won't let us follow you.

TN: But how can they beat people up?

J: They thrashed us mercilessly.

TN: How will you guys get out?

J: We don't know. It seems they have told the hotel not to unlock the door.

Eventually, I tried asking the police again where they were taking me to in Delhi and if there was a place that had been designated. There was only one officer in the group, thick moustache and thug-like demeanour, who could answer questions in Hindi, though it did not seem he was interested in answering any of mine.

P: No. You have to arrange for the place. We will just escort you to Delhi.

TN: You will hand me over to the police in Delhi, right? As in, hand me over to a security detail?

P: We will take you to whichever address you want to go in Delhi. Do you know the name of the hotel?

TN: But I don't have an address in Delhi!

P: What do you not have?

TN: Address!

I finally decided to call Mr B, the only high-ranking bureaucrat in the Bengal government I knew. A very busy and influential man, before he could ask anything, I informed him of the entire sequence of events.

TN: They sent me away from Kolkata. I reached Jaipur last night. Now, early in the morning, they are taking me to Delhi. I have been asking them to let me fly back to Kolkata. I don't know why I am being sent to Delhi so abruptly. They are saying they haven't spoken to the Delhi police regarding anything. They are asking me where I want to go.

Mr B assured me he would find out everything about Rajasthan, why I was being sent off to Delhi and let me know very soon. He never did, unfortunately. Instead, his secretary called to inform me that I should tell the Rajasthan Police officers to drop me off at a police station in Delhi where Mr B's men would pick me up. 'Then let them take me to the airport directly. I will catch a flight to Kolkata,' I said to Mr B's secretary. 'This is ridiculous. If they don't want me to stay in Jaipur for two days, then they might as well just let me get back to Kolkata. Wouldn't that solve every problem? Now I have to go to Delhi first, and then to Kolkata. Was all this necessary?' The secretary simply made a non-committal noise. I continued, 'Is the airport very far from Delhi city? I don't remember too well. I can catch a flight today itself, can't I?'

'Reach Delhi first. We will take it from there,' she replied.

Yet again, the car stopped en route and the officers left abruptly, this time all of them. They came back a while later, now dressed in plain clothes. As I sat wondering why they had taken their uniforms off, my brother informed me in a hoarse whisper that they had taken off the number plates of the cars too. Turning around on my seat, I realized that at least the car in front and the one behind were also missing their number plates. At the same time, I could overhear two stocky officers telling the others to hide their rifles so that no one could guess they were carrying firearms. This done, they turned towards us menacingly to tell us to switch our mobile phones off. Before I could protest, one of them shouted, 'You still haven't switched it off? Do it right now!' The policeman who was driving glanced back, and I could not figure out if the gaze was predatory, resentful or plain angry.

The long day passed and yet Delhi was nowhere in sight. Suddenly, glancing at the signposts by the road I realized that we were, in fact, going the other way, away from Delhi. Eventually, the car turned off the main road and took a circuitous route through fields, ditches and farmlands, navigation almost becoming impossible. My throat was already parched from a paralysing fear that had begun to take hold, and I started to suspect that these men were not police officers at all but goons who had kidnapped me. Were these agents of the ISI (Inter-Services Intelligence) or something like that? They had kidnapped me from Jaipur by some clever ruse and were taking me to a jungle in some distant village where they would dump my dead body; I would rot there and no one would ever know—a million such thoughts were racing through my head.

We had long since turned away from Delhi and it was obviously not possible to find out where we were being taken. The men were talking to each other in Rajasthani, glancing at us from time to time. The driver was still staring at me as if he could eat me alive, also making sure if I was where I was, if the other men were where they should be, if the car following us was fine, and if there was any other vehicle in pursuit. I was convinced by then that these men were my soon-to-be assassins—my phone was switched off, my brother was scared stiff, I was silent, the cars had no plates, and the laughing policemen were not in uniform. There clearly was no point in asking them anything and I could not send a surreptitious text to anyone either. Discussing anything with my brother was already out of the question. Soon we reached a lone, desolate house in the middle of nowhere. Not a single other human being in sight, we were led inside a room and asked to wait. Feeling my blood pressure rising ever so gradually, I stole into the bathroom and made a furtive distress call to an acquaintance of Mr B: 'I think I have been kidnapped. I'm sure these are Islamic radicals. They have brought me to this abandoned house in the middle of a jungle, far away from Delhi, to kill me. I'm so scared.' The acquaintance consulted Mr B and informed me after a while that they did not believe I had been kidnapped, and asked me to remain calm. Their words somehow managed to reassure me and I took a deep breath to calm myself. For the past few hours, fear and anxiety had ravaged my nerves. I let go of the breath I seemed to have held back in the car and tried to relax.

One of the men came back to inform us that a few police officers were on their way from Jaipur to meet me. The mortal fear I had felt at the sight of these men, like a vulture perched on my head and boring into my skull, was no longer there. At dinner, they informed me that they had taken off the number plates and changed their clothes to evade the journalists who had been following us, to ensure that no one could identify the car I was in. They also explained why the plan of taking me directly to Delhi had been altered. I must admit I could not fathom the reason for this degree of secrecy that made it necessary for all this to happen without my knowledge.

I have never been good at subterfuge. Besides, linguistic barriers can be a huge impediment to human interactions.

We set off for Delhi quite peacefully, accompanied by four officers. One of them, fortuitously, turned out to be Bengali and I spent much of the journey talking to him, learning a lot of things I had previously not been aware of—especially about the BJP-led government in Rajasthan and its female CM, Vasundhara Raje.

The car finally came to a stop in front of the Rajasthan House in Delhi. Despite the security precautions taken to avoid the journalists, there was still a sea of cameras we had to wade through as I was escorted out of the car and taken to a suite on the first floor of the building. There I was to stay the night, before being moved to a safe house the day after, or so Mr B told me over the phone. He also informed me that someone was already on their way with clothes, etc.

TN: Why clothes?

B: Won't you need some? Have you got any with you?

TN: No, I just have my laptop.

B: You will be provided clothes and anything else you might need. The officers will reach you shortly. They will take care of you.

TN: But I am supposed to return to Kolkata. I don't need clothes or anything else; I can return tomorrow if that's all right. I can pass this one night in what I have.

B: No, you can't come back to Kolkata right now. You will be taken to another house tomorrow. We have made all the arrangements.

TN: Another house?

B: Yes, a safe house.

TN: But . . .

B: Stay there. The food and everything else will be good, I assume. There won't be any problems, and call me if you need anything.

TN: Fine.

The food was indeed good. All of us sat down for dinner in the drawing room of the suite booked for me.

The next morning, a couple of central government officers arrived as promised, some old and some young. It became apparent soon enough that the officers from Jaipur were not taking very kindly to the new arrivals, picking fights and skirmishes constantly. My brother had immersed himself in television, especially the Bengali news channels where constant news updates of me were being telecast, and burning questions were being asked about my well-being and whereabouts. I was asked by Mr B's officers to stay strictly away from the media, warning me of the possible dangers if I revealed anything to the journalists. On the other hand, the officers from Jaipur had drawn me aside to tell me to talk to at least a select few journalists from the many who had been camping outside my doors for over a day. Dazed and confused, pulled in two directions by two opposing demands, I decided to stick to what Mr B's officers had asked me to do, simply because of his involvement.

The officers from Jaipur had initially told me that they would go back to Rajasthan the next day, after my departure for the safe house. The next day, however, the officers from Delhi came and informed me that it would take them another day to find a suitable safe house. Forced to stay behind, the entire set-up around me too—the police, the journalists stationed outside, my brother parked in front of the TV—fell into a simple routine. While most of the news telecasts were primarily discussing my plight and how I had been driven out of Kolkata, Star Ananda had apparently sent a team to Bangladesh, to interview my family and relatives back in Mymensingh. My brother, already overwhelmed, looked equally elated and saddened on seeing his wife and children after such a long ordeal.

The central government officers, meanwhile, had been persistent in their warnings against interacting with the media, just as their Jaipur counterparts were trying to make me do the opposite. At one point, taking advantage of the former's absence, the latter had allowed a photographer to enter my room under the guise of an official photographer for the Rajasthan House. I have later seen in newspapers the photos he took. Similarly, without even asking me, they allowed Barkha Dutt of NDTV inside my room in the dead of night—knowing fully well that I had refused all the other journalists without a word, had stopped taking phone calls or listening to people's requests. Shocked at the sudden intrusion of a journalist and a camera in my room, I firmly stood my ground and refused to give in. Needless to say, the officers from Jaipur were surprised that I could not recognize Dutt, one of India's most well-known journalists. To be honest, I did not recognize her, just as I had not known who Karan Thapar was before meeting him. When Karan had initially asked for an interview, I had bluntly refused and he had had to travel to Kolkata instead. Not even during the interview had I realized I was talking to someone renowned. It was not until later, after I had heard more about him, read his columns for the *Hindustan Times* and seen his show *The Devil's Advocate* on CNN-IBN that I had gathered how famous he was.

Barkha tried her best to convince me to speak to her—it would help if people knew the truth, it would garner public support for me, and so on. While I was sure that I did not want to go against what Mr B had told me, it became a little awkward nevertheless because of the constant pressure I was being subjected to from the Jaipur crew. After a lot of requests, while I was still not ready for an interview, I agreed to speak to her just to make one statement: 'I want to return to Kolkata.'

A BJP politician came to visit but no real conversation took place. On the other hand, Tara Gandhi, Mahatma Gandhi's granddaughter came to see me and we ended up having a long chat. She had brought a handwoven bag as a gift for me and though this was the first time we had met, she assured me that she would keep in touch. I had only known her brother, Gopalkrishna Gandhi, the Governor of West Bengal, socially, having read poetry to him once at Raj Bhavan. He had appreciated and praised it and we had later spoken when I had been put under house arrest. I remember him being very angry back then; he had asked me to alert the Centre about everything immediately. Back then, any talk of the Centre used to mean only one thing to me—Mr B. He had always been the person I would talk to, and share everything with. I had shared this too with him and he had assured me he would look into it.

On the very first day, CM Vasundhara Raje had declared that I could live in the Rajasthan House for as long as I wished to. The officers, too, had assured me of the same. Three days later, the same people informed me that I would have to check out of the Rajasthan House immediately as per the CM's orders. I straightaway called Mr B's men to alert them about the ultimatum. I may be worldly-wise but I have never been politically savvy. For my life I could not fathom why the men, who had thus far been so courteous to me, were now so angry that their voices had hardened and their behaviour towards me had become visibly insolent. I did, however, manage to understand that they were not happy with the fact that I had listened to the officers from Delhi and avoided speaking to the journalists. Their motivations were simple: in the worst of times, when even the media was completely willing to take my side, why was I hell-bent on alienating and upsetting them? If the media were to support me, no government or political party would be able to harm me, but if there was no support, then anyone could play any sort of political games with me. They wanted me to tell everyone how the CPI(M) had driven me out of Bengal, to reveal everything in order to garner public sympathy and support. They tried very hard to convince me that the people of India loved and supported me and that I should use the media to get close to them. Consequently, the implications at that point were simple: that I had been wrong and that I should have spoken to a chosen few journalists.

I never listened to them. The only person I consented to meet was Sheela Reddy from *Outlook* magazine, not for an interview but as a routine visit. I had written a series of articles for *Outlook* previously. She repeated the same thing to me, that as long as the media was by my side the government would not be able to do anything. However, what I could not come to terms with was the fact that despite having welcomed me as a guest, these people could ask me to leave so abruptly just because I had refused to give interviews. Perhaps there had been some other reason that I will never know.

Yet again, I was ushered out through the back gate in the dead of night. Another officer dressed in a burqa had already been escorted out through the front gate in full view of the media people to throw them off the scent of the real Taslima

Nasrin. While the journalists set out in pursuit of the decoy, I was driven straight to the cantonment where I stayed for two days before being moved to another cantonment. Thus began my exile, my days of living incognito. I was provided with everything I might need—mobile phone, Internet, clothes, toiletries, whatever I wished to eat, furniture and television, and two government officers as my guards and companions. I had everything except for the one thing I craved for—the freedom to go somewhere on my own or to meet someone of my own accord. The officers would often express their sympathy, saying, 'It is indeed horrible to have to live without freedom.' I would silently let the words wash over me as they studied me, perhaps to fathom how I was holding up, if my skin had started to wrinkle, if my nerves were still throbbing, and if my muscles still had strength left.

My brother, meanwhile, had grown restless and agitated about returning home, and it became impossible to placate him any further. Would he be so unkind as to leave his own sister behind at such an hour of need? What if I died? Irrespective of what I said, no amount of reasoning or tearful pleading could change his mind. Perhaps he too had been preparing himself mentally to bid me farewell. With barely concealed relief, one fine day he went back to Dhaka via Kolkata, leaving me behind as price for his freedom. My struggles have always been mine alone.

Poems from a Safe House

1.

The truth makes some people furious. Henceforth, don't speak the truth, Taslima. We are long past the age of Galileo, and yet, even in the twenty-first century, the truth can drive you to exile; sometimes, it can drive you out of your country. The State incarcerates you, punishes you, so don't speak the truth.

Rather, tell a lie, say that the sun revolves around the earth, that the moon's light is her own, that the mountains have been nailed into the heart of the earth. Say that the woman has been carved out of the man's ribs, claim how some bone in her neck is perennially bent out of shape. Say how on Judgement Day the dead will rise from their graves and ashes and rotten bones, to wake up as freshly minted men and women to live out their eternities in heaven or hell. Lie, Taslima. Say that the numerous planets, satellites and solar systems are nothing but lies; that gravity is as much a lie as the journey to the moon was.

The lie will set you free, will give you back your land, your friends, your freedom—unfettered, you would be able to walk in the rain and the sun. No one will abandon you to be consumed by the darkness. Lie, Taslima. And live.

2.

What I had thought to be my city had never been mine. Rather, it belongs to the wily politicians, the dishonest businessmen, the smugglers of women, the pimps, the scoundrels. It belongs to the rapists. It's a city that belongs to people who will not bat an eyelid when someone is murdered, raped or tortured; people who live behind masks, who can casually walk by starving people, who can cross over dead beggars on the pavement, who run at the slightest whiff of danger despite living in houses built on lies. It's a city of people drunk on fantasies of this world and the next, a city of astrologers, con artists and opportunists.

This can never be my city, this city of thugs, liars, cheats and narrow-minded, selfish zealots. In their city, there are only a few of us left who think, who are rational, who protest; a few decent, honest people living in perpetual fear.

3.

Nowadays when I wake up at three in the morning, I no longer get annoyed. People say a restless night invariably spoils the day. But how does that even matter? As if my days and my nights have a reason for being! They laze about quietly instead, one snuggling into the other, nearly indistinguishable. When the boundaries between life and death become blurred, petty things like time and space hardly make sense. I would not be able to pry life apart from death now, nor would I be able to coax death away from life, even if I tried.

4.

I am stranded amidst soldiers with guns. They don't know me, and they keep staring at the unarmed woman from time to time. They cannot fathom the reason for my being here. I may not have the dirt and the grime, the tattered clothes, the wild, unkempt hair, but they can still sense the shackles on my feet, the ones that keep me at bay. I can see this terrible awareness in their eyes, an awareness that their guns and boots inspire fear. It hurts them that I am not afraid, and I have no right to hurt them I suppose. Perhaps they will send word to their masters—that I am not afraid, that I am trying to break the chains. Surely the authorities will hang me. They will fix the date and throw me a feast of fish and prawns.

What if I tell them I don't want to eat! What if I don't sigh even once at the gallows! What if I can be fearless even after they tighten the noose around my neck!

5.

For the past few years, I have been standing very close to death. I have been standing in stunned silence in front of my parents and some of my loved ones. After all this time, I have even lost the sense of whether I am dead or alive, the line separating the two having frayed to a fine silken strand. The ghastly mute creature that has inhabited my body these few years has outlived its last spring. So if I die tonight, do not say a word. Simply plant an epitaph under the night-flowering jasmine—my own epitaph, written over these years with so much care, with white ink on white paper.

6.

Has a poet ever been put under house arrest? Perhaps many political games have been played with poets. Perhaps they have been pelted with stones or set ablaze. But nowhere in the world has a poet ever been put under house arrest. Twenty-first-century India had first embraced the poet and then immediately cast her aside for the sake of religion and politics. She is innocent and yet under siege. She has forgotten what the sky looks like, what people look like. They have cast her into the shadows, promising never to return for her. It has been 155 days of not knowing whether there is anyone with a heart still alive in the world, of not knowing if this is life or death. The poet sits in the darkness wondering if someone will make up for her lost days and bring her back to life. At least reassure her, falsely if need be, that all those who had come before her had been poets too. Just so her darkness lightens a little.

7.

I had only wished to cure people of their blindness, purge the darkness, violence and intolerance from their hardened hearts, and fill them with love. My beloved India has punished me for my wish.

8.

How do I stop worrying in this state of exile? If you abruptly force a free spirit into a cage, can you really expect it to be calm? Will I ever be able to walk out of the cage, will I be able to go back to the hustle and bustle of humanity—these thoughts will not let me rest! People of light cannot survive for long in the shadows. My distress stings me like a wound; as long as the cage remains, the wound will remain too.

9.

Last night, a lizard, I do not know from where, fell on me as I slept and clambered up my arm, past my neck, and finally came to rest in my hair. There, content in the darkness, it sat and stared at another lizard for about two hours, after which it climbed back down by the ear to go and sit on my spine. The other one had been lying still the entire night a few inches below my right knee. Unable to move them I did what I usually do—lie still with my eyes shut, counting back from 100 again and again.

The bed that I have been sleeping on has gradually transformed into a pile of sundry rubbish—dirty clothes, unwashed plates, tea-stained magazines, filthy combs, stale puffed rice, medicine wrappers, inkless pens. Besides, a colony of big, black ants has taken over the bed recently, painstakingly building their new city.

They are taking over my life. They are so tiny and I feel that every passing day I am shrinking to their size. Surprisingly, not a single ant, despite roaming all over my body, has bitten me till date. I believe they think of me as one of their own! I feel safer in their tiny world than in this world of people.

10.

Days have passed since I have taken a shower. I have begun to stink and yet I just don't feel the urge to bathe. A strange apathy has taken hold: what will be the use of bathing? Thrice a day, people arrive with food which I eat whether I want to or not. What if I didn't have to! I would have told them not to bring me any more food.

Sometimes, before going to bed, I get afraid. What if I don't wake up? I manage to fall asleep only to wake up again and again, unable to recognize the alien room. This exile is simply a bad dream and nothing else—that's what I keep dreaming all day. I don't sleep, lest I wake up and this dream breaks too.

The directive is unequivocal—move if you have to, but only within these four walls. The room forgotten, I sit silently in a corner stunned by the order, wondering when this vast earth became so very miserly.

Even jails have certain provisions for visits. I do not even have those. It is as if I do not even have the right to have a family or loved ones. Everyone silently ignores my daily pleas for jail privileges.

11.

If I wish to stay in this country, I must obey their dictums. I must be quiet and stay how they want to keep me; in a prison, alone. For how many years? No one knows for certain, and neither is it clear if I will ever have my life back.

But why is the room locked? Because there will be death and devastation if I step out.

I flinch. People will die because of me? They say yes. I tell them to let me go, to prove how wrong they are. People believe all these arrangements are for me, that the security is to keep me alive. It is perhaps a universal rule that some people always have to lose their way in the darkness for others to feel secure. My incarceration is making some people feel secure; it is making them feel extraordinarily safe.

Sometimes I feel the urge to find out who these people are. Are they from the streets or from the colourful town houses? Are they real people or just a catalogue of customs in human form? For whose safety do I challenge death every single day?

12.

I live in a safe house where I have no say about anything that I do not like. A safe house where I can get hurt but I cannot cry, where I have to lower my eyes always so that no one can see my pain, where my desires are brutally slaughtered every day at dawn and the remains have to be buried before nightfall.

My sighs tear through the silence of the safe house, the only sound in the vicinity. I live and sleep in fear, conversing with my shadow for as long as I stay awake. It seems as if a venomous snake slithers out from somewhere in the shadows and hisses at me. Writhing all over me, it asks me to leave, to go across the border and the mountains, away from human sight, for good. Friends, pray for me that I may safely leave this safe house one day. Pray that one day I am fortunate enough to live in an unsafe house.

13.

Please let me look at people for a while. Normal people on the streets, walking, laughing, taking a wrong turn, or in the fields, in the theatres, in a market—people in buses, trains and trams. People running, or people in love, who live in houses, who love, dream and think.

They have told me to live out my days feeding on the stray glimpses of the sun and the sky through the cracks in the windows. No human beings will be allowed. I must live without craving for life.

14.

Who can give you a country once your own country has rejected you? Aren't all these nations similar, right down to their rulers? They will cause pain in equal measure, hurt with the same glee, be similarly elated by your misfortune. By whatever name you call them, you will still be able to perfectly recognize them in the dark—their whispers, screams, footsteps making them stand out. When you run with the wind, the wind will whisper their names to you. All rulers are after all the same, aren't they?

You might try telling yourself that the rulers do not own the country, that it belongs to the people who know how to love, people like you who have made this land, who have etched its contours with their own hands. Where can you go if the rulers drive you out? Which country welcomes someone who has been driven out of another?

You are no one now, hardly even human. With nothing left to lose, now is the time when you can drag the world outside and demand they let you stand out in the open. The no man's land beyond the frontiers, the one that no one cares for, let that be your nation henceforth.

15.

Since before I was born, India has been part of my history. A history of strife and hatred, a history that seeks to reach out to all unsure possibilities, while nursing the deep scars on its soul—a history of blood and death. India has given me language, culture and dreams. It can as easily rob me of my history, my self and my home.

Why should I let it tear me apart? India has given birth to saints too; saints who have reached out to a helpless, tormented and banished soul such as me. Their reach is greater than the powers that be, over and above the confines of the nation and its borders, these hands lovingly shield me from all cruelty. I call them my home now.

16.

My nation has been savouring my pain for well over a decade. It has seen me in captivity in various other countries, has laughed at my misfortune, with millions of people cheering at my ruin. They were not like this earlier. They had a heart, they had humanity. Now the country is just a lifeless tableau of still rivers, cities and towns, a few stray trees, shops and houses. And, amidst the desolation, roam some almost-human creatures.

Once upon a time there was life, there was poetry. Now no one bats an eyelid when a poet is exiled, when a poet is dragged out in the middle of the night and lynched; instead, millions of people revel in the little carnival of death. My nation used to know how to love; now it has learnt to hate and to intimidate. It has taken up arms—guns, tanks and bombs—and forgotten how to sing.

For over a decade I have scoured this earth for a home, nearly driven to insanity. For over a decade I haven't slept. I have reached out blindly, standing at the frontier, to touch my home. I have been warned that if they ever get their hands on me, that would be the end.

17.

Neither West Bengal nor Bangladesh is any longer what it used to be. Its golden sheen is now dim, rusty and hapless. Fundamentalists dictate terms and the scared populace walks by with their heads bent—a land of ghouls. Bravery and honesty have been banished, and Bengal is now full to the brim with cruel overlords, cunning flatterers or the unconcerned multitude. They endure, lifeless, as trash.

I will cry my last tears for Bengal with the hope that one day the land will again be fertile enough to grow people. So that one day it might again be fit for life.

18.

When I die, take my corpse to the mortuary of the medical college in Kolkata where I have donated my body. The city will not accept me alive. Hopefully, my beloved Kolkata, you will welcome me in death!

19.

Minu is not just a cat, she is my daughter. I have had to leave her behind in Kolkata. She has been waiting for me for a long time, still sits listlessly by the window, counting days. She had to spend the winter alone this year without my blanket and my warmth. Hopefully, the summer would be different. She wants me back, wants those uneventful days back!

The stray cat, found at Gariahat, had gradually become a part of my soul. I was her only family, her only refuge. My little girl sits in the cloying darkness alone, her home, her warm blankets, her sunny terrace, and her toy mouse— everything has been taken from her. Kolkata, you never gave me a safe haven. Please keep my daughter safe.

20.

Even when the narrow-minded populace is against you, when the fundamentalists are baying for your blood, and the ghouls have cornered you, some Good Samaritan will always stand by you. But when the State drives you out, when the rulers turn enemies, and the administrative machinery is against you at every turn, these people too turn their backs. The well-wishers seek a safe corner, all institutions abandon you, the smaller players look for the closest hole to slither into, and the celebrities turn blind. The so-called friends suddenly become very busy. Only a few people are still there, a few genuine ones, friends who stand beside you with honesty and courage, their only sources of strength.

They are marching in protest, holding candlelight vigils, demanding justice. Who says this fight is mine alone? The right to free speech is for everyone, not just me, just as every thinking individual in this country must join this fight. Such times of distress do not just affect me, they affect all and sundry. If freedom and rights emerge victorious, my personal triumph will pale in comparison to the collective victory.

This is not about me. They are not standing beside me. Rather, it is me who is standing beside them, beside India, in every vigil, every picket and every protest march. I stand with them even from my distant, dark, uncertain prison.

21.

I am still alive!

22.

They have snatched your home away, forced you to turn away from your life and locked you in a ballot box. There is not a single soul or a single loved one that you can reach out to—you cannot even choose to live your life according to your wishes. You are someone else's property now whether you admit it or not, left to make do with just regrets, while freedom is nothing but a distant fantasy.

They want to drive you insane. If your nerves are too strong for that, then you must leave, go into exile—this is no longer your country. Eventually, we all must let go. How long can anyone survive surrounded by so much hatred, so much violence and so much disgrace? All they desire, if you cannot be mad, nor will you leave, is that you die at the very least.

You have informed them explicitly that none of these options will be good enough. You have thanked them politely and told them you owe them for fortifying you, for helping you endure. Now all they can do, even if they set you ablaze, is to cast you in steel.

23.

I was human; I had a family, and dreams. I too had my terrace garden, my markets, my afternoon theatres, and friends' houses. Suddenly, in the blink of an eye, because of a handful of people, I became a forbidden object.

What had I ever done to them? With nothing except my dreams by my side, I had always endured, like the countless others in this crowded, jostling city. Was that trifling life too much to ask for?

The king's men have managed to put the banned object six feet under. Now that the dissenting witch has finally been caught, they have sent out drummers to spread the word, a feast has been ordered, and the fundamentalists and terrorists are making merry.

I am not a plaything! This is my life! Is there no court of the people anywhere in this world?

24.

How are you, my darling house? Do you feel lonely? Trust me, so do I. Do you not get afraid, especially at night, when the window opens on its own or if someone comes knocking on the door? Do you not feel afraid that someone will steal into the house and hide in the shadows? Thieves and robbers have become so bold! Not that the wind cannot force open the window! But then, perhaps it is me who visits, who prowls about from room to room in the dead of night. Do you see me in the dark? Do you recognize my footsteps?

Keep my study safe, my darling. My entire life I have left behind there, my life's worth of writing, nine cupboards bursting to the seams with books, and my whole world. And I am meant to be fine being away from that world! I am almost certain it is me who visits, a spectral presence that cannot seem to let go of an unfulfilled promise, that of a home and a life of one's own. Who will water my plants? Since there is no one to take care of them, will my tears suffice? I can cry a river for them, even a sea I can send your way, if you so wish, my darling. Not a moment passes without thinking of you, my beloved. The cat is not there; neither are the people. Still, please wait for me, my darling house! Wait for me and I will come back and clean the layer of dust that has settled over you with my own tears. You are not just a house, but a fragment of the land I have lost, and my mother tongue. For over a decade, I have nurtured you within my heart, an enduring dream that now sustains me. Keep the dream alive, my darling house, and keep me alive too.

25.

All my hopes have been washed away in tears, despair settling like a cloak around me. Separated from every last friend in this exile, I have been indicted of a crime that I never committed—indicted and sentenced to death. I spend my days and nights absurdly waiting for hope, half expecting it to wander into my cell through some nook or cranny. I stay up nights, crawling on the floor trying to find a tiny fragment or speck of hope in the dust. And yet, there is nothing. I have spread out my life to you, wishing for you to bring me some hope. Even if what you bring me is barely enough; even if it is false.

26.

Criminals have a splendid life in India. They strut their way about, perfectly content in their power and the safety it brings, constantly planning their next attacks, all their fraudulent dealings thriving.

While they go scot-free, I am being punished for the crimes they have committed against me. They have threatened me and asked me to leave; for the past seven months, my exile has been planned. Their hateful fatwas and demands for my head have repeatedly broken the State's laws. It seems I have been punished for that too.

I know I am innocent and so I am waiting—waiting to see how my country can uproot my world and banish it in one fell swoop. To see how long it takes a billion people to finally discover their humanity.

I make this demand because of my love for India; not simply because this country is the land of my ancestors, or the place which has nurtured me, or the culture that has enriched me. Even if the state condones the pardon of those who are truly guilty, let it not pardon the torture of innocents.

27.

No one visits me in the comatose silence of the dark safe house. I gaze at the moon with longing, perfectly aware of how well we have taught her the art of deception over the centuries. She plunges our lives into darkness, turns and flees with her light, leaving me to chase her in despair. She hardly cares. Why should she care when people, our loved ones, find it even easier to turn away?

A restless wind blows in from the south and breaks the stillness, my last resort in this desolation. But the squall has also taken my last remaining trinkets. It has upturned my life, leaving behind more anguish; such is the terrible travesty of these times. I wish for nothing from the sky. What can it give me except emptiness? Emptiness, in this exile, I already have enough of.

28.

Each one of you must try to find out what is wrong with me. Go on, tell me what it is. You have to, or something horrible will happen to you! Tell me why you have banished me! Have I caused an epidemic somewhere? Have children died, or women been raped, or have there been mass executions? There must have been strong reasons for sending me into exile! Unless you can find that perfect reason, unless you can show the world the true face of the monster, will you be able to forgive yourself? Perhaps even I would be able to breathe easy knowing what I have done. Perhaps then I would be able to come to terms with my exile. I want to know what I have done; I want to embrace you again, knowing you were only ever looking out for me.

Tell me why you have cast me out of society. Tell me about my crime so that it can absolve yours. Find the perfect reason for having brought back the Dark Ages or would you rather have history frown at you in disapproval? And if you cannot tell me what my crime was, if not for my sake then at least for yours, let me go.

29.

Annada Shankar Roy[28] had once said, 'Bangladesh is Taslima's mother, while West Bengal is her aunt.' The aunt is supposedly dearer than the mother, or so the ironic proverb goes.

I had crossed forests and rivers to come to my aunt after having lost my mother.

Now the aunt too has turned her back, my tears causing her discomfort, my very presence a source of displeasure. The sight of me now causes her disgust, and she constantly urges me to leave, wishes for me to die. Tell me, where should I set out now to search for my mother?

30.

I am not well, Kolkata, but I wish you all the very best. I am not well because it is impossible to stay well in this banishment that you have put me through. You crush me under your feet every day, choke me because I have dared to speak, cut off my hands because I have dared to write. I have never killed anyone, nor harmed anyone in any way, never pelted anyone with stones—you detest me simply because I have spoken a few uncomfortable truths in favour of humanity. And for that you have taken from me my language, my country, my people, you have taken my history, and my home, my last refuge in this world. So what if I am not well! I wish you well, Kolkata, the city of poets and wordsmiths, the city of high philosophy, the most progressive city in the country, a touchstone of culture. Be happy, Kolkata. Dance and make merry. Laugh and let the world witness your greatness.

31.

While I was living in Kolkata, I used to receive a bouquet of roses every day from a veteran freedom fighter. Back in the day he had been part of the Nationalist Movement, had fought for democracy and the freedom of speech. The powerful people who have cracked their whip, who have made me bleed and shattered my dreams—they do not know how they have hurt him too. They do not realize that his roses were brighter than the blood they had drawn. Even now, even in this vast unknown, it seems as if he sends me his tears to put on my wounds. The faint memory of the smell of roses dispels the cloying air of this place and helps me breathe.

I am a banished woman hiding in a safe house in an independent nation. Even a revolutionary can do nothing for me any longer. Freedom too seems a distant possibility in this lifetime.

I will name the roses, 'freedom'. And the tears too.

32.

I wait for the book fair the whole year. I wait to lose myself in the crowded, dusty lanes and the heady smell of new books, to soar in delight like a kite without a care in the world. It keeps me alive, secretly keeps my dreams alive, protecting them from being consumed by the dark dankness of every day. I have no rituals, no festive occasions, no special dates I commemorate. I come to the fair to see people, my only pilgrimage and the one spell of happiness I allow myself. The certain certainties of cultural life—the craft expos, the costly card games, the evening cocktails—hold no meaning for me. The fair is the only thing I have, the place where I can lose myself in the multitude. It is my childhood, my adolescence, and all my memories of belonging to the land by the Brahmaputra. It is my language, my mother's touch, and her legacy. It is a sliver of my life.

India, how could you deprive me so! Why have you pounced on me like a relentless, insatiable beast, with your teeth bare and your claws wicked, and robbed me of my last measure of joy? Your vicious teeth have torn apart what was left of me. Do you still have a heart, India? Does it still beat?

33.

If Gandhiji had been alive, he would have rescued me somehow. He had a generous heart; he would have taken me back home, I know this for sure. He would have stood by and smiled, a warm, indulgent smile, seeing my jubilance at having been returned to my tiny, carefully preserved life, built of a thousand laughs, a million dreams and a lot of joy. He had a heart; I know he would have smiled. He would have been relieved to see me living my life on my own terms, of that I am sure.

If Gandhiji had been alive today, the state of the nation would have broken his heart. He would have called for non-cooperation again, to make a last stand against the terrifying sentinels of intolerance that have raised their ugly heads today. Not just me, he would have saved India.

34.

Let us talk about tigers or, better still, about beautiful blackbucks. Let us not talk about humans—they are too vicious. You threaten a tiger or a buck and you will surely be in trouble. Humans, on the other hand, you can threaten them all you want—you can blow them up too if you want. And those who argue, who try to reason, who try to inspire other people to ask questions—they are not human, they are fire!

Of course, fires must always be put out. The ones which are the most like animals—well behaved, obedient, productive and normal—keep them alive. These people— the ornate, decorative ones who never stop to think—let everything be their legacy. Let them live and prosper. The others, the ones who think, seize them; kill, if you can.

Let us not talk about them. Let us talk about beautiful blackbucks or something like that.

35.

They are all waiting. They are waiting for me to say it. They wait in the hope that, terrified, frozen in fear, I might finally utter the two astounding words—Goodbye, India! Days have rolled into months, and hundreds of pairs of furious, watchful eyes have been trained on me all this while, and a hundred eager ears waiting to hear those two sweet words. I am not uttering the words, not yet. Instead, I choose to believe in truth, honesty, beauty, art and compassion.

The day I have to utter the two words—when collective shame will bring forth a deluge, when the flag of intolerance will cast a shadow over the land, and vultures will fly over my corpse floating in a pool made by my own blood—let it be so dark that I do not have to see the face of this nation, that I don't have to look at all I am leaving behind. Let it be so that I forget I ever belonged here. I am yet to utter the two words; I have steeled my tongue against them. I still dream that love will triumph.

36.

I spend my days in this dark abyss, where each moment lasts an eternity, so that one day I may be reunited with all my loved ones. I have renounced my home, my life, my family and my society; for them, I have broken my body and soul into a thousand tiny fragments. I have shed tears of longing in solitude, waited and let age pass by, slowly building up the moment of reunion to immeasurable heights in my head. But do they ever remember me? Am I ever on their mind, even as a passing thought? For whom have I wrapped myself in battle gear, a speck ready to take on a behemoth? Can they love like me? Can they love at all?

37.

One of these days India will banish me to a land of ice. In my frosty exile, when there is not a single kindly soul to provide me warmth and succour from the cold, I will wrap my memories around me for comfort.

Every day in the afternoon, Susmita would turn up at my central Kolkata house, carrying something or the other for me—a bit of *rabri* or some coriander chutney. She would narrate stories of her struggles, of how she had come to be where she was. Swati and Sapna were young girls, their youthfulness and infectious energy reverberating in the house. Sarmistha would come and read out poetry to me. There were so many others—Shibani, Sharmila—all gentle, loving souls, who would never fail to visit. Jayaprakash, shy and bashful, would turn up suddenly from Burdwan with packets of delicious *sitabhog* and *mihidana*.[29] Ranjan would narrate funny anecdotes from his life. Those monsoons spent with Sumitabha or the days in Subrata's company! Giyasuddin would come from Jangipur and Muzaffar from 24 Parganas— each and every one of them bringing me a plethora of dreams of incredible beauty. As my days in exile threaten to freeze over, the memories of these moments will keep me warm.

My brother would visit, carrying on his shoulders memories of childhood and fragments of our old home, the smell of hasnuhana wrapped around him. The heady smell of those flowers will give me warmth in my distant, frozen exile, where only memories will keep me alive.

38.

I have rarely, if ever, fraternized with the famous. Well-known people have usually carefully avoided me, or I have stayed away from them out of fear or reluctance. This is why I could live on my own the way I did—live with the people, among them. I have always considered these simple folks as my own—the vendor, the vegetable seller, the fishmonger, the young boys cleaning and packing the fish, the sober man from the tea shop, my laundryman Sanjay, Mangala from Mallikpur or Saptami from Sonarpur, the beautiful Muna,

Gargi who used to visit from Kalyani, or Manasi, or my old gardener who I would ask questions about the wild flowers only for him to inform me with a smile that the flowers were nameless. As far as the eye can see, there is a field of dreams full of similarly nameless people. Where would I go leaving all of them behind?

39.

My sentinels often stare at me in wonder, trying to fathom why I am languishing here all alone, away from the world. When they fail to understand, they shed a tear or two in compassion, and whisper in my ear—how does one survive without freedom? Waiting in the darkness, my bones have begun to crumble. I have learnt to be patient, amassed so much of it that it brooks no challenge any longer. The true test now, however, is for the government—to see when their wounds finally start to fester and become infected. Now is the time for the reaping, the gathering of the fruits of intolerance and dogma they have so lovingly nurtured. Some will nibble, while others, ravenous like whales, will gobble things down. I will wait, with fledgling hope, for the day when they begin stocking their ill-gotten gains in their cavernous barns. For, their spoils will beget serpents, and monsters that will consume the very masters who created them! Such a day is in sight, when faced with their weakness, and their lack of foresight, they will finally realize how they have inadvertently been lying to themselves.

40.

It makes no difference to anyone if I am in jail or not—so many people are put in jail, many of them innocent like me;

so many are sentenced to life, so many who die every day. My fate then is hardly special. Many states are known to have put their writers through hell; jail is hardly something to write home about in comparison. Or at least, that's what the important people say to each other. If one fine day news of my sudden, mysterious death reaches them, I suspect they will be quite relieved. I wonder how many people will try to find out how it happened; will there be people at the protest march? Experience has taught me to recognize power. However, exile has taught me to recognize people. Sometimes, I feel ashamed to have lived and loved in this spineless nation. Except for a handful of honest and brave people who will live in my heart till the end, I expect nothing from this country any more.

41.

If only for the sake of the experience, everyone should live in exile at some point of time in their life. It is only in enforced captivity that one can truly learn to appreciate freedom. I have been fighting for that freedom since I was a child, so I understand just how necessary and valuable it is. I have seen what life can be and so I have fought for my right to live; otherwise, I may as well have given up like so many others and chosen to live in servitude. Even those who revel in their freedom do not know its true relevance. And those who lived and died ignominiously as slaves never understood how truly hapless they were.

I have fought to teach others how to fight, to show others what freedom is, that one must break one's shackles oneself without depending on others. The theocracy has chosen to celebrate a lie by punishing me. Numerous women are caged by patriarchy inside their own homes; numerous people are sacrificed to the cause of fundamentalism. Freedom is a very rare commodity in this wretched country.

42.

You are playing these political games with a simple, honest individual because you cannot condone her speaking the truth any more; nor can you stand her honesty. You have driven her out of the country, scared her into a plane, forced her to leave her home and everything else behind—the book she was reading is still lying open, her notepad left askew, the ink perhaps has begun to dry from the pen. You are trying to silence an author's voice. You don't wish to let her return home, having incarcerated her as if you have caught a murderer. You have kept her like you would keep someone on death row, hidden her away from the world and even herself.

You do not wish to allow a writer to think, do not wish to let her write, or even let her live. Your actions are brazen enough for the world to see. But you hardly have to worry! After all, it is your pet authors and historians who will write a golden history for you!

43.

I live in a room where the windows are barred. I cannot open them even if I wanted to, cannot part the drapes to peer outside. In fact, I am not allowed to open the door, cross the threshold and venture outside. The only other inhabitants in the room are two lizards. No human, not even a humanoid, is allowed to enter this room. I live in a room where I often have trouble breathing.

The room is silent, except for the occasional sound of someone desperately banging their head against the wall. There is no one to take note, except for the lizards who keep staring. I often wonder if they feel sad for me—perhaps they do. Do they cry when they see me cry? I live in a room where I don't want to be, where I am forced by democracy to spend my days in darkness, uncertainty and anxiety. In this room, secularism is killing me, bit by bit, every day. My beloved India has forced me into this room.

The day they clean out from the room the remains of my body—putrid flesh, crumbling bones—will these busy people pause for a second to see? Will death finally set me free? The lizards will stare in bafflement the entire day; perhaps they will be sad. Government officers will wrap my body in the flag of democracy and bury me. I will finally have a room of my own where there will be no thresholds, and where I will finally be able to breathe.

44.

If you ever face exile, if someone ever wishes to put you in shackles, remember me. Remember me if you ever find yourself behind locked doors, when there is not a soul around to hear your cries for help. When you try to speak but cannot seem to form words, or even if you do, no one bothers to stop and listen, remember me. Just like you, I had cried for someone to come and unlock the door and take off my shackles. No one came. And those who did were too afraid of the consequences to bother going ahead.

When you are desolate, remember I had been desolate too. No matter how softly you tread, darkness might consume you regardless. At that moment, you and I, we will be echoes waiting in vain in the gathering dark for an answering call.

45.

So heinous am I, so treacherous, such is the magnitude of my crimes against humanity, that I do not even deserve a country. So you, my country, have set out to rob me of my home. I have travelled from one corner of the globe to another, across nations, forests and oceans, across cultures, grasping at straws and blindly searching for a country to call my own. And when, weary of my quest, I have finally come back to you, you seize my last refuge in one violent attack and cast me out! Tell me, my country, by what name do I call you then?

You choke me with your boots, gouge out my eyes, tear out my tongue and whip the skin off my back. You break my feet and crush my skull, put me in chains, all the while wishing for my death. And yet, my country, I remember you only with love. I am a traitor because I have spoken the truth; I am a traitor because you wish to march in a cavalcade of liars. You have warned me about my humanity, asked me to bury it or spread it in the air, and told me I will never have a country. You, my country, have broken the spirit of the nation within me.

46.

Then let them be free. Throw open the arsenals for them to stock up on guns and swords and bombs and the holy word of Islam. Let them go out into the world and behead the sinful non-believers. Let them kill the women or let them put the women, heads bowed, in burqas and force them back inside. Let there be rape, often, to ensure that only sons are

born. Let all men, from Argentina to Iceland, from Malaysia
to Morocco, from Bangladesh to Bahrain, anoint themselves
as Taliban. Let our statesmen pay homage at the holy altar of
Islam and crown each and every terrorist. Let our statesmen
fold their hands in prayer and let the fundamentalists absolve
them of their sins.

Excerpts from a Diary

24 November

There is an interesting article by Karan Thapar in the *Hindustan Times* (11 March 2008), 'Do we pass the Taslima test?': 'The India I would be proud of would welcome Taslima Nasreen and grant her sanctuary. The India I'm embarrassed by wreaks violence on the streets of Kolkata, vandalises art schools in Baroda and threatens peaceful worshippers in Sirsa. Alas, that is the India I live in.'

A wonderful article, it had begun on a different note though: 'Taslima Nasreen may not be a great novelist. She may even be motivated by a quest for publicity. And many say she deliberately and calculatedly compromises other people by revealing their personal secrets. But those are literary or moral judgements. No doubt each of us will accept or reject them as we deem fit. The question is, do we have a right to silence her voice because of them?'

It is easy to guess that Thapar has not read my writing, but he has nonetheless chosen to take a stand on behalf of a writer's freedom of expression. Those who have read my works, who know me personally, are aware of what I write about and why. Rumours have always been fanned—ever since Bangladesh—that I write to garner publicity, that I am not an author of any consideration, that I write simply to stir trouble. After all, there is not much difference between India and Bangladesh, at least not in the air we breathe. Consequently, it would indeed be very difficult to throw off the spell that is in this air and encourage a new set of beliefs and convictions. Some choose to undertake this difficult endeavour, while others give themselves up to the spell. If I had ever been unduly concerned about myself, about my image, then I might have shown that same care for my writing and would perhaps have made the effort to get it translated into English and other languages. Unfortunately, I have always been a bit indifferent to such things. I have never been able to keep any literary agents. Pirated copies of my books have been sold all over India and Bangladesh; people have done whatever they have wished to with my books. So many people across the world have wanted to read my books but have never had the opportunity.

27 November

'. . . all decisions had already been made to have Taslima Nasrin expelled from West Bengal. This decision, and the way it has been implemented, is completely unethical and unwarranted. Firstly, there was no need to send Taslima to another state for the sake of her security. The government could as easily have arranged for the same in this city. It would not be a stretch then to assume that the reason cited for sending her away is simply an excuse to cover up the fact that she has been expelled to appease the sentiments of her fundamentalist protestors. Secondly, the way this expulsion has been handled is nothing short of offensive. This nexus between the government, political parties and powerful members of both, has been an enduring legacy for us and it points towards a larger sickness that has enveloped society and which is completely contrary to the ideals of a modern, liberal democracy. Thirdly, these actions have made it amply clear that we have surrendered to the unjust demands of the radicals, and this perhaps is the most worrying aspect of the entire thing. The rulers of West Bengal have, time and again, boasted about their secular world view, but when push comes to shove, they invariably and happily bow down to Islamic fundamentalists. The recent incident with Taslima Nasrin has further foregrounded this dangerous trend. The "secular" rulers of West Bengal are, in fact, not appeasing Muslims at all; they are appeasing Muslim militants instead. The valued advisers of the party believe that this strategy will help them in guarding the Muslim vote bank. However, fanning such illegal and dangerous actions for the sake of vote bank politics can only end badly.'—*Anandabazar Patrika*

Whether they stand by me otherwise or not, *Anandabazar Patrika* had been steadfast in its support ever since I was sent away from West Bengal. Star Ananda (now ABP Ananda) too had been constantly reporting about me, and holding discussions and debates about the issue; in fact, I was recently interviewed by their anchor, Suman Dey. In another such interview by Milan Datta of *Anandabazar*, the latter wanted me to tell him everything, starting from the time I returned from Hyderabad— how I was confined to my house, what was said to me, how I was turned out of Kolkata, and all other relevant details. He kept asking me questions and I kept answering till a slowly increasing din of voices abruptly interrupted us. News arrived that Milan Datta was being summoned. He went, consulted them, and

came back to inform me that Aveek Sarkar has asked for
the interview to be stopped after having a word with foreign
minister Pranab Mukherjee. The latter had requested that
news related to me or my interviews not be telecast for some
time, assuring all and sundry that he will be getting me back to
Kolkata in another fifteen days.

Star Ananda has consequently stopped all discussions
and debates, thereby ensuring the natural demise of any
possibility of developing public opinion in my favour.

28 November

'I would urge everyone, especially the Muslim intellectuals,
to pause and consider one point about the controversy
surrounding Taslima Nasrin. The woman has not pelted
stones at those opposing her; she has not set cars on fire,
or threatened to commit murder either. A section of the
intellectuals believe that what she has written about the
oppression of Muslim women is un-Islamic. However, if
she is not allowed to write what she believes, how will her
critics be able to aptly respond to the un-Islamic accusations
she has levelled at their faith? This will only jeopardize the
democratic machinery and the worst fallout of that would be
felt invariably among the minority communities. Thus, it is
quite obvious that Taslima's struggle for being able to freely
write and express her opinions is ultimately a struggle for
preservation of the ideals of democracy.'—Sunando Sanyal

Since yesterday, news reports had stated that Pranab
Mukherjee was supposed to speak about me in the Lok Sabha
(on 28 November 2007). I waited to hear him, and this is
what he said: 'Throughout history, India has never refused
shelter to those who have come and sought our protection.

This civilizational heritage that is now a government policy will continue and India will provide shelter to Ms Nasrin. Those who have been granted shelter here have always undertaken to eschew political activities in India or any action that may harm India's relation with friendly countries. It is also expected that the guest will refrain from activities and expressions that may hurt the sentiments of our people. While these guests are in India, the Union and the state governments provide them protection—this policy will also apply in Ms Taslima Nasrin's case.'

'A seasoned diplomat,' my brother commented.

A drowning creature will always grab at reeds. The news that seemed the biggest to me was I would not be turned out of this country; that I would be allowed to stay. I had hoped for another stand though, something that would sound somewhat like this: 'India is a generous and welcoming nation that has welcomed, from time to time, people of various cultural backgrounds, enriching itself in the process. Taslima is an oppressed and banished author, this is her motherland, and we honour her desire to spend her life, if not in the East, then at least in the western half of Bengal. India is a secular country, the world's biggest democracy, and its people have the freedom to express their opinions in a democratic fashion. What happened on the streets of Kolkata on 21 November was nothing short of barbaric. The first and most important condition of a secular democracy is the freedom of speech and expression. Like everyone else, Taslima too has the right to partake of these. Thus, it is necessary that the government take adequate actions against those who took to the streets to loot, plunder, commit arson and create a law-and-order situation in order to rob her of her fundamental rights. The government must also ensure that such incidents do not recur in the future, and that the ideals of a secular democracy are not put at risk. There will be an investigation as to why Taslima had to be removed from West Bengal without her consent, and those at fault will be punished. The rioters of 21 November will also be given exemplary punishment. Tomorrow, Taslima will be sent back to Kolkata from Delhi and the central government will ensure her complete security along with the state government, not just in West Bengal but elsewhere too. Not just Taslima, but every citizen and guest in this country, and anyone who seeks asylum here, will be governed by the same rules.'

This is what I had hoped would happen. I am not entirely sure what exactly happened instead. The only relief is that perhaps I will finally be granted a residence permit.

30 November

'The issue surrounding Taslima Nasrin has ripped off the hitherto carefully maintained secular façade of the CPI(M), which had survived Singur, Nandigram, years of police violence, and the party-endorsed tradition of seizing power through the point of a gun . . . Let her wander, in various states, in various foreign nations, while we sit here counting our ballot boxes. Let us measure till the final decimal what is more convenient for us—to let her stay in Kolkata or to keep her in exile. Whatever it is, it should help us win the Muslim votes. Only through the litmus test of elections can we determine when we should assist the extremists and when we should march in protest against them.'—Ashish Ghosh

Enamul Kabir called from Birbhum this morning. No political party has yet condemned the CPI(M), however. No one has criticized their actions, or stated that it had been unethical to drive an author out as they had.

I deleted a few lines from *Dwikhandito* today and the devastating news was published with much pomp and fanfare across the nation.

2 December

The chief of the cantonment, a seemingly decent and educated individual, had come for a courtesy visit a while back. He confessed to have never even dreamt that he would one day meet the author of *Lajja*. That is how most people know me: as the author of *Lajja*. There is hardly an educated Indian who hasn't ever read the book, and Penguin has even declared it the most sold book in Indian publication history.

The officer's surname was Sen. Quite obviously, and with a surge of joy, I had taken him to be a Bengali, only to learn later that I had been mistaken.

4 December

'She does not have any choices. She is just like a person who has now got the protection of the mafia which is the state in some way. She has nowhere to go. She has no protection. She just has to blunder her way through this kind of humiliation and I really feel for her.'—Arundhati Roy[30]

Today was my brother's twenty-fifth wedding anniversary. Every year he usually celebrates the day but this exiled life in Delhi has made it impossible and useless to observe festivities. Instead, he was ready early in the morning, packed and raring to leave immediately after lunch. He is going to Kolkata. The flight will reach the city at five in the afternoon. We had come away together but he is going back alone. I could not go with him because it is not possible. When he was leaving I could not even look at him, my heart was about to burst out of my chest. Perhaps he had been sad too. But what would he have done staying here? Does anyone like being in hiding?

5 December

'Secularism is not appeasing fundamentalism and terrorism. The November 21 incidents could have led to communal riots in Kolkata. Fundamentalism, whether Muslim or Hindu, is a challenge which must be taken very seriously. The Taslima Nasrin issue is no longer about Taslima Nasrin the writer. It has revealed a much larger conspiracy in the making.

'It was a test case, and the CPM's decision has conveyed to the Islamic fundamentalists that they have won the round one.'—Bhaskar Roy[31]

Three things of note today: the editorial in *The Hindu*,[32] an op-ed article in *Anandabazar*, and a book by Sarvepalli Radhakrishnan in which a photo of Muhammad Nabi had caused such outrage in Kolkata that the Delhi-based publishers have had to apologize. The editorial in *The Hindu* has pointed out how the section 295(A) had also been used against me in Bangladesh. For the past fifteen years, I have been trying to get this draconian law against the freedom of speech revoked, but no one wants to listen to the voices of the few of us who dissent.

The *Anandabazar* op-ed piece has simply astounded me. Such complete reversal of position over the space of only a few days has left me dazed and confused! Kalyan Sanyal has written against me, or perhaps he has been made to write. If he has done so simply for the sake of a debate, I might try and understand it, but if these are indeed his genuine views against the freedom of speech, then it is a matter of grave concern. I believe *Anandabazar* will not write or publish anything in my favour for the foreseeable future. Sanyal has opined that not all art is pure, just as not all forms of politics are dirty. The politics practised by the CPI(M) is thus not dirty, just as my writings are not pure. Since my writing is tainted, those in positions of power have the right to drive me out and there is nothing unethical about it. Sanyal has gone on to state how he detests what I write as well as my style, and consequently he sees nothing wrong in my exile. He had protested the government's actions in Nandigram but in this issue he has nothing but support for them.

I have gradually come to the conclusion that most artists, writers and intellectuals share Kalyan Sanyal's views. Otherwise, why have there been no protests against the injustices committed against me by the CPI(M)?

6 December

Today was the fifteenth anniversary of the demolition of the Babri Masjid. I had written *Lajja* fifteen years back. How time flies! Bhalobasa[33] was born fifteen years ago, on 6 December 1992. Apparently, some members of the party Harkat-ul-Jihad have entered Delhi in a car today through Deoband in Uttar Pradesh. Their objective—to cause massive bomb blasts in certain key, heavily populated areas in order to intimidate people. As far as I remember, the Harkat-ul-Jihad had originally been formed in Bangladesh at the height of the Islamic radicals' protests against me. I am

yet to fathom how taking innocent lives benefits the agenda
of these people.

I spoke to Prasanta Roy over the phone for a long time.
He is hopeful about protests on my behalf in Kolkata. I had
to remind him that protests would have happened long back
if they were meant to. Everyone saw how I was treated, how
I was driven out, how I was mentally tortured for days before
that—there was not a single protest march despite all that.
Only a few of my friends marching, holding placards! Do
I not have anyone? Even if not for me, is there no one to
protest against an act of barbarism? There have been a few
stray articles in some newspapers, but they have not been
powerful enough to incite people to protest.

Tapan Raychaudhuri[34] had called and I broke down over
the phone. I begged him to take me back to Kolkata, and
if that was not possible, if West Bengal refused to take me
back, then to send me back to Bangladesh. Quite possibly the
activists and religious leaders would just come and murder
me one day. That would be the best for everyone. If nothing
else, it would absolve me of the sin I had committed by
hoping that a foreign country could ever become my home.
At least it would save me from having to see the people I love
laughing at my misfortune.

My head is about to explode in pain. It is increasingly
becoming impossible to bear. I had begged my captors to cast
me back into Bangladesh, to wait for the final verdict there.
They heard, their voices urging me to confess more as if they
had been waiting for a long time to get me to this place. It
reminded me of a similar incident when, like them, a top
government official in Rajasthan House had told me I should
always stay where I would be safe. I had asked him where it
would be safe. He had replied that there was no dearth of safe

places in the world. 'Do you mean in the West? In Europe or America?' I had asked. He had nodded and said, 'Why not!' I had been scared but I had told him firmly, 'I will not go abroad.'

7 December

Sharmila called from Kolkata in the morning to tell me about an article written by Joy Goswami[35] for the weekend supplement of *Sangbad Pratidin*.

> How does it feel when an author is forced to withdraw her work? I can but imagine the immense pain Taslima is going through because of this decision. None of us has ever had to live in exile for days on end, in foreign countries, surrounded at all times by security personnel. None of us has ever been driven out of our own homes. None of us has ever had to witness our books being banned systematically even before they can reach the public. None of us knows how it is to live with a death sentence dangling over our heads.
>
> We can criticize Taslima, discuss what she should or should not have written or said, and even whisper about how all her actions are motivated by a lust for publicity. Yes, we can allege that even after being fully aware that an insane, obsessive fanatic might attack her any day, she has done everything to garner publicity. We have said as much.

Joy has gone on to compare my situation to Galileo's, who had been threatened with being burnt at the stake till he was forced to capitulate under pressure, recant his ideas and admit that the church had been right all along about the sun revolving round the earth. Galileo may have buckled under pressure, he may have admitted that the earth was stationary, but it did not necessarily mean that the earth too gave in under pressure and followed suit.

I called Shibnarayan Ray and found out that he was not doing too well, neither physically nor mentally. He told me he had been too unwell to write and I advised him to consult a doctor and have his blood pressure checked. It seems enough care is not being taken of him, and like most people in old age, he seems to have shrunk, saying things like, 'It's been long enough, this life.' I reminded him that he was only eighty-six while Jyoti Basu was nearly ninety-three. I also asked him what I had done to deserve this fate. He replied, 'Who has told you only crime deserves punishment? You have hurt the self-interests of the ruling elite, and so you have been punished.'

An article in the *New York Times* made me very happy today. There was a report of a girl in Saudi Arabia who had been kidnapped and gang-raped. According to the laws of Islam, of course, the rapists were not punished but the girl was—lashes and jail, the usual story. Indeed, such heartening news! In Sudan, a school mistress was punished because she had named one of the class teddy bears Muhammad. I was punished because the fanatics did not like what I had written in a book somewhere. Apparently, most Muslims are not religious fanatics! A handful of extremists have hijacked the entire faith and except for them, there is no dearth of goodness in Islam. I have the same question as the author of the article: where are these moderate and modern Muslims? Why don't they ever take to the streets to protest against the riots, violence, rape and pillage committed by the zealots? How is it possible that only a few Muslims are behind all these incidents and the majority of the population is just silently observing everything? Sometimes I feel that the 'moderates' do not even exist. There are two types of Muslims: the believers and the non-believers. Since most are believers, the non-believers are much fewer in number. Some of the believers wear robes, fez caps, long beards, while others wear different clothes. Some of them regularly visit mosques and observe fasts during Ramadan, while others do not. That is all there is to it. Hence, when some believers commit a crime against humanity, there is no protest against them from the other faithful. The moderates, consequently, are absent. They are absent because they do not exist.

Many people called today—Keya from Patna, Enamul from Birbhum, Muzaffar from 24 Parganas. Besides, I received a letter from a friend that has made me very happy. Panchu has written a letter to me, an email, after months without any news. A close friend, the sole reason behind this long gap had been my hurt. He has written: 'I know you are safe. But it pains me to think how devastated you might be. Will our world then be ruled henceforth by religion, dogma, and electoral politics only? My blood runs cold thinking what degree of state-sponsored terrorism you must have faced to have decided to withdraw three pages from your book. I can only hope that these dark days will pass, that you will be yourself again, and your words relentless and undaunted. Take care, as much as is possible in such dark times.' I wrote back: 'Even in this pain, your letter has brought me some amount of joy. I don't know what will happen. I want to return to Kolkata but the progressive city is not willing to take me back. I am drowning in uncertainty and despair; perhaps, they secretly wish to prolong my agony to such an extent that I will be forced to leave the country or commit suicide.' He wrote back: 'Which city are you calling

progressive, Taslima? The Kolkata where a party carrying red
flags shamelessly uses fundamentalism as a tool to control
Muslim votes? The city where the other parties with red flags
cannot create a powerful united front to protest against the
atrocities committed or condoned in the name of politics? The
city which fails to understand the severity of state-sponsored
terrorism that can force a writer to tear up three pages of her
writings? Will you call such a city progressive? You will be able
to find justice one day for these terrible crimes. Even amidst
this growing darkness, I believe that fundamentalism cannot
have the last word.'

It cannot? In Bangladesh it has been thirteen years that
fundamentalism has had the last word. I have not been able
to return home, and what's left for Bangladesh to say? West
Bengal too has gone silent, and it does not matter in the very
least what its last word is. Silence, rejection, disdain, insults
and fundamentalism—these are the last words.

The room that I inhabit now has a sliver of a balcony
attached to it, next to a terrace. I generally do not wander on to
the terrace for fear that someone might see me and something
might happen. In fact, I have been told not to go to the terrace.
That is fine; I am used to being under house arrest. I have
spent days, months like that, both at home and abroad. There
is hardly an ordeal I have not been through in the name of
security. In order to be able to write about breaking shackles, I
have had to wear them on my feet, always!

8 December

'I think the Taslima Nasrin case has tested, and will test,
the integrity of the Left intelligentsia even more than
Nandigram.'—Ramachandra Guha[36]

Buddhadeb Bhattacharya had gone to attend a programme organized to commemorate the fifteenth anniversary of the demolition of the Babri Masjid. He told the people gathered there that Ram was merely an idea, a figment of the poet's imagination. The mythical Ram-setu had been a natural one, and the controversy surrounding it was simply madness. I was left astounded hearing this on television yesterday. Only a few days back he had bowed down to the dictates of Islamic radicals, had not uttered a peep about their barbaric acts all over the city, had in fact defended their right to protect their religious sentiments. Instead of punishing the guilty he made sure that an innocent person had to leave the city. And here he was, hurting the religious sentiments of the Hindus!

9 December

'The greatest, most fundamental right promised to any thinking individual is the right to not agree with the status quo. You cannot dictate to an author—you can write thus far, and no more! It is the same as telling them not to write. In the end it boils down to the simple fact that you have the freedom to speak and express your opinion as long as you don't step on the toes of those in power. After that, no more! Freedom cannot exist without this perpetual threat, this covert permission to pace in your designated cell.

'There can be no threshold to the freedom of speech, no frontiers. Otherwise, any powerful group, be it the state, a religious sect or any random upstart, will be able to reassert its thresholds, at its convenience declare any work of art anywhere in the world as something that has hurt someone's religious sentiments, and then let the bullets loose.'— Chandril Bhattacharya

I wrote a letter to Buddhadeb Bhattacharya. It will not be possible to send it to him, of course, but I still felt like writing one.

Dear Mr Buddhadeb Bhattacharya,

I hope my letter finds you well. We have previously met, and at one point of time, we have also had a few conversations. I have always known you to be an absolutely warm person. I remember one time in Nandan, when you had warned me against flying to Paris via Mumbai, suggesting I fly via Delhi instead. The reason? A group of Islamic radicals had been protesting against me in Mumbai, threatening to burn the airport down. I had almost agreed to it when people like Shabana Azmi, Javed Akhtar, Javed Anand and Teesta Setalvad began insisting that I must not cancel my Mumbai visit to take a stand against the unjust demands of the radicals, to show them that I was not willing to cower under fire. Otherwise, it would be like handing the victory over to them. Realizing that you had convinced me otherwise, they had approached you to convince you how important it was that I fly via Mumbai. You had understood and relented.

We have only met a couple of times since then, at Nandan. Once while attending a sarod recital by Ustad Amjad Ali Khan, when we exchanged pleasantries and Ustadji warmly welcomed both of us before beginning his performance. That was back in 2002 when, certain that I was going to spend the rest of my life in Kolkata, I had been searching frantically for an apartment. You had told me that there would be no problems in my buying the flat allocated for the state minister Gautam Deb in

Udita. I had been ready too, paperwork had been sent
to Delhi or Mumbai, and the Reserve Bank was going
to give its approval. The approval had never arrived, no
paperwork had come, no apartment, nothing. Our paths
never crossed after that and I could never reach you again.
Your friends, who had been my friends too, had suddenly
grown distant.

I remember those days, and it is still incredible after all
these years how much things have changed. I remember
back then I had been at Harvard, pursuing a fellowship
on secularism, when news reached me that you had
banned *Dwikhandito*. I had been shell-shocked and had
asked my friends back in Kolkata if it was true. They had
assured me it was. I have been brought up amidst leftist
ideology. I have grown up reading the great leftist Russian
authors. In *Dwikhandito*, I had written about my fights
against fundamentalism, about feminism and women's
rights, about equality! So, how was the book contrary to
the Left's stance? I had heard you admit that a handful
of intellectuals told you to ban the book and you too had
arrived at the same conclusion after reading the book
yourself. Is that so? Had you meant what you had said,
that what I had written had been wrong? If you hadn't,
then what had made you so anxious that there could be
a riot in the city? There had been no sign of a riot. After
the ban was revoked by the high court, the book had
sold for months and years. There were no riots! Not a
single Muslim came out in protest! One of the reasons
cited for banning the book had been that it would disrupt
communal harmony and cause widespread communal
violence. When the high court found this insufficient
reason for a ban, stating that the two communities were

in no way involved, you had come up with yet another reason—that my book would hurt religious sentiments. A three-judge bench had still voted in favour of my book. For your kind information, Mr Bhattacharya, the verdict had not been pronounced by me. I had never appealed to the court against the ban in the first place. Despite your role in the banning of my book, my respect and admiration for you never declined. I have tried meeting you, but in vain. You have kept all the avenues barricaded. People close to you, who had also been close to me, became strangers suddenly, but I still did not lose my faith in you. I had formed a cine club called Bhalo Chhobi (Good Films), hoping to screen some good films I had collected from across the world, for the cinephiles of Kolkata. Anshu Sur had assured me the possibility of screening these films at Nandan. However, after collecting nearly 2000 brilliant films, I was informed that I was prohibited there. As foolish as I was, I understood quite late in the day that I was prohibited from all government spaces. That I had no right to attend any festivals organized by the government, let alone participate. I became so very lonely that day!

May I ask what the reason behind such hatred was? Was it because I had written about Islam? Tell me, do you truly believe this is about Islam? The people who are crying foul about insults to Islam, who are burning my effigies, calling for my head, demanding my exile, do you really believe they are good and honest people? Do you think their demands are justified? If you don't, then why do you not say anything? When Hindu fundamentalists make ridiculous demands, cause furore over the Ram-setu issue, you don't like it. Unequivocally, you term this religious madness. In front of the Muslim fundamentalists, you had apparently called me a horrible woman and promised to have me leave the state. In beliefs, ethics and ideology, I had believed you would find me an equal, and yet you had sided with them, the people who wish to drag society back to the Dark Ages where women get tortured relentlessly, and where there is no place for the ideals of justice and equality.

What crime had I committed to deserve such punishment? In the journals run by your party or its allies, I was insulted in the worst ways over the years. Lies were written about me. I read all of it but I never reacted. Everywhere, people were protesting about Nandigram and Singur, about Rizwanur, but I was not able to say or write even a word about them. I had been told that since I was not a citizen of the country, I had no right to comment on its politics. Friends had warned me that you would unleash the worst consequences on me if I ever took to the streets, that you would drive me out of Bengal. It has never been in my nature not to stand up to injustice. And yet, I had stayed quiet, shamelessly, because staying in Bengal had been that important. If Bangladesh had not driven me out, had not sent me into exile, I would have lived there. I would never have sought shelter here. For eleven long years, I wandered from one European country to another, without being able to form an attachment with any place, or call another country my own. I was given a lot of respect in those countries, no conditions were placed on my freedom of speech, and no one told me to speak in measured tones because I had been given shelter. Yet, I wished to return to my country, to my parents, my family and my friends. During my years in exile, suffering from depression in Europe, I

had turned to India for shelter after my cries for help had
fallen on deaf years in Bangladesh. India had responded
but it had taken them nearly six years to do so. The few
days I was given in the meanwhile I would invariably
spend in West Bengal, to revel in the taste of home. My
relatives would even travel from the other side to meet me.
I was allowed to live in India only three years ago and the
moment the approval had arrived, I had moved to Bengal.
Living in West Bengal for me had never simply been just
about living as if in any other place.

For the three years I was in Kolkata, I never harmed
a person. I spent most of my time at home, writing, or
sometimes I would meet friends and chat. Unconcerned
about others, unaware of politics, my quiet, unassuming
life could not have been such an eyesore for someone,
could it? My home in West Bengal had not been simply a
home; it had been so much more for me. I was desperately
trying to recreate my home in Bangladesh, the one I had
already been exiled from. The dream had consumed me,
but it had been impossible to find that in an alien culture
and amidst an alien language. After an eleven-year-long
search, I had found that home finally in West Bengal. I
have never seen Bengal as two different nations, and so it
had been quite easy for me to adopt Kolkata as my new city
and West Bengal as my new country—a long-lost dream,
a dream I had had to leave behind, and a sense of comfort
and belonging after years of struggle. My mother had
hoped to see me back home. My exile had caused her much
heartache, and she had prayed I would be able to live with
my family again. That had never happened though, and I
was never able to return to Bangladesh. However, if she
had been alive that day, she would have been glad to see

me among Bengalis again—if not home, at least as close to it as possible.

My life in Kolkata was peaceful, and I was writing regularly. Suddenly, I was attacked by radicals in Hyderabad. While the general public expressed their sympathies for me, you, Mr Bhattacharya, did not even think to spare a glance. Whether I was beaten up or killed, it would have meant nothing to you. You never condemned the incident. No, I did not utter a single word about religion in Hyderabad and yet the barbaric incident happened. The fundamentalists had made it possible. After that, instead of support, your city allowed these men to declare, in broad daylight at Esplanade Crossing, a reward for my head. None of them were arrested or prosecuted. I am used to fatwas being declared on my head, my life has never walked the beaten track. I have had to live with numerous threats, fatwas, tortures and prohibitions. So, I was not afraid of this new fatwa either, and you had kindly arranged to have a security detail posted with me. The thought never crossed my mind that I might be attacked in Kolkata. So many times, I let go of my protectors and went out on my own, to Gariahat or to shop at Jadubabur Bazar, or to simply walk among the crowd. No one attacked me. Those who approached me did so out of love.

All of a sudden, I was told I could not go out. Why not? The guards had informed me that they had received missives from above, forbidding me from leaving the house—no markets, or long walks, not even friends' houses. I was not allowed to go out even in secret, or with my security officials in tow. It had taken me a while to feel the shackles on my feet. For a while I had even assumed

everything to be true, that there indeed was a plot to kill
me. The day Prasun Mukherjee had come over and spent
a couple of hours trying to convince me that I should
not go out lest the radicals find me and pursue me to the
house to kill me, that Kolkata and West Bengal were no
longer safe for me and that I should leave immediately
for Europe, America, Thailand or Singapore, or even
Kerala or Madhya Pradesh, that there would be a riot if
I didn't—even that day I did not realize that the entire
thing had been an elaborate set-up to frighten me into
leaving West Bengal. My security had only been a ruse.
Prasun Mukherjee had called quite often after that to
ask me to leave, sometimes to threaten. The last call I
received from him, he had freely admitted that the CM
had instructed me to leave as soon as possible, that all
arrangements had been made for me in Kerala, and that
the Kerala governments would now give me security.

Trust me, Mr Bhattacharya, not for once did I
even imagine that you had deployed Prasun Mukherjee
to convince, threaten or frighten me into leaving
the country, or at the very least West Bengal. I had
asked to be allowed to tell people everything, that
the Government of West Bengal was unable to give
me security and was asking me to migrate to another
state, lest there be further repercussions once I moved
to Kerala. I had wanted everyone to know that I had
not gone to die in Kerala of my own accord. Prasun
Mukherjee, however, insisted that I leave secretly and
tell no one. Not just him, you had asked some of your
friends, people I had always respected, to ask me to
leave too. I had been stubborn, perhaps I had been at
fault—I had refused to leave. I refused, thinking you

were genuinely concerned about my security and this was why I was being asked to leave. In a peaceful city, I had been clueless about what security issues might arise. And then, one fine day, the peace was broken. It was not meant to happen, but it had.

My punishment had been implemented in Kolkata already. I used to go mad while under house arrest, trust me! Did you ever imagine yourself in my place? If you had been kept locked up like that, how would it have been? How would you have felt if friends you wished would visit had kept away because they were wary of the policemen who stopped them to note down names and addresses for future reference? How would you have felt having to sit alone in a dark room, for months on end? Would you have felt suffocated? When one finds oneself locked in, without any strength or trick in the arsenal to unlock the door, there is a deathly silence that pervades everything, a mix of helplessness and misery. Tell me, Mr Bhattacharya, in those dark days, did you ever spare me a kind thought?

After Prasun Mukherjee, his responsibilities had been passed on to Mr Vineet Goel. He used to call often too but unlike Mr Mukherjee, he never suggested a bouquet of places for me to go to. From the very beginning, he had told me to go to Jaipur, where he had assured me all arrangements would be made for my stay for two days, a resort would be booked and a cook specially hired for me. Why did I have to go? To save myself because Islamic radicals in Kolkata were planning my assassination! Under house arrest, and my captors were telling me I was free to make my own arrangements if I was not willing to listen to what the government had

planned for me. I understood much later why Jaipur had
been chosen, after Sundeep Bhutoria began calling me
up. It was obvious the responsibility of 'managing' me
had been passed over to him, and he had begun by trying
to convince me to trust him that all arrangements would
be taken care of in Jaipur. That everything was ready
there for my reception, and I was to spend two quiet
days there, away from everything, while things calmed
down in Kolkata. Prasun Mukherjee had been unable
to find someone I knew who could be used to convince
me to leave. Vineet Goel had first dedicated himself to
finding that very person before dealing with me. So,
both Mr Goel and Mr Bhutoria had been quick to assure
me that all arrangements for travel, stay and security in
Jaipur had been taken care of. That I had committed a
grave error having risked my life to stay in Kolkata, and
that I would fly to Jaipur immediately if I had even the
tiniest bit of common sense left in me.

On 15 November, the day of the bandh called by
Siddiqullah Chowdhury and his ilk, the day the police
had been wary of and for which they had been asking me
to leave West Bengal, I was escorted hurriedly to another
house early in the morning only to be left there alone by
the police. Where had the officers gone? I called and got
to know they had all gone back to the police headquarters!
I had called Vineet Goel to ask when I should return
home. He had been so angry with me because I had not
escaped to Jaipur, because I had repeatedly turned away his
messenger, and he could not even speak to me properly.
That entire day I had spent in abject terror, thinking I
would have been better off left alone at home where at
least a dozen security guards had been posted for that

day. The terror had taken root a couple of days before 15 November, on realizing that my security had been abruptly decreased. The reason that had been cited was that those men had been transferred to proper police stations. There was to be a traffic barricade in the afternoon, organized by Chowdhury's Milli Ittehad Parishad (MIP), to protest against Nandigram, Singur, Rizwanur, the Sachar Committee Report, and me. I watched a group of protestors burning my effigy not too far from my house. Anxious that the fervour might reach me, I had called the undercover officers, who had been posted in front of my house since 9 August and were now sitting in the police station, for help. They had come, but only for a while. By the time they left, around fifteen minutes later, the effigy had not finished burning.

Nothing was supposed to have happened on the 21 November. And yet it had. I had underestimated Idris Ali and his front, especially since the other twelve had failed to create much stir. However, the scenes I witnessed on TV that day were astounding. I sat dumbfounded trying to make sense of the boys I saw, mad in their righteous rage, demanding I leave their city. Who were they? They were not the familiar faces from College Street I had expected in the protest! How could I have hurt their religious sentiments? Had they been brainwashed for a long time, or had they been deployed specifically for that day? I remember feeling suspicious about the whole thing being a set-up. The boys were lifting their lungis and flashing the policemen, making rude and obscene gestures, some were beating up cops, and I remember wondering whether they even knew me, whether they had read my books, whether they had even read the religious book they were meant to be champions of. Were they pelting the police with stones and setting cars on fire because someone had told them I was un-Islamic and had to be driven out of the state? Looking at their faces, their hatred for the police had shone through. Were their actions also motivated by a desire to avenge Rizwanur's murder? At the same time, it did not seem Nandigram was one of the things they were protesting against. I remember feeling my blood freeze on seeing the police stand as silent witnesses to the carnage. They had been forbidden from shooting, and when the army was deployed, they too were given the same instructions. If the mob had marched to my house that day and murdered me, the police would still not have done anything. They had been asked not to, they had been asked to get hit but never to hit back.

Sundeep had come to me again that night. Of course, to say the same old thing: 'You know I have made all the arrangements in Jaipur. The moment you land there, I've already had a word with the government, you will be provided with security. Go for a holiday. Eat, rest, do some sightseeing. Here, they might kill you any day. Why are you being so foolish?' For the umpteenth time, I had firmly refused.

From early the next morning, the news channel Chabbis Ghanta (stylized to 24 Ghanta, i.e. twenty-four hours) had begun airing live updates of a gathering mob at the Park Circus seven-point crossing. People were shouting they would murder me, even at the cost of their own lives. The scenes were so horrific and barbaric! I spoke to Vineet Goel over the phone in the afternoon. He informed me that the attack would be set in motion after the Friday prayers the day after. When I had suggested that I move to someplace within the city—Salt Lake, Belgharia, Behala or even Golpark—for the day, he had firmly told me that I would have to do so on my own without any security. Security arrangements would only alert the mob, I had been told. Without security, of course, it would be impossible for me to stay. The implication had been clear—I had to agree to go to Jaipur to survive because there was no way I would be alive in Kolkata. They would come, the very next day, after their prayers, champions of faith, to kill me! That day, Vineet Goel had finally succeeded in his campaign of terror and fear, nearly four months in the making. Frightened, and with the desire to live and write driving me on, I had consented to fly to Jaipur for two days. In moments, a white Ambassador had been sent to drive me, with only my laptop in tow, to the airport. The police handed me tickets at the airport and that is how I had bidden farewell to Kolkata. Perhaps Stalin used to banish people to the Gulag in a similar way. Stalin used to banish those who were staunchly anti-Stalinist. Me, I had never been anti-Buddhadeb, Mr Bhattacharya!

It was only after reaching Jaipur that I had realized that everything Vineet Goel and his messenger from Jaipur had told me had been nothing but a pack of lies. The police there had been informed that I was going to attend an event. Consequently, I was put up in a seedy hotel which had apparently been booked by the eponymous messenger. Late in the night, I was informed by the local police that I had to leave Rajasthan immediately to avoid a potential law-and-order situation.

Terrified again, I had immediately resolved to go back to Kolkata. However, early next morning I was taken from the hotel and driven, not to the airport or Kolkata, to Delhi. Again, I came to know later that the Government of Rajasthan had been trying to pull the same trick that the Government of West Bengal had already played with them—to foist me on the other without any prior news. West Bengal had obviously replied this time with a curt refusal to keep playing the game any longer. Alas, when I could not be dumped on any of the available courts, the only option had been to pack me off to Delhi. So the police had driven me out, a stateless, orphaned, helpless refugee, to some distant no man's land, hoping to return to Kolkata someday. You had already informed the Centre that you were not responsible for me, had washed your hands of me, so to speak. The simple truth is that the decision had always been yours to take—and you had decided you wanted me out of West Bengal.

Rumour has it that you, Mr Buddhadeb Bhattacharya, had been afraid of losing the Muslim vote by keeping me in Kolkata. Everything had been done to secure that vote. I have always written against religious fanaticism. So, how could you not take my side that day? How could you condone the actions of those fundamentalists? You helped them win! Do you believe they love you? Are you certain that, like Frankenstein's monster, they too will not demand your head one day?

I have left everything behind in Kolkata. My home, my work, my life—I feel disconnected from everything. I am not sure I know where I am. I am not sure how long I will have to wait here for your approval so that I can go back home. The depression, uncertainty and restlessness are slowly driving me towards insanity. I can feel my blood pressure steadily rising, the anxiety goading me to commit suicide and end everything once and for all. Just so that you are happy, I have agreed to remove the lines which had most offended you in *Dwikhandito*. No, I did not agree to it because I am afraid of the fundamentalists. I agreed to it because I am more afraid of you, your secular democratic political parties, and the codes of conduct you have determined for those whom you grant asylum. I am afraid of how numerous intelligent individuals have shamelessly remained silent. I had to leave Bangladesh because there had been no freedom of speech and expression in my country; I had migrated to India hoping to find these here. If the world's largest democracy cannot guarantee these rights to me, who else can? When I was asked to keep quiet, when I was asked to disavow my own writing, when I was forced to destroy my own book—was it me who was being demeaned? Or was it something else that lost face?

Mr Bhattacharya, I don't believe your party will lose any votes on account of me. Your party is all-powerful, so I am certain it will come up trumps in any election. Despite that, if you are sure of earning a few extra votes because you have managed to drive me out of Bengal, then I wish you all the success with these gains. Perhaps after the election is over and you have won, you will let me return home? I will wait for your consent. I have never tried to harm you, and neither do I wish to do so in the future. All I wish is to be left to my own devices so that I can write as I please. I am not your adversary. It is the fundamentalists you have embraced as friends who are the true enemy here, they who wish to consume our world through their narrow-mindedness, superstitions and intolerance. I don't believe you are not aware of this.

If you do indeed believe in terms like secularism, equality, honesty and courage, then it should not be difficult for you to accept me as a friend. Elections cannot be the last word to everything in the world, there are still things like humanity to consider, and ethics too. If we end up losing these, then what else is left to redeem? So many kings win, yet so many fall from grace, but do we judge a king's character by how long he managed to hang on to his throne? Shouldn't a king be judged solely by his actions?

Yours sincerely,
Taslima

10 December

'. . . Taslima has suffered too much and has gone through prolonged distress and agony. This must be brought to an end without delay. She should also, without much ado, be allowed to return to Kolkata, her preferred place for stay. Moreover, she should be granted Indian citizenship before her current visa expires so that her creative work does not suffer and she is never again rendered fugitive and stateless. The award of citizenship would also make it easier for her to protect her rights. In urging this, I am not alone; hundreds of millions of Indians desire likewise.'—Muchkund Dubey[37]

It is International Human Rights Day today and I am in a deeply pensive mood as I reflect upon my life. I have been in exile for nearly two decades. I am yet to win back the freedom to go back to my native Bangladesh and settle there. The Government of Bangladesh, on its part, has never bothered to inform me why it has revoked my citizenship.

It is International Human Rights Day today and I am languishing in a godforsaken place far away from my beloved Bengal. Both the eastern and western halves of Bengal have banished me, making any refuge anywhere in either state impossible. No one would know where I am; not that anyone is supposed to in the first place. No one is allowed to meet me and neither am I allowed to see anyone. My days and evenings and nights thus pass in solitude.

It is International Human Rights Day today and I have spent the entire day thinking about a life that is devoid of all rights. An orphan, helpless and mute, denied the right to speak. Isn't the freedom of speech and expression a fundamental right too? Sometimes, not having spoken or expressed an opinion in a while, I feel I might summarily forget how to speak, how to think. I might forget that just like my own, there are contrary views that I must be open to. I might forget the true definition of human rights. Today's date will come and go but it will no longer make a difference to me.

My captors came to visit me in the evening, usually a sign of new developments. What they told me boils down to this: Gunnar Svensson is coming from Sweden to meet me but I am not allowed to host a foreign national in my safe house, and neither am I allowed to go and meet him at his hotel. I have also been informed that if I wish to meet Mr Svensson, then I would have to ask for approval in writing. If the powers that be are fine with my request, then both of us will be separately taken to a neutral space for a couple of hours so that we can talk. I have been asked to not expect anything more. My captors are not gods. They are far more powerful.

I have given countless lectures across the globe, on different platforms and in various universities, on personal freedom and the freedom of expression. So many people in so many countries have come to listen and be inspired. And here they are, having confined me to a room, dictating what I can and cannot do. The people who are so busy with the shackles on my feet and the blindfolds on my eyes, have they even heard about me? Have they ever been privy to my history?

I was supposed to be in Kolkata now, and Svensson was supposed to visit me there! If I had been in Kolkata, he could have easily visited me in my home, and perhaps even stayed on as my guest. I know for a fact he has a Stockholm–Kolkata ticket, bought in advance a few months ago. His itinerary has been changed on hearing that I am presently in Delhi. I have told him over the phone that I am more or less under house arrest in Delhi, so I cannot say for certain how I will meet him. Svensson was obviously not happy hearing this. He tried explaining to me that I should not let them coerce me into everything, that I should fight against the arbitrary rules made especially for me—like how he would not be able to visit me or stay with me. Despite being aware that it is not possible for me to fight, Svensson has not cancelled his trip. Besides, there are no refunds on cancelling cheap tickets, so it makes sense he continue his trip!

What manner of life am I supposed to live in this exile if I am not allowed to meet even a few chosen friends? I will eventually suffocate to death if things go on like this! At least when I had been under house arrest in Kolkata, friends had been allowed to visit. Now I have been cut off from the entire world. What my captors told me had a lot in common with what Prasun Mukherjee had said to me: 'If it is so important to meet him, why don't you go and do so in Sweden?' So, is that what they want? That I leave this country?

Indeed, it is International Human Rights Day today!

11 December

I would have surely perished if not for my computer and the Internet. I had initially thought to myself, why take the computer along for a two-day trip? It's not as if I was going to work too much! Then I thought to myself, at least I might write a poem or two. So, I had set out with only my computer.

Work has kept me alive. I remember helplessly crying at the sight of the small cell in Robben Island where Nelson Mandela had had to spend eighteen of his twenty-seven years of incarceration. I remember crying at the thought of what he used to do besides his work in the limestone quarry, only to realize that the tiny lock-up had books and some sparse stationery. Perhaps one can momentarily forget a lot of suffering if one is only allowed the freedom to read and write.

I frequently get calls from Kolkata where people read out articles that have been published in solidarity with me in the Bengali newspapers. These days it is Enamul Kabir who has taken on this task. In the morning, he read out Suranjan Dasgupta's editorial from *Aajkaal* where he has cited numerous instances since 1947 where political asylum has been granted to various people, never with any preconditions or prior promise of obedience. Dasgupta has unequivocally declared that it will surely be a condemnable incident if the same is not made available to me in this secular democratic country. I have never met Mr Dasgupta. Yet, so many people like him, people I do not know, have stood by me through this ordeal and have taken a stand against a grievous injustice.

I received a text message from Arundhati Roy: 'Am in Kolkata. Everybody I meet wants you back here. I am sure it will happen. Stay strong. Am in a crowd. Will call when I can. Lots of love.' So few words and yet they have brought me so much joy. I had spoken to her on the very first day in this 'safe house', all thanks to Karan Thapar. I had told her everything—Hyderabad, my return to Kolkata, the ensuing house arrest, the commissioner's visit to my house, 21 November, and my forced farewell the very next day. Karan later interviewed Arundhati on his show, *The Devil's Advocate*. Arundhati had been fantastic! She confessed that if all the things that had been done to me had happened to her, she would have given up writing to do something else. She also admitted to being suspicious that the entire controversy was a carefully manufactured diversion meant to deflect public attention from the uproar surrounding Nandigram and Singur. The protest rally at Park Circus had been nothing but a rehearsed performance to provide the perfect excuse for driving me out of the state. Already the news of the death of another Muslim youth, coupled with the embers from the Rizwanur murder scandal, had been threatening to upset the Muslim vote bank that had always staunchly supported the Left in Bengal. Afraid of losing their fiefdom, the drowning Left Front government had grasped at the nearest straw they could find—me. They had known it would be easy to tag me as anti-Islamic and drive me out forcefully, just so the Taslima-hating Muslims keep voting for the incumbent government.

Ever since our last conversation on the night of 23 November, I have not spoken to Mr B, even though he had assured me I could call him whenever required. But he is such an important man, I don't wish to bother him. I called him today at long last because of Svensson's visit; I wish he stays nearby during his visit here. Mr B told me to write a letter. He also informed me that the fundamentalists had not simply targeted me; they had also caused him trouble, though he was a little fuzzy about the exact nature of that ordeal. I would assume the Muslims have abused him because he has taken me on as a responsibility and has been feeding and keeping me alive instead of driving me out of the country entirely. I asked Mr B when I would be able to return to Kolkata, the same old uncomfortable question. He could not say for sure, only that the entire thing was at the mercy of an impulse. What had happened had been impulsive, and as soon as there was another distraction, the people would shift their attention from me and things would automatically calm down. Till then, however, I would have to stay away from West Bengal.

I am an unwanted creature. The Government of West Bengal does not wish me to be back, and it seems, neither do the people. Some do perhaps, but not strongly enough for anything to change. Never in my life did I imagine that something like this would happen.

12 December

The days pass, though I am not entirely sure how. They have bought me a black sweater; my skin is dry and peeling in the cold. The dermatologist Mr Malakar has advised me to use a cream called Venusia for my skin. They have bought me that too, besides getting me two new pairs of socks. It's the same type of food for breakfast, lunch and dinner. It works, in a way. I am called and I go and eat. Not that I feel too hungry, so I am not exactly certain why I eat. The senses are gradually withering, as if death has taken root somewhere in my body. A few days ago I had sat and howled, prayed to my overlords to fetch me some poison. They have surely taken that request quite literally and dispatched it to the department concerned.

A slew of stony faces surround me day and night, my protectors and captors, I am no longer sure which is which. I keep oscillating between being under house arrest and being under surveillance. The stones have become impatient, half expecting me to burst out one day with a sudden 'That's it! I've had it. I'm leaving!' If something can reanimate these stones, this surely will. They will promptly ask, 'Which country, ma'am? Do you want a business class ticket, or would economy do?'

I cannot breathe and no one seems to be noticing. No one seems to be sensing any unease, my gasping sounds are inaudible too. Wrapped as they usually are in silence, such sounds are mostly faint and are rarely ever heard.

I cannot comprehend our times any more. I also do not know if I will ever be able to go back home. West Bengal might forever remain a distant dream or even a nightmare.

Joy Goswami has written a wonderful article about me. I spoke to him over the phone and he told me they were proud of me back home. Aparna Sen[38] called in the afternoon to express regret that the true miscreants had been spared while an innocent person had been punished. Yes, that is what had happened. So, what were they going to do about it? She assured me she was trying her best to come up with something. Jayashri Dasgupta called to express her grief. However, throughout the conversation it was obvious that she had assumed I would be staying away from Kolkata. Jayashridi, I want to go back home! Dolly and Saugata Roy called later in the night. Saugata told me, 'The CPM doesn't want you back. And we don't have the power to bring you back.'

'Then? Will I never be able to return to Kolkata? I have to go back!' 'Let me see what I can do. I will try and have a word with Priyada and Pranabda.'

'You haven't tried calling them yet?' I asked, trying to hold back tears. I could understand he was a little mortified. Clearly, back in Kolkata, everyone has gotten used to the certainty and finality of my farewell. They will express appropriate sorrow when the topic arises, some will confess to missing me, others will show pity. The rest will simply blame the entire episode on my bad lot.

Of course, those who do not know me, who do not read my work, who do not understand me, they will allege that I had set the entire thing up to garner fame, boost sales, and manufacture publicity. But they will not be able to list out the crimes I have supposedly committed. Some will find peace in denouncing the literary merit of my writings, since that can clearly be reason enough for the state to banish a writer with complete impunity. Anxieties concerning communal unrest and violence can also serve as equally effective pretexts. Either way, the outcome remains the same.

13 December

If you are alone, then that is all that you are. All you have then is solitary confinement and a room full of misery. When you are alone, you are completely alone. And you have no one else in the entire universe.

14 December

Eminent historian Tapan Raychaudhuri has been calling quite frequently from Kolkata. He is a revered man, an established writer and a Padma Bhushan awardee. During one such conversation he confessed, after reminding me that I was not supposed to ask for names, to have spoken to a high-ranking official from Bengal.

TR: Things are quite grim!
TN: Grim? Where?
TR: Back here.
TN: But why are things grim? I don't see anything that's wrong!
TR: You have no idea. The Lashkar-e-Taiba is bent on killing you. They are looking all over for you!
TN: I haven't heard anything like that!
TR: It's come out in the *Telegraph*.
TN: I don't think the *Telegraph* has written something like this. Have you heard of the HuJi in Bangladesh? A few years back, they had made elaborate plans to kill me. Now no one has any such plans. The antisocial ruffians who violated the streets of Kolkata on the 21st have not read my books, of that I am sure. So, there was clearly a scheme behind their involvement.
TR: Let us negotiate for now. We are trying to find out what the fundamentalists want, whether you have to tender a written apology or something like that. Whatever their demands are, it will be best if we can come to an understanding accordingly.
TN: I have already excised certain sections from the book. Their top-rung leaders had declared the matter closed.

So, what is this now? Why should I have to pander to any random demand anyone might make?

TR: A written apology might go a long way.

TN: What do you mean by a written apology?

TR: One stating to the public that you have removed certain offensive sections from your book.

TN: But all that is done! It was shown on TV for the entire day. In fact, a new edition has already been printed without those deleted sections.

TR: They are not willing to understand.

TN: Who has told you that? They are perfectly willing to understand. It is Mr Biman Basu who isn't. He has said I have written more. What he means by that is more of my work should be erased. Ultimately, if they do not wish to understand, then nothing will convince them otherwise, not even a written apology. If someone deliberately wants to be spiteful, there is very little that can be done to stop them.

TR: Things are uneasy though.

TN: Things are uneasy if you want them to be uneasy. Or else, they are perfectly peaceful. Who has told you about this trouble?

TR: They told me! They told me that the fundamentalists are creating a racket.

TN: They are creating a racket because they are being encouraged to do so. If the media keeps giving them free publicity and the politicians keep bowing to each of their dictums, this is what they will keep doing. They are not doing anything right now, you would have noticed if they were. Have there been any protest marches lately? The imam of the Tipu Sultan Mosque has mentioned not liking something a few times. If he had been reprimanded, he would have stopped. The last time he had issued a fatwa against me, Prasun Mukherjee had called him over and reprimanded him, or bribed him perhaps, and the imam had emerged from the meeting having completely reversed his stance. In fact, he had denied having issued a fatwa in the first place! You see, the problem is with intentions. Right now, no one wants to stop the imam. The people who could have easily handled the situation just don't want to do it.

TR: I understand that. But these people are playing political games. How can we call ourselves civilized! They're all scoundrels.

He informed me that he would be meeting someone very important very soon, to talk about me. I asked who it was, but he did not want to say. 'I won't take names, but I know he is the only person who can help you. In fact, he can save you from this dangerous predicament.'

The assurance gave me hope. I knew Tapan Raychaudhuri has always been fond of me. However, the news I received, of the meeting with the 'very important' man, left me flabbergasted.

TR: So, I spoke to him. He told me it would be best if you leave the country for a while. You won't have to spend any money. The Government of India will sponsor your travel and stay abroad.

TN: What? Who has told you this?

TR: I can't say who it is. Don't ask me his name. But he is someone very important.

TN: So they truly want to drive me out of the country?

TR: Absolutely not! You will leave only after your visa has been extended. So, you don't have to worry about that. If you have a visa, you can always return.

TN: They can stop me in the immigration even if I have a
visa.

TR: No, that's not possible.

TN: Yes, they can. They absolutely can. They can if they
have orders to do so.

TR: Things like that don't happen in India. I have never
heard about it.

TN: Have you ever heard about a writer being thrown out of
a state within India's borders?

TR: No.

TN: Didn't it happen with me? I have a residence permit. I
have a right to live in Kolkata. Have I been able to go
back?

TR: No.

TN: If I leave India, I will never be allowed to come back, just
as I have not been allowed to go back to Kolkata. Besides,
have you ever considered why I should have to leave at all?

TR: I was simply trying to negotiate. I told them you are like
my daughter. You want to go back to Kolkata, get back
to writing, and we are willing to do anything to make
that happen.

TN: Negotiate what?

TR: Your return.

TN: Then I will return to Kolkata. Why should I have to go
abroad?

TR: They want to consolidate their vote bank.

TN: Hasn't all this been enough? They drove me out of
the state. They forced me to tear out pages from my
book. The fundamentalists are finally satisfied and have
gone quiet. What other demands are they trying to
appease now? They are still not sure about their vote
bank? For that I have to leave India? Next, the fanatics

will demand my death in exchange for votes. Will they
send men to kill me then? There are no limits to certain
demands and there is no limit to appeasement either.
Let me tell you, these are imaginary demands which
they are trying to take the credit for handling—just to
fool the uneducated poor into voting for them.

My captors came later in the night with the answer to the
request I had put in as per Mr B's advice. They had passed
it on to the authorities for consideration and I had been
waiting ever since for the reply. The answer was unequivocal:
my Swedish friend would not be able to visit me and neither
would I be able to visit him. If we have to meet, it would
have to be somewhere else, which would not be decided by
us. I would have to put in another request and if the higher
powers approve it, my captors would make all the necessary
arrangements. Why would I not be able to meet him here?
Why would my friend not be able to visit me or I would
not be able to visit him? My captors had no answer to these
questions. They were following orders as usual.

　　The more I tell my captors that I cannot bear this, that
no one can survive like this, that I want a normal life where
I can breathe freely, go out, visit people or have friends come
over, the more uncomprehending they become. Their faces
devoid of expression, they stare me down. It would be more
fruitful to try and converse with robots since my captors are
way more lifeless than them. Or perhaps they are like walls.
If you bang your head against one, the only thing you can be
certain of is the possibility of a cracked skull.

　　They called me again after a while to ask me about the
writer I had been speaking to over the phone, his name,
address and other useless details.

TN: Tapan Raychaudhuri.

Captor (C): Oh yes. What else did he say?

TN: I have told you everything.

C: He spoke to you about the negotiations.

TN: Yes, but I have refused. I won't give in to demands that I should leave India.

C: Why not?

TN: I won't because it is unreasonable to ask me to leave the country first in order to be allowed to return to Kolkata.

C: Unreasonable?

TN: Yes, completely unreasonable. Tell me, do you understand how exactly does it get easier for me to return to Kolkata by leaving the country? Perhaps you do, but I don't. Besides, I am not a child. I have gone through this before and the wounds are still fresh. I had been told to leave for a few days and then come back. It is only people who wish to kick you out who use words like 'abroad' and 'later'. Those who don't wish you to leave, allow freedom without restrictions. They don't lock you up or try to disrupt your life.

15 December

I was taken to another safe house in the morning where a man had been called to draw blood for tests. His name on the official papers was Miku Srivastav.

16 December

Days have been passing, somewhat like how a dying animal lingers till the last breath has left its body. It is Victory Day in Bangladesh today. The long revolution to save the Bengali language had finally ended in war. On such a day, a writer from Bengal who has always written in Bangla finds herself caged. There is no victory for me to commemorate. I had written to Hameeda Hossain[39] of the Ain o Salish Kendra,[40] who had been steadfast in her support during the toughest of times in Bangladesh: 'It's been years. I hope you are well. My misfortunes have not ceased their pursuit of me. There is not a moment when I do not wish to return to Bangladesh but will that ever be possible? It can only happen if the cases against me are withdrawn, if the government provides me with security and if I am not stopped from returning. I would be eternally grateful to you if you could help me find my way back home.'

She wrote back: 'You must not forget that even if all the cases are withdrawn, there will always be a group of people who will march in protest simply for their own petty gains. I am sure you have heard about the cartoonist from *Prothom Alo*. He is in jail now, fighting for bail. We don't know what is in store. See, we don't yet have the freedom that will allow us the freedom to say whatever we wish to. It's become a part of the cultural script to use religion for the benefit of politics. Writers and journalists have to remain vigilant. It's becoming clear that we are gradually becoming increasingly reactionary, both culturally and politically.'

I knew about Arifur Rahman. The poor man is in jail for his cartoon for the supplement *Alpin* (The Pinprick). An old lumberjack meets a poor little boy walking with his cat and asks, 'What's your name, boy?'

'Babu,' answers the boy.

'Don't you know that you have to add Muhammad before your name?' snaps the man.

Seeing the boy shrink in fear, the man asks again, 'What's your father's name?'

This time the boy answers, 'Muhammad Abu.'

Pleased, the old man asks again, 'What do you have there in your lap?'

'Muhammad Cat,' replies the boy.

In all probability, it had been a harmless cartoon meant to underscore how a lot of the poor and uneducated people erroneously believe in adding 'Muhammad' before every name. However, nearly 25,000 people had marched in protest against the cartoon. On top of this, Motiur Rahman, an ex-communist and editor of *Prothom Alo,* did something extremely shameful—he fired both the cartoonist and the editor of the supplement, and apologized to the citizens. He did not stop there. He went on to apologize to the *khatib*[41] of the Baitul Mukarram,[42] crouching on his knees. As the saying goes, when communists begin to rot, they rot badly and the stench is enough to smother a nation.

I do not accept a nation that does not guarantee the freedom of speech as my own. This Bangladesh is not my nation. Thirty million people did not give up their lives and two million women did not get raped for the independence of this Bangladesh.

17 December

Svensson called from Ashoka Palace to complain about his hotel room. There are rats roaming in the room. The air is apparently heavy with the stench of kerosene. The bathroom window is open and it cannot be pulled shut.

My captors have told me that Svensson has been given all facilities. They were careful enough to inform me that it was they who had received Svensson at the airport, who brought him to the hotel, and who were feeding him and showing him around. Despite all this, Svensson was not only refusing to show any gratitude, he was also constantly trying to find faults. Svensson has never been fortunate enough to have been a guest of a government anywhere in the world. If it had been somewhere in Europe that people had escorted him from the airport, put him up at a five-star hotel, showed him around and fed him, he would probably have been in a half-bow of gratitude throughout. If he is given just an ice lolly by a white man, we would probably spend an eternity praising both the white man and the ice lolly. However, if someone black or brown were to give up even their absolute everything for him, he would still scrunch his nose in discontent. A closet racist through and through, it is a side of Svensson that I have been aware of. I wanted to meet him and I put in an application for him to stay here with me, not so much for him but for the sake of my freedom.

Around noon, I was again taken to the other safe house where they had drawn blood for the medical tests. Svensson was brought there too. My captors informed me that they had extended the duration of the visit for my sake, from one hour to three. I could not help but wonder what they were expecting— that I bow my head in gratitude? Am I a murderer or a thief? Have I been jailed? It stuns me to think that someone else other than me is going to take decisions regarding how long I can be out and for how long I can talk to my friends.

Arrangements were made there for lunch, again by my captors. It was a quiet and desolate house, a government property usually used for covert meetings. A spread was laid out for us on the dining table so artfully that one would not be able to guess that nothing there had been cooked at home. I do not know much else about the house, especially because my captors refused to answer any of my questions.

In the evening I suddenly had an absurd urge to cry my eyes out, thinking about the state of my life. Till late in the night, I could not stop crying.

18 December

I could not sleep well last night. I woke up with a start finally at around dawn. While surfing the Net, I chanced upon the happy news of Gloria Steinem's visit to Kolkata. There she has spoken about me, stating, 'This is an outrageous violation of her human rights. She has a right to be safe.' On the news of certain passages being removed from *Dwikhandito*, she has said, 'It is one thing if a writer excises passages from their writing of their own free will, but if they are forced into doing it then that is another concern altogether.' How easily she can voice the truth! Steinem has always been someone whose words would compel one to pause and reflect. She has written about me in her magazine, *Ms*, and has also published my writings, and has spoken about our previous meeting in Delhi at the South Asian Writers' Conference. I too have written so much about her work. If only I had been in Kolkata, I would have invited her over to my house to truly commemorate her visit.

Gloria Steinem was one of the leading icons of the feminist movement in the late 1960s and early 1970s. When I began writing back in the 1980s, I remember feeling the same pain, protesting in the same language, arguing similar viewpoints and reflecting on similar opinions and reasons, as her work two decades back, without ever having read her writing prior to that.

19 December

I received an invitation for dinner at Khushwant Singh's house, 7 p.m., Saturday evening. I dutifully passed on the invitation to my captors for approval. I also gave them

Khushwant Singh's details, address, telephone number, etc. and the request was forwarded to the authorities concerned. As usual, it has been turned down. I had also fixed a meeting with Brinda Karat of the CPI(M) but that too has been turned down.

The first time I spoke to Brinda Karat, she said, 'The final decision regarding your return to Kolkata rests solely on the Centre, not the state.' Obviously, this had terrified me. So many people have told me so many different things that sometimes I cannot understand what I should believe and what I shouldn't. I tend to believe everyone, especially since I have trouble believing that someone would deliberately misguide or lie to me. Even after so many lies that have been spoken to me, I have not learnt my lesson. I do not understand the complicated equations between the Centre and the state. I simply know the truth that I have done no wrong and that I have been unfairly persecuted.

I can also sense the inexorable passing of time. Previously, journalists would incessantly inquire about how I was, about what I was doing or thinking. Now the phones do not ring as often, although back when they used to, I would usually never take the call. Similarly, I would refuse to talk or give interviews. My captors would often warn me against the media and journalists, how greedy they were, how each and every one of their actions was motivated by money or fame, how they would all abandon me once they were done without even glancing back to see if I lived or died. I must admit though, my captors are not always wrong.

I have received an email from Gloria Steinem: 'Please, please tell me if I can do anything—and you always have a room with me in New York.' The words have lifted my spirits immeasurably. The world has still not been damned because there are still a handful of good people left in it. Despite all the limitations, the severity, the injustice and the abuse, hope springs eternal.

What happened today should not have happened in this country. This is a democracy, which makes it necessary that everyone enjoys the freedom of speech in this country. This nation has always boasted of being large-hearted and generous, after all! A senior officer from a top ministry had come to talk to me today. He did not reveal who he was but for some reason told me his name—let it be Sanatan Sengupta. He seemed a lot like my captors. I knew his name but that was about all that I knew, though I cannot say why he should feel the need to hide his identity from me. So, I assumed he had been sent by Mr B. And why had he come by? Mostly, to repeat the things that Prasun Mukherjee had once narrated to me back in Kolkata:

SS: You should go away.
TN: Where should I go?
SS: Go away from India.
TN: But why?
SS: Why are you here? Is it because you want to go back to Kolkata? Isn't that what you are waiting for?
TN: Yes, it is. Kolkata is my home. I have left everything behind there, my house, my books and my things.
SS: But you cannot be allowed to return to Kolkata.
TN: Why not?
SS: They will kill you. Besides, we have to save our people too.
TN: What do you mean?
SS: It means people are going to die because of you!
TN: How is that possible?

SS: Do you want a bunch of people to die because of you?

TN: Why on earth would I want that? I believe in humanity, I write about it. I write about life. Why should I wish for people to die?

SS: There will be protest marches because of you. Guns will be fired. People will die.

TN: I don't believe any of that will happen. I see no signs of protest marches. No one has declared one recently and there is no reason to do so either. Even if there is a protest march, why should people have to die?

SS: Do you want an old person to die because of you?

TN: Why would I want that? But why would they have to die in the first place? Who would kill them?

SS: Do you want innocent children to die because of you? You want to be responsible for their deaths?

TN: So strange! Why should kids have to die? And why would I want something like that to happen?

SS: If you don't want that then you must leave!

TN: I don't want a single life hurt because of me. However, I don't believe that in order for that to happen, I have to leave this country. If there is going to be a procession, it will happen regardless. People march in protest against so many things. Do all of them have to leave the country after that?

SS: This is not your country!

TN: I know it isn't. I am living here because of a residence permit. I am here today because of the permit. If I don't have the permit, tomorrow I might have to leave.

SS: Yes. So then, leave. If you are anxious that you will not get a residence permit if you leave, then I am assuring you that won't happen. It will be renewed as usual. I am giving you my word. I am sure you want the safety of the people of this country.

TN: I won't leave. I am not harming anyone. I have done no wrong, committed no crime. I am a completely honest person. I have lived in Kolkata for years. No one has come to murder me, and neither has anyone died because of me during that time. Send me to Kolkata if you can. None of you have to worry so much about me any more.

SS: You won't go abroad?

TN: No, I won't leave India.

SS: This is not your country!

TN: Despite that, I will live in this country. Not because my ancestors hail from this country, but because I love this land and its people. If you wish to manhandle me and physically throw me out, please go ahead and do so.

20 December

Arundhati Roy had advised me never to trust politicians. She had said, 'They don't think of you as a person, they think of you as currency. They want to use you for their business deals. They have no intention of loving you.'

I have been in a terrible mood the entire day. My captors came in the evening, probably to find out my decision after my conversation with Mr Sengupta yesterday. Just as I had told him, I informed them too that I would not be leaving any time soon. Writers don't instigate riots and pogroms. Other people do, politics does. There are other nefarious reasons behind the murder of innocents. Writers and artists write and paint. They don't riot.

21 December

It is the 21st today, a month since the terrible events of November. It still seems so fresh, as if it was just the other day

that those non-Bengali ruffians had caused pandemonium on
the streets of Kolkata. The days seem to be flying by! Even
now, the moment I close my eyes, I can see those uncouth,
disgusting men dancing on the street, their macabre glee
apparent in each exuberant gesture.

I could not control myself any more. Mr B has not been
receiving my calls, though I understand why a busy man
such as he might not be able to take my calls. I usually don't
send him messages. If he is so busy, he would probably not
read those either. Yet I wrote to him: 'You have already
done so much for me and I am immensely grateful. I depend
on you and I want to tell you how difficult it has been to
endure this life of captivity. At least in Delhi, can I not have
a normal life? If I don't meet my friends, don't spend time
with them, how am I going to survive? Can we please meet
one of these days?'

22 December

'In response to demands from a few religious fundamentalists,
India's democratic and secular government has placed a
writer of international repute under virtual house arrest.
Shorn of all cant, that is what the Centre's treatment of
Taslima Nasreen amounts to. She was forced into exile from
her native Bangladesh because of the books she had written
and it looks as if the UPA government is about to repeat the
same gesture by placing intolerable restrictions on her stay
in India.

'She is living under guard in an undisclosed location.
She will not be allowed to come out in public or meet
people, including her friends. Without quite saying so,
the government is clearly sending her a message that she

isn't welcome in India and ought to leave. Earlier, she was turfed out of West Bengal by the state government. It's not quite clear who's ahead in the competition to pander to fundamentalist opinion, the Centre or the West Bengal government. Earlier, Left Front Chairman Biman Basu had said that Taslima should leave Kolkata if her stay disturbed the peace, but had to retract the statement later. Now External Affairs Minister Pranab Mukherjee echoes Bose by asking whether it is "desirable" to keep her in Kolkata if that "amounts to killing 10 people". In other words, if somebody says or writes something and somebody else gets sufficiently provoked to kill 10 people, then it is not the killer's but the writer's fault.

'That is an astounding statement for the foreign minister of a liberal democratic state to make. The Greek philosopher Plato thought that artists were dangerous people and exiled them from his ideal Republic. But such views can hardly be reconciled with modern democracy, which survives on tolerance. Democracy also accords a valuable place to the arts, where boundaries are pushed and new thinking becomes possible. Taslima's views on women's rights may seem threatening from the point of view of patriarchal codes governing society. That would explain why the animus towards her is not confined to Muslim conservatives, but includes Congress and Left luminaries.

'The ministry of external affairs must think through the implications of what it is doing. If it forces Taslima out of the country, India will be placed on the same platform as Bangladesh, which is close to becoming a failed state. At a time when India's image is ascendant in world affairs the official guardians of that image must not act like weaklings who cave in to every illiberal or fundamentalist threat to this public's constitutional values.'—*Times of India*[43]

Yesterday, there was a protest meeting in Kolkata demanding I be allowed to return to the city. Some have said there were around twenty-five people in the procession and some have reported a thousand. The other side's meetings have always been well attended. Last year, there had been nearly one lakh people at Siddiqullah's meeting and apparently there had been around ten to fifteen thousand boys on the road on 21 November. Usually if traffic is not disrupted, and stones are not pelted, no one notices a big rally. Enough words have been spent and enough has been written. Has anything actually happened?

23 December

I get into trouble whether I speak to journalists or not. If I do, people say I do it for publicity. If I don't, the newspapers and journalists I avoid write whatever they can concoct about me. Today, I read an article in *DNA India* that when Narendra Modi had been in Delhi a while back, I had met him and requested him to give me asylum in Gujarat. I remember how Mumbai's *Mid-Day* had taken a random photo of me off the web, superimposed dark clothes and the Mumbai landscape on to it, and had published a hoax news item that I have stolen into Mumbai in a burqa. Scores of people had believed the news too; just like how normal people believe everything they see in print.

My captors, displeased, have warned me not to play 'political games' while I am in India, though I am not sure which games they were referring to. What I do not comprehend is why people keep thinking the worst of me. Is there something in me that gives off this invincible vibe that I can play with something as complicated as politics? Mostly

simple, quite laid-back, slightly stupid and a little silly—
that's me! If someone can assume that a person like me can
play political games, then they have played these games so
much that it has spoilt their sight and everyone now appears
as players to them.

The *Telegraph* has simply been printing lies, citing 'an
official' as their nebulous source from within the government.
It has been reported that I have been driving my caretakers
up the wall for a hairdryer, because I cannot do without one
after shampooing my hair. Another lie printed on the basis
of 'unofficial sources'! Besides, I have apparently become
crazy about eating fish and have been demanding the most
exotic varieties which the poor government has been running
helter-skelter to arrange for me. With all this and more, the
picture that has been presented to the public is that I am
living my exiled life not just as a king, but as a despot, driving
people insane with my demands. I had asked my captors:
'An official source would mean that someone from your
department is passing this information on. But who could
that be!' My captors had denied it, saying no news could
ever have leaked from within the ministry. 'They make these
things up!'

That had left me puzzled. A prestigious newspaper like
the *Telegraph* would keep writing a pack of lies about someone
for days? I had later gotten to know from a journalist friend
that these articles were written as per instructions from the
ministry, with the only stipulation being the use of 'an official'
as the formless source. That way it gave everyone plausible
deniability, and ensured that no one person got singled out
as the source of the 'leak'.

Let's say this was what the lesser-known, less courageous
journalists were doing. The senior ones were by no means

lagging behind. Noted journalist Vir Sanghvi has written a scathing indictment.[44] I have always put maximum effort in rising above the petty and the immediate, but when people who do not even know me express their judgement about me, they do not usually accord me the same courtesy. Instead, they form their opinions based on their own petty political and social moorings, and the self-serving unscrupulous impulses that guide them and their cohorts. Neither do they ever realize their mistakes, nor do the mistakes ever get rectified. None of them ever get to know the real me, nor do they get to see my real life at close quarters. One can only imagine what unholy joy Vir Sanghvi may have found by writing a pack of hideous lies about me. A helplessly trapped person, living under a dark cloud of uncertainty, under house arrest, who herself has been a subject of political intrigues, is being accused of orchestrating everything to make it to the headlines! Apparently, I do not even have the time to write any more since all my time is being taken up by phone calls to journalists! Once upon a time, the radicals in Bangladesh used to make similar allegations. They would accuse me of doing everything to garner fame, whenever something I had written stung them like a whiplash.

Quite possibly, Sanghvi has heard from Barkha Dutt and Karan Thapar about my calls to them. I had called them for news, to understand which way things were headed. The day the government officials had irrevocably informed me that nothing could be done, that I could not return to Kolkata nor could I live a normal life in Delhi, that I would not be allowed to visit my friends, and that I would have to go out of sight, possibly out of the country, it had seemed the earth had caved in under my feet and my entire world had come crashing down. There was no way I could have stood in combat against the powers that be. I have seen the world abroad and I do not wish to live that life again. With all doors to Bangladesh shut, India had been the final beacon of hope. And now that light has begun to flicker, threatening to go out and plunge my life into darkness. I had called Karan Thapar and Barkha Dutt, people who know and deal with politics far more effectively than I ever will, to take stock of the situation—why was everything happening? Would hundreds of people truly die because of me? Are these claims, regardless of whoever is making them, true?

Karan had wanted to interview me for television but I refused. Instead, I requested him to speak to Manmohan Singh or Sonia Gandhi about the incomprehensible things the government officials were telling me. Karan told me they would not even speak to him about this. That evening I received news from CNN-IBN that a meeting had been held that very day at the ministry of home affairs between the secretary and the Intelligence Bureau (IB). The officials had discussed my situation and come to the conclusion that I would either have to stay in Delhi as dictated by them or leave the country. The news shattered me completely. When asked for a reaction, I told them all that the government officials had said to me and confessed that I was practically under house arrest.

The primary reason behind Vir Sanghvi's ire is perhaps the fact that I have admitted to the media that I am under house arrest. Hence, a laundry list of complaints. I am getting so much exclusive coverage that I don't have time to go to the bathroom. I am getting the best security because I am a foreigner, and a huge amount of money is being wasted on me. A group of literary critics from West Bengal have told him I am a bad writer, not that he has read any of my work to find out. I am constantly asking my captors to save me and then talking to the media about them when their backs are turned. How dare I, being a foreigner, say anything against them? I have created these controversies to stay in the newspaper headlines.

I laugh and think to myself, how have I really created controversies? I was living peacefully in Kolkata, without bothering anyone. It's your government who drove me out, who put me in the headlines! Your government has kept me confined to this house, has forbidden me from meeting anyone, has not let anyone come and see me! You make the headlines, not me! The political terrorism that you have unleashed on me has put me in the headlines! You have made me a pawn in this game between politics and religion. You have thrust your own pawn into the limelight. The victim never wanted to be victimized; she wanted to live with her head held high. You have used something she wrote five years ago to make her a headline. The honourable high court had simply reaffirmed this notoriety by repealing the ridiculous and draconian ban. Your fanatics then pounced on the book, and your secular liberals pounced on me to please them. Your controversies, not mine, have made me into a headline. The readers were perfectly content with my book and it had been in circulation for quite a few years already! No one had had a problem before! You create trouble but you blame me for it. You complain about me being a foreigner and about the money being spent on me!

I was miserable the entire day.

Later in the evening I was informed by a friend that Mr B had instructed Vir Sanghvi to write the article. He had also instructed many other editors and journalists that he no longer wished to see my name in print anywhere.

I don't know why people blame religious fundamentalism. One should be more wary of the politicians, journalists and intellectuals who do not even spare a glance at victims of intolerance but are always very concerned and sympathetic to the plight of the fanatics.

24 December

I asked to meet Svensson but it was turned down. I asked him to meet my Hindi publisher, Arun Maheshwari, who has taken care of everything thereafter.

Meanwhile, I have been in deep despair, as has become a constant for me it seems. Although a slew of phone calls has managed to lift my mood a bit today. Bibhutibhusan Nandi, Sunando Sanyal and Debabrata Bandyopadhyay called to express their solidarity. One of them even told me to think of Nelson Mandela who had been in jail for nearly two decades. All of them assured me that such circumstances would not continue for long and they asked me to keep writing, reminding me how writing was my one true refuge from everything. As if I did not know that already! But whenever I sit down to write, a feeling of despair settles on me. I keep staring out through the window, drowning in my own sighs.

Sheela Reddy of *Outlook* magazine called to tell me about the writers and intellectuals who had signed a petition in support of me. She also informed me that Brinda Karat had refused to sign.

Madanjeet Singh, the UNESCO goodwill ambassador, has written a letter to Jyoti Basu, attaching an editorial from *Times of India* and one of my articles for the Bengali newspaper *Ei Samay* with it. Mr Singh is a truly remarkable man. I have never had the chance to have a proper conversation with him, and yet he has been doing so much for me!

Arun Maheshwari has told me that his writers have come together to protest. Some friends from Kolkata want to come to Delhi to start a hunger strike but I have firmly asked them not to. They help nothing, these things. In a country of a billion people, unless at least a million people are seen walking in a procession, the grievances and hunger strikes of a handful are tantamount to nothing.

I was in a good mood the entire day but it got spoilt at night. The English translation of my article 'Nirbasito Bahire Ontore' (Banished Within and Without) has been published by the *Statesman* without the date I had mentioned at the end. Instead, they have added an editorial comment about the article being an expression of my annoyance at the Delhi government's shenanigans. I am equally annoyed at the *Statesman*'s shenanigans! For some reason, they have convinced themselves that the readers will not read the piece if the date is mentioned. Does history mean nothing then?

Tui Nishiddho, Tui Kotha Koish Na (Don't Speak, You Are Forbidden) is a collection of my writings that has just recently been published. The first article had been written way back in 1993 and the last is as recent as this year. The rest were written at various points of time while in Europe or on a visit to Kolkata, whenever I have thought of home. Without mentioning any of the dates, the publishers had wished to give the impression that the entire thing was written in the past year; that I simply happened to end up in Delhi and sent them the manuscript from here. Is this anything else except fraud? I cannot tolerate this sort of dishonesty at all.

There is a big, round moon in the sky tonight. Is it the full moon? Even if it is, how does it matter? Would I be able to bathe in the moonlight and dance with someone ever again? One can perhaps watch the moon from one's room too, listlessly. The moon, after so many days! Both of us, the moon and I, are so alone. Amidst this cloying, swirling darkness, we stay awake together.

25 December

They took me back to that house again today, to meet Svensson, and to meet Asesh and Muna. Asesh and Muna have come down from Kolkata to see me, a suitcase full of things sent from home in tow. Since no one is allowed to visit the safe house, my captors had arranged for them to meet me in that house and hand over the things to me. They were picked up from the hotel and taken through circuitous alleys and dingy by-lanes before being brought there, just like everyone who was to be taken to that secret house. Besides, Asesh and Muna had been allowed to meet me simply because of the suitcase. Though, in the end none of that even matters because the final decision rests with the people who are acting as liaisons with my captors, without whose approval even my captors cannot do anything. If the latter had the power to take a decision for me, they would have long since sent me back to Kolkata.

There was an ornamental tree and various related paraphernalia for decorations, as gifts for Svensson courtesy of the Government of India. There was also a gala lunch, followed by chocolate cake, again thanks to the government. Even the book I gifted him was arranged by them. I never told them to make these arrangements. I had just requested them to let Svensson spend Christmas with me. Svensson is not a religious person, but I have seen him always celebrate Christmas.

Decorating a tree and giving gifts to each other is more than a set of religious rituals, it's perhaps a bigger social event.

Asesh and Muna had a train to catch for Kolkata and they left soon. I kept staring at their departing figures, thinking about the home I had left behind in the city. Unlike them, I have no way of going back. Kolkata is accessible to everyone—animals, humans, criminals, everyone—but me.

However, the biggest Christmas gift was delivered on television. A friend called from Kolkata to tell me that Jyoti Basu has publicly welcomed me to Kolkata, and that it was being telecast on all the TV channels. To be fair though, immediately after welcoming me, he also made it clear that all arrangements for my security would have to be the Centre's responsibility, just as the other leading communist leaders like Buddhadeb Bhattacharya, Biman Basu and Sitaram Yechury had often pointed out previously. Nevertheless, hearing Jyoti Basu say 'welcome' and 'I have heard the poor girl is depressed' touched my heart. Whatever he said after that was obviously politically motivated, meant to shift the entire onus on to the central government. How can an atheist make statements to the effect that whatever I have written in *Dwikhandito* might hurt the religious sentiments of the Muslims? Can only Hindus, Buddhists, Christians and Jews then be atheists? Do only they have the right to be critical of religious dogma, and not Muslims, because Islamic fundamentalists cannot tolerate any critical interventions? A backward, abject community cannot be reformed through customs and traditions alone; they have to be brought back to life, made aware of their situation, through intermittent shocks. Unless that happens, how can they ever hope to take stock of how much they have regressed! Besides, to be truthful, I have never written out of a desire to lead Muslim society out of the Dark Ages. I write what I believe in, I write about my convictions. When I write I am not preoccupied with thoughts of a particular community or a particular gender. I see people as human, and not as components of warring communities. If one can manage to shed all moorings of religion, community and superstitions, it is perfectly possible to view everyone as equal.

My captors came back in the evening, signalling my return to the safe house—the place where I hide away from prying eyes, not for the sake of security but for reasons which are entirely political. I understand that politics but I cannot come to terms with it. On our way back, my captors gave me just one piece of information—I will not be able to meet Ram Mirchandani because my appeal has yet again been turned down. Who turns these appeals down is something my captors never tell me, and nor have I ever asked them. They had once told me that they simply pass my requests on to the higher authorities, and obediently follow any instructions that are sent back.

My captors left without even a farewell. That in itself is completely out of character, though I understand the reason for it in this case. They were angry because I had given my reaction to Jyoti Basu's comments to the television channels. Many journalists have been calling and to one of them, whom I knew, I had said, 'I feel delighted hearing what Jyoti Basu has said. Hopefully, one day people will wake up to reason and I will again be able to return to my beloved Kolkata.' Why shouldn't I be allowed to say even this much! Jyoti Basu has always been fond of me. Why must I keep quiet even after he has welcomed me to Kolkata? Why can I not express my desires aloud? My captors had sternly instructed me to stay away from the press, because the press is bad through and through. I have tried to live firmly by this decree from the very first day. However, the more I know of my captors and their overlords, the more I become convinced that none of them are the gods they would like to believe they are.

27 December

This evening I was talking to my captors; in the background the Times Now headlines were focused on Pranab Mukherjee telling the media that while it was the state government's responsibility to take care of someone's security, the Centre would graciously step in if the former made a request for aid. In the middle of this, breaking news started filtering in from Rawalpindi about a bombing at an electoral meeting of Benazir Bhutto. My eyes were inevitably drawn to the television—to a mass of dead bodies, half-blown skulls and mangled carcasses, people running, screaming and wailing. So terrible! Such a devastating sight! The ticker was giving live updates. Benazir was safe, a minute later she was injured, another short while later, she was unconscious! Half a minute and the biggest breaking news exploded—Benazir was dead! I sat there, stunned, unable to fully process what had just happened. Was it possible? Could it have truly happened?

Yes, it could. Anything is possible in a country like Pakistan. Is there any reason why it should be a sovereign nation any more? No other country in the world has perhaps successfully manufactured so much terror and so many terrorists as Pakistan. The real anxiety now is what would happen if a madman there manages to get his hands on nuclear bombs. They would incinerate the world within the blink of an eye!

Benazir had written to me twice this very month. I replied to the first letter quite some time later, suspicious as

I had been regarding who had truly written it. Why would she, in her busy schedule, write to an apolitical person such as me? Especially since in the secret political playbook of the subcontinent, supporting me was akin to losing Muslim votes. I was afraid she would be in danger if people got to know she had been in correspondence with me. This was the first time in my life that I had received a letter from a political luminary. My first thought on seeing the Hotmail address had been that this was a prank or a nefarious plot to cause me harm. I never mentioned the letter to my captors, with whom I usually talk about everything, about every single thing I do or think. I wrote a reply to the first letter after a couple of days had passed, a simple answer expressing my gratitude. Within two days, the second one had arrived. I did not even reply to that. Even if I could have come to terms with the fact that a big political leader would write to me via Hotmail, I could not come to terms with her use of 'Sonia'. Being a politician herself, would she call another by their first name instead of referring to her as Mrs Sonia Gandhi or simply Sonia Gandhi? I was convinced this could not have been Benazir and that someone was pulling a fast one on me. What I could not reconcile was why someone would go to such lengths to crack such a joke. Benazir Bhutto never got a reply from me to her second letter because she had been guilty of calling Sonia Gandhi by her first name.

These are the letters. They still make me waver between believing for one instant that Benazir had written to me and then immediately thinking she had not. Perhaps she had truly written the letters. They are hardly eight or nine days old and I had surely been wrong in not replying to the second one. However, the letters do not really matter at the end of the day. The woman had been speaking against terrorism only a few minutes ago. She finished her speech, walked off the stage and got into her car. The car took off and moments later she was shot dead and a suicide bomb was detonated. How could the assailants have come so close to her car? They could because Benazir did not have the sort of strict security detail that was made available for Pervez Musharraf, the President of Pakistan.

First letter:

> Dear Ms. Taslima Nasreen,
>
> I have been impressed by your courage and determination in the face of such backwardness and fundamentalism. I was not able to contact you before due to my pressing engagements at home. I would extend my unflinching support to you. I have contacted Sonia and have urged her to provide you with all legal avenues of protection. I was saddened to know that you had to make amends in your book. Your prose and poetry have been an integral part of my collection and I would like it to bloom further with fresh and bold ideas like yours. Keep up the struggle but please remember that sometimes discretion is the better part of valor.
>
> With warm regards,
> Benazir Bhutto
> Chairperson—Pakistan People's Party

Second letter:

> Dear Ms. Taslima Nasreen,
>
> I am so glad that you are fine. I know what it is like to live under the puritanical yoke of our backward looking societies. It is like trying to find fresh oxygen in a room

filled with smoke. I hope you reach a safe and functional
destination soon. I am sure Sonia will chalk out something
for your safety. Congress should enhance its liberal image
by extending all support to you.

Remember dear, home is where your human soul
finds resonance.

Wishing you all the best.

Sincere regards,
Benazir Bhutto
Chairperson—Pakistan People's Party

I have heard Zardari is a complete idiot. I have heard many
people wonder how an educated woman like her could have
married a corrupt fool like him. Hadn't I married someone
like that too, someone evil and stupid? Anyone can make
mistakes. The difference between Benazir and me was
that I had divorced all the senseless elements from my life
while Benazir hadn't. Besides, Benazir had made many
compromises with the radicals for the sake of votes, while I
have never agreed to any settlements with fundamentalists,
regardless of what has been at stake.

28 December

'Taslima Nasrin, the fearless, ingenuous, renowned Bengali
writer, has been living under solitary house arrest in Delhi
for quite some time. Despite having had her work translated
into numerous regional and most of the major international
languages, Taslima's mother language is Bengali and it is in
this language that her true literary might is evident. She has
been banished from Bangladesh due to her fearless admission
of the truth, due to her unyielding stance that art is simply

not just for art's sake. With this in mind, she has always been
an advocate of larger social and cultural transformations, and
investing both processes with ideals of freedom, equality,
justice and morality. For her, language is but a wondrous
tool that she uses to contest limits set by human hands,
and to inspire the oppressed with renewed hope.'—
Shibnarayan Ray

The statement by the intellectuals has finally been
published. Sheela Reddy has written the statement using
various things I had told her, especially during some of my
most vulnerable moments. I feel deeply hurt by what she has
done. Is this why she never shared the piece with me before
it was published? She knew I would have refused. Authors
Khushwant Singh and Arundhati Roy, director Shyam
Benegal, playwright Girish Karnad, M.A. Baby and Vinod
Mehta (the editor of *Outlook*)—only these few have signed
the document. Sheela had told me a number of people would
be signing. They should have written their own statement.
What they have published simply makes it seem that the
fight for the freedom of thought and expression is my fight
alone. I had not expressed those qualms to her for them to be
put in the declaration! If the authorities decide to come and
raze this safe house to the ground because of my apparent
complaints against the government, who will come to my
aid? I have been depressed the whole day because of all this
and more.

I cannot forget Benazir's death either. Today the Al-
Qaeda has accepted the responsibility for the assassination.
Will they kill me similarly one day? Back in Bangladesh
when Al-Qaeda had yet to become a name, when there was
no Osama bin Laden to terrify the world, there had been
a rumour that a group of Bangladeshi Taliban militants,

having trained under Osama in Afghanistan, were planning to kill me. Soon, Osama became a well-known name and the militants forgot all about me preferring bigger targets, sparing my life in the process. The Harkat-ul-Jihad al-Islami was on the rise then in Bangladesh and one of their first demands had been to ask for my head. Now they are notorious throughout the world as HuJi, a leading terrorist outfit based out of Bangladesh. Not just in their native country, the HuJi is responsible for quite a few local acts of terror in India too, which have claimed numerous lives.

Will a radical Islamic terrorist organization come and kill me one of these days? I try not to believe it, but I cannot help but morbidly anticipate the bullet passing through my heart or the suicide bomb tearing me apart. Perhaps that is how I will die, one way or the other. But does that mean I have to hide in a hole like vermin, waiting for it to happen? If I have to die, does it mean I cannot live now?

At night I read online the statement made by the imam of the Tipu Sultan Mosque. The imam, accompanied by Idris Ali, had called a press conference to declare that were I to return to Kolkata, the city would be set ablaze—that neither did the police have as many bullets, nor did they have jails big enough to contain the Muslims. They have not taken kindly to Jyoti Basu's comments and they do not want me back in Kolkata. Apparently, my crimes have not been absolved by simply deleting the offensive sections from *Dwikhandito*. I would have to apologize for every single insulting thing I have ever written against Islam before reading the *kalima*s and being rechristened. Idris Ali too has joined the fray, declaring proudly that a horde of Muslims would descend on to the streets if I return to the city.

Which country am I living in? Is this Pakistan or Bangladesh?

Had they wished to, could the CPI(M) and the Congress not have been able to handle these religious fanatics? It is common knowledge that the imam's loyalties are with the CPM, while Idris Ali will do whatever the Congress tells him to do. However, has either party said anything to them in censure? No one has condemned their actions! Rumour has it that these people are being used instead to stir further trouble, and to cause riots to ensure that I do not return to Kolkata. In one fell swoop, it takes care of the anxiety of alienating the Muslim vote bank.

The Congress leaders visited Idris Ali in police custody, the same man they had expelled from their party for his complicity in the 21 November incidents. Not only has he been accepted back into the party, it has been done with a fair bit of pomp and show. If this is how it is, if this is how people like him are going to be encouraged to do whatever they desire, is it really strange that he should issue such public threats?

29 December

How did I spend the entire day? No, I did not do anything. I spent it doing nothing. I do not see my situation as being under house arrest. When someone is under house arrest, at least visitors are allowed even though the person might not be allowed to leave the country. If I wish to leave the country, they will gladly drive me to the airport.

I do not call this a jail either. In jails too, there are visiting hours which I do not have the luxury of here. Jails have an address; I do not. Those who are incarcerated know when their sentence is supposed to end. I have no idea when my term ends.

This sort of a 'safe house' is usually reserved for notorious criminals, for the police to be able to use any number of extrajudicial methods to extract information out of them. However, even criminals are not kept for as long as they have kept me, despite having committed no crime, nor having hidden anything they would need to extract. When I am asked about phone calls, about the conversations I have had, I hide nothing from my captors. I cannot imagine a scenario where someone eavesdrops on someone else's conversation. However, a number of friends have told me without a shadow of doubt that my phone calls are being monitored. Since then I have tried to find out the truth myself. Gradually, I have realized that whenever a call is transferred to me, the voice I hear is usually quite a few decibels lower than when my captors talk to me over the telephone. Is that what a wired phone sounds like?

Am I being kept under watch or under house arrest? The overlords have already assured everyone that I am not being kept confined to the safe house. Not that anyone will be able to come and verify how I have been kept. It is impossible to reach me and no one would ever know. I would probably perish here, my corpse abandoned to rot. I cannot explain to anyone why I have been imprisoned, or in fact, how it has been done; it's not as if I understand it all too well. Sumit Chakraborty (of *Mainstream*), Sheela Reddy and others call me regularly. They are so much more aware than me and so I ask them all my questions. I had once asked Sheela Reddy why I was being kept here instead of being allowed to return to Kolkata. She had glibly replied that it was meant to exert mental trauma on me to force me to leave India. 'But they have

declared in Parliament that it is the nation's custom to give
shelter to guests!' I had continued with a catch in my voice, 'I
have done nothing wrong!' 'You have committed an offence.'
'What offence?' 'You have provoked the fundamentalists,'
Reddy had replied with a mysterious smile.

Why subject me to psychological torture? What is the
use of this charade? They might as well drag me by the hair
to the airport and dump me there. I would have no choice
but to leave. Besides, if my visa is not extended this February,
I will have to leave regardless.

I asked them to bring me cigarettes, which I had quit
nearly four years back. By asked, I mean I gave money to the
person who brings me my food. He will get me cigarettes
the next time he comes around. For the past four years, I
could not even stand the smell of cigarettes. Now amidst
all this emptiness, will cigarettes be able to lessen my pain
a little bit? We will have to wait and see, though whatever
has to happen must happen in front of my captors—my
movements, conversations, pauses, everything is monitored
by them. The only things they cannot survey, or smell, touch
or record, are my emotions.

My captors are always here, their duty spanning all twenty-
four hours. They live in the rooms adjacent to mine and the
ones on duty leave the next day to be replaced by new ones.
Thus, the wheels turn, day and night. I have developed warm
and cordial equations with almost all of them. They are all
quite courteous, sympathetic and polite, normal people like
me. I am privy to their joys and their sorrows but I can never
know what they actually do or what their last names are.

I cried again today. I called Abdul Gaffar Choudhury[45]
to request him to use his contacts, if any, in the government
to help me get back to Bangladesh. I told him I was willing

to give in to any demand. My country, where I have been born and raised, where my parents and my family reside, do I not have a right to go back there? For how long must I roam from one country to the next? Unfortunately, Gaffar Choudhury could give me no reassurance.

I can no longer stand this captive life. I can no longer live here. My telephones have been tapped, unseen strangers eavesdrop on all my conversations, perhaps finding joy in my tears and in the knowledge that I am contemplating leaving this country. Why are people so heartless? Why do they not show even the smallest sliver of kindness to a helpless person?

I feel myself gradually breaking, my dreams slowly crumbling to dust, and the ground slithering away from under me. Where can I go? Without my home, without India, I have no ground to stand on.

I spoke to Shankha Ghosh but even he could not give me any hopeful news. While on the phone, I could not hold back my tears. Why was I crying? I do not remember ever crying like that. I had cried after hearing about my mother's deteriorating health but that was the last time. After what seems like ages, Panchu called too. He told me that no one knew how exactly I have been kept. Everyone is convinced that I am well. Not a single person has even the faintest idea how I have been, and what shackles have been put on my feet. Panchu told me this was nothing short of barbaric, that I was not a victim of fanaticism but of state-sponsored terrorism.

A strange fear seems to have taken hold of me. If the fundamentalists had not railed against me, the government would perhaps not have bothered with me at all. The overlords can punish the fundamentalists if they wish to; or they can covertly encourage their activities. The latter approach obviously harms me. Till date, all my misfortunes—losing my home, my nation, my world, my people, my friends and my family—have been wrought on me by the State and not the zealots. It is the state's representatives who have expelled me from my home, who have cast me into a mire of insecurity, and thrust this life of emptiness upon me.

I do not know if there is any true difference between fundamentalists and those who pander to them.

30 December

'Taslima has been advised to be careful, to avoid saying something that might offend or hurt someone. Then why is this honest advice being imparted only to her, why is it not being shared with the fundamentalists too? The long-term, in fact even the short-term, consequences of this bias can only be devastating. There are always people who get upset when someone speaks something contrary to the majoritarian opinion. Once upon a time many devout Europeans were deeply offended by the assertion that the earth revolved round the sun. Every new strand of knowledge offends someone to begin with. Taslima has managed to establish her human identity way above her communitarian or religious one. She deserves all our respect for precisely this reason. Let us reserve for her nothing but a cordial and steadfast welcome.'—Amlan Dutta

The way I have sustained, that can in no way be called living. I have done nothing wrong and yet I was kept under house arrest back in Kolkata for four long months. Constant pressure was exerted on me by the government to ensure that I decide to leave. Yet, I stuck to my guns and refused. I did not wish to abandon Kolkata, my beloved city, my painstakingly set-up life, and my home. I did not leave because I knew there would be no riots because of me and no one would have to die. Kolkata, I knew, would be the safest place for me to be in. It was the city where I could go out alone without any security, where no fundamentalists ever approached me, and the only people who did, did so out of love. The few times some Islamic radical leaders spoke out against me, their words were mostly politically motivated. Their words were meant to provoke, it had not even an iota of faith in it. I believe my writing had nothing to do with the incidents of 21 November. If there had indeed been a connection, then the controversy should have died down after the contentious passages were removed from *Dwikhandito*, and I should have been free to return to Kolkata.

I am certain that the boys who had taken to the streets on 21 November have never read any of my books. Their hatred and anger, which propelled them to pelt the police with stones, was due to some other reason and not because I was living in Kolkata. Their zeal had been carefully implanted in them.

The events of 22 November succeeded in bringing to fruition the long-nurtured conspiracy to drive me out of the country, or at least the state. What have I done? Why was I under house arrest? Why was I driven out of Kolkata? What have I done to deserve this forbidden life in Delhi, filled with uncertainty, depression and loneliness, where I am not even allowed to step out of the safe house? Why are my friends and family not allowed to see me? For what crimes have I been confined to this suffocating life? The central government claims that I have been given security. So, is that what this is, security? Have I been kept captive for my own security or for someone else's? There are visiting hours in jail, and the prisoners know when their sentence is supposed to end. I have neither here. I do not know when I will be free from this unbearable solitude, from this terrifying insecurity and deathly stillness. In Kolkata, my house arrest had been geared to force my hand so that I would leave the country or at least the state. This new form of confinement in Delhi, is it meant to now finally drive me out of the country? Otherwise, why have these shackles been placed on me? Why have I not been allowed to go back to Kolkata even after numerous requests? Why have I not been allowed to lead a normal social life in Delhi?

There have been no processions or meetings against me in Delhi. No threats have been made against my life. In fact, the truly secular and socially aware people of the city have marched in solidarity with me and written in support of me. Why must I then live in captivity? If someone had made threats, then this security could be justified, as is the case with so many people in this country. (Abroad, I am provided security everywhere I go even though I am not a citizen of the country concerned. Isn't India too a part of the United Nations?) Have people's lives been disrupted? Are they sitting at home? If not, then why should I be the one to go through this?

It is not as if I have not been allowed to meet anyone thus far. However, the way it has been done is truly preposterous. They probably follow similar protocol for notorious criminals or those on death row. When I wish to meet someone, I have to tell my captors about them, detailed information about their address, their life, and who they are. This information is passed on to the higher authorities along with my request. The process typically takes a few days as the authorities then decide and let me know whether my request can be granted or not. Most of the requests are rejected. When they do decide to let me meet someone, they usually decide the time, date and duration on their own and I am simply informed about it. Then, on the stipulated date, I am packed inside a car with tinted windows and taken to a neutral place where I am allowed to meet my friend for as long as has been fixed by the authorities. Of course, constant watch is kept on what we talk about. It is indeed thrilling, this entire adventure of meeting another human being. What is it all aimed at? That I remain in constant fear, anxiety and shame, and eventually die? That I get exasperated and choose to leave this country of my own volition? It cannot surely be anything else!

I will not leave this country, though. I will not leave because there is no other country in the world which I can think of as my own. I am not the most threatened person in this country; threats are a reality in every part of the world. I have been wandering from one country to another for the past thirteen years. More than the fundamentalists, it is the politics that seeks to submit to each of their demands that has caused me harm. The radicals did not oust me from Bangladesh, the government did. That I have not been allowed to return till now is also their doing. I do not believe that the government is concerned about my security. The Government of Bangladesh has always been more preoccupied with their own safety and sustenance.

I do not wish to think of India as Bangladesh. I truly believe that the government here is capable of letting me live my normal life with the minimum amount of security that I might require. I believe that it is baseless to assume there will be riots and deaths because of me. There were nefarious reasons behind these rumours, reasons that still persist. There have been no riots anywhere in the world because of me. Writers do not cause riots. Some fanatics have been offended by certain passages in *Dwikhandito*. Before it was banned, and after the ban was repealed, the book sold freely everywhere and no one protested. Instead, I have been threatened with riots so as to drive me out of my home. I will keep repeating—I have done nothing wrong. In fact, I have even stated that I did not write anything hoping to hurt someone's sentiments and I am truly sorry if that has inadvertently happened. After I cut out two passages from my book, even Maulana Madani of the Jamiat Ulema-e-Hind, who had spewed venom against me previously, had admitted that the matter was closed and that I could live anywhere in the country, in whichever city I chose. Which powers are then obstructing my way back to Kolkata?

Imam Barkati and Idris Ali had had so much to say because they had been encouraged to do so. Back in 2006, the imam had happily issued a fatwa and put a price on my head. Prasun Mukherjee, the commissioner of police, had called the imam to his office and after the meeting Barkati had summarily denied the entire episode. In fact, he had come out of the room and denied ever having issued a fatwa at all! Why isn't there anyone today to teach people like Imam Barkati and Idris Ali that no one has the right to oppose democracy, human rights and the freedom of expression? In a democratic nation no one has the right to issue fatwas, create terror or cause riots. If they are felicitated after every act of terror they commit, why will they ever refrain from violence and terrorism?

What crime have I committed? I see everyone as human first—be it Hindu, Muslim, Christian or Buddhist. Is that wrong? I desire equality among all and I write tirelessly on behalf of humanity and equal rights. I write about the people and for the people despite much opposition from fundamentalist, conservative, narrow-minded factions. I have always been steadfast in my support of the poor and the downtrodden, those deprived of education, health and civic amenities, whose human rights are violated because of differing religious beliefs. That is how I have stood by the Muslim population of West Bengal, how I had stood by the Hindu minority in Bangladesh. The self-serving fundamentalists who wish to use Islam for their narrow political gains cannot be considered suitable representatives of the Muslims of Bengal.

Is it not time yet to ascertain who the true enemies of society are? Is it not time yet for my freedom from this irrational captivity? Have I been completely foolish in trying to spread the word of humanity and free thought in India? What am I being punished for? Do the people of India simply desire to see me wither away from this pain, suffering, depression and dark emptiness that I have been subjected to thus far? That I should die, homeless, stateless, without a society or any friends? What am I being punished for in this secular democratic country?

I have never been actively involved in politics, nor do I understand it. I demand that these political games being played with a writer be stopped. I demand a space where one can write, where free thought is encouraged, where there is no fear or coercion. This is my ardent request to this nation, a nation which has provided shelter to the needy since time immemorial. I am proud of India's liberal heritage and I wish I can continue being proud of India as an author, for the rest of my life.

Those of you who have stood by me, who have been resolute in the denunciation of the injustices committed, you have my undying gratitude. I beg of you to rescue me, to free me from this relentless psychological trauma. You are my friends, the only family I have left, my last stand. I continue to endure because of the faint hope that one day I will be free. That is the only light left in my otherwise dark world.

1 January

'Buddhadeb threw Taslima Nasrin out of Kolkata only because he wanted to appease the fundamentalists.'— Mahasweta Devi[46]

I was supposed to meet Svensson today and the meeting finally happened. The poor foreigner, he does not know the roads of Delhi! He was led from one place to another, through forests and what not, taken round and round, before being brought to this secret place designated for the meeting.

We spent a fair amount of time together. A lot of good food had been arranged for us and we were also allowed to go for a stroll in the field nearby. It seemed like the entire world was being handed over to us! Since August last year, I do not remember having touched the earth even once.

2 January

The Association for Protection of Democratic Rights (APDR), a human rights organization in Bengal, held a seminar today in the Mahabodhi Society Hall demanding I be allowed to return to Kolkata. Mahasweta Devi was the chairperson while Dipankar Chakraborty, Sujato Bhadra, Shuvaprasanna and Ananya Chattopadhyay spoke at the assembly. Shankha Ghosh, Aparna Sen and Shaoli Mitra were also supposed to attend the event but could not make it in time due to various reasons. Pratul Mukhopadhyay sang at the programme; I heard it over the phone. Such a stunning song he had composed for me! I have been an ardent fan for a long time though we have never met. We will surely meet one day in Kolkata.

Today was Svensson's last day in India. We spent the afternoon together though I cannot say I truly feel anything for him. If it had been someone else in my place, someone with a smidgen of self-confidence or awareness, that person would probably have never spoken to him again. After he left, I kept thinking what an odd man he was. He had quite unapologetically enjoyed the hospitality extended to him by the government. Would I have been able to do the same in his place? Perhaps not, since I would have died of mortification if a country had had to spend on me against their wishes. I would have tried to live within my means just like I have always done whenever I have been abroad. Till date, I have never accepted a foreign nation's pity or charity, though I was entitled to it as someone seeking political asylum. My captors have taken Svensson around to the Taj Mahal, and to Jaipur and Delhi. The government has also paid his hotel bills and other expenses. I had told him he should be paying these bills, but he had told me to let it be. I accept that I had requested my captors to show him around a bit, to help and guide him a bit, since I was not able to do it. My captors did more than I had asked for. I wonder why they did though. They treated Svensson like a valued guest; perhaps to make me happy they took on every responsibility related to him. Had they assumed he would see my terrible circumstances and convince me to leave India, even take me with him to Sweden? Whatever my captors may have thought, Svensson should not have taken such advantage of their hospitality. He should have politely thanked them and told them he would be covering his own expenses. Some people will even eat shit if it is for free! There is a popular assumption that foreigners, especially Swedes, don't cheat or cause trouble for other people. It is a completely false piece of information. If allowed, they will drain your veins dry. They are perhaps less devious to each other but the moment it is someone else belonging to some other nation, they are relentless. I have seen this trait of selfishness more among foreigners than I have among people of our nations. Among my own people, I have mostly found kindness, generosity and selflessness.

It is undeniable that there will be positives and negatives in every culture and a lot depends on the individual person one is meeting and working with. The amount of money that has been spent on Svensson is truly startling and I want to pay it back any way I can. Money is already being spent on me. Separate arrangements would obviously have to be made if my friend is not being allowed where I have been kept. However, Svensson should have offered to pay on his own. I was the one who became overtly emotional and foisted him on someone else. He had known he would not be able to stay with me even before he started for India. So, why should I have to take on the entire responsibility for his visit? Why am I so naïve? It is not as if I have not been on the receiving end of Svensson's selfishness and narrow-mindedness. He too has made me cry, he too has taken advantage of my helplessness. This grand welcome and generosity, he does not deserve any of it. Whatever he has been offered, he has taken with both hands. I know for a fact that if I tell him tomorrow that I have to take care of the expenses of his stay in India, he would just silently listen, nod in agreement, and let it pass.

My mother's traits are in my DNA and I can never run away from it. I have always forgiven the scoundrels of this world. Just like my mother, forgiveness and love have forever tainted my blood. My mother has only ever been hurt by people in return. The same fate probably awaits me.

3 January

Except for *Dainik Statesman*, no other newspaper has reported the event held yesterday. The *Statesman* has been resolute in its opposition to the CPI(M), which explains why the newspaper has continued to write about the abuse I have faced at the hands of the party. Of course, one must admit that this is truly a courageous stand! Even Mamata Banerjee is against the CPI(M) but till date she has not uttered a word on my behalf. She has been known to raise a hue and cry over the smallest of indiscretions by the government, but in this case she has been remarkably restrained. Not even once has she said anything critical about the CPI(M). *Anandabazar Patrika* too has capitulated, though I am not sure if it is only surrender or an accord is in place. They have been silent for a long time and they have not written about the Mahabodhi Society assembly either. Doubts about *Anandabazar*'s integrity had begun to form ever since they went against popular opinion and sided with the government on the Singur and Nandigram scandals.

Prasun Bhowmik had requested me for a statement that was to be read out at the assembly. I had promptly written one. This has been a persistent habit. The moment there is a request, I can finally get some writing done. I had told them repeatedly that the report was only meant to be read out, not published. However, the moment it was read, Mahasweta Devi declared that it was going to be published in the *Statesman*.

That can only mean one thing. The account will spread like wildfire, as journalists usually pounce upon anything I say which can be perceived as being critical of the government. They never pause to think how a report like that affects me. Did the journalists in Jaipur not reveal my hotel room number to the media despite being aware that fundamentalists were after my head? For every honest and forthright journalist, there is another who is corrupt and morally bankrupt. A fellow from the Press Trust of India (PTI), with whom I shared a very cordial equation and who had justifiably been very anxious about how I was doing, had nonetheless refused to go to the Mahabodhi Society event. He would rather write citing secondary sources, firmly ensconced behind his desk, that too on facing pressure from Delhi. Besides, I am usually just a phone call away. Instead, most journalists merely report many things attributed to me, instead of verifying what I have actually said. They expose potentially anti-government statements, never pausing to hear my arguments for them. What they crave is a bomb for the headlines.

Tapan Raychaudhuri came to Delhi for a few days and asked to meet me. My captors made arrangements in the same old place yet again. It seemed they were far more excited about the meeting than even I was. It was a delight meeting Tapan Raychaudhuri. He has always been very fond of me, or else why would he wish to meet. Apparently, he had come to Delhi for two specific reasons: to meet Mr B, which he had done immediately after his arrival, and then to meet me. The primary reason, of course, had been to talk to Mr B about me. I was justifiably excited to hear what Mr B had had to say about me. When was he going to allow me to return to Kolkata?

Instead of answering any of these questions, he kept staring at my captors for a long time before stating:

Tapan Raychaudhuri (TR): They seem to be RAW agents.
TN: RAW agents? I don't think so.
TR: I am sure they are RAW agents.
TN: They are good people. They have taken good care of me. However, what I need the most is to be allowed to return to Kolkata, to be allowed to lead a normal life like before.

The more I insisted on knowing about Kolkata, about the possible dates when I could return, the more he kept trying to evade my questions. Instead, he kept telling me about how dangerous a threat the fundamentalists still were, how their pistols were poised and their swords unsheathed, ready to strike me down.

People who have spent a majority of their life in a secure environment abroad get scared easily. He was probably thinking that a very powerful, radical Islamic group had me on their kill-list. He was probably thinking about my security. Anyway, after his conversation with Mr B, what he had understood was that there was no way I was going back to Kolkata any time soon.

4 January

I sit out in the sun every afternoon, often simply staring blankly at the trees. It's a familiar scene, the sad tale of my empty days. Today, I was speaking to Sheela Reddy, narrating to her my conversation with Tapan Raychaudhuri. It was not as if I volunteered all the information. Sheela too asked me, about how things were going, about what I was doing or thinking. She advised me, 'You must tell him to help you. Even if you can't be sent back to Kolkata, you should at least be allowed to have a normal life in Delhi. He must speak to Mr B about this.'

Sheela also asked me to call Shyam Benegal and request a meeting with him. I have never been very comfortable calling up famous people, especially if I am not on very friendly terms with them. Sheela, though, is much like a clever psychoanalyst; she has me completely in her thrall. Whatever she says, I do, sometimes even when I don't want to. If I don't call Mr Benegal, Sheela will tell me that I do not really wish to extricate myself from my predicament, and this explains why I do not try. Previously, whenever I have ignored her advice, this has happened. The day after the advice is given, she usually calls to check if and how much I have acted on it.

I could not reach Mr Benegal. He called me back later from Mumbai and I thanked him for signing the petition. He would only be back in Delhi around the middle of February, so we are probably not going to be able to meet at least for now. I would have to content with meeting my friends and well-wishers. At least, it gladdens me that he has been sensitive enough to spare me some thought! He has assured me that he will talk to someone from the government; he has even said he will let me know by tomorrow. Even M.A. Baby had promised to let me know but he still has not gotten to it. It is as if there is nothing left to inform me about, no assurances or hopes to give.

Whether Shyam Benegal lets me know or not, he will always remain my favourite director in Indian cinema. My respect for him will remain the same.

5 January

I have written two poems today, after a very long time. Gautam Ghosh Dastidar had sent me an email from Kolkata requesting poems for his independent magazine *Rakta–Mangsha* (Flesh and Blood). These days I cannot seem to write unless someone has asked for something. Only if there is a request, I can get some writing done. I started crying while writing the poems. I kept crying, and kept writing. 'Long live democracy!' 'Has a poet ever been incarcerated?'

6 January

Bangladesh is possibly a forgotten name for me now. It is only alive in my memories, both happy and sad. I cannot imagine that my parents are no longer in Bangladesh, that their houses lie abandoned. I cannot muster up the courage to face these thoughts and so I don't. Whenever such thoughts trouble me, I force them aside. I feel so empty sometimes, so alone that it becomes impossible to endure. Which is why I never think of the absence of my parents. I constantly strive to forget it.

Something strange happened today. I was on Google in the morning, sifting through new information about myself, when I chanced upon an article in the *Daily Star* on K.M. Sobhan. The writer had mentioned that Sobhan had stood beside Taslima in her hour of need. The past tense immediately put me on edge. Did that mean Justice Sobhan was no longer there by my side?

Soon after, I received a call from Kolkata telling me about an article by Justice Sobhan which has been published in *Dainik Statesman*. K.M. Sobhan, former judge of the Supreme Court of Bangladesh, passed away last Monday. This was his last article. The last thing he wrote was about me. The thought sat heavily on my heart and I could not speak through the grief clogging my throat. K.M. Sobhan had been one of the few intellectuals in Bangladesh who had taken my side.

In the article he has said, 'The fact that Bangladesh could not hold on to Taslima Nasrin will be a thing of enduring shame for all Bengalis. Bangladesh had failed to secure this Bengali writer her constitutional rights . . . and the Left Front government had chosen to compromise and bow down to the fundamentalists.'

Sometimes I feel so angry that I have wasted so much time on useless things when I could have used it to keep in touch with these people. I call so many people around the world, why did I never find the time to call K.M. Sobhan? He would have felt happy too. Who am I so angry with? People like him have been steadfast in their support of me, even though they had no power of their own to get me back to Bangladesh. Shamsur Rahman too is no more and neither is Wahidur Rahman. Wahidur Rahman had been very fond of me. I have heard he used to speak of me often, and his last article for *Janakantha* (Voice of the People) had been about me. I cannot hold back my tears when I get to know these things. The Government of Bangladesh has forcefully alienated me from such generous and kind people; its filthy politics has deprived me of their love and affection.

There is nothing but a vacuum all around. Zillur Rahman Siddiqui, Khan Sarwar Murshid, Kalim Sharafi, they have all gotten on in age. I often feel very anxious about when they will not be around any more. Even now, we are separated by thousands of miles. I keep remembering Samim Sikdar, Ruby Rahman and Ferdousi Priyabhashini. Does anyone understand how much I want to go back? Does anyone care why I cannot? Sometimes I wonder why I left the country. If death had been my fate, it could gladly have happened in Bangladesh. All these years, as I have wandered from one country to another, have I died any less?

These people were forever by my side in Bangladesh. In Kolkata, there was Annada Shankar Roy, who is no longer among us. Shibnarayan Ray too has been steadfast in his support, as has been Amlan Dutta. Most of the people here have gotten on in age and I fear without them I would be quite alone. There would be no one left in the world to take my side. I have noticed that younger or middle-aged people do not understand what I try to say as much as the seniors do. Not that seniority is a big factor. One has to have the sensitivity to want to understand.

I am completely alone. I have had to live away from my parents, and my family, from those who love and care for me, not out of any choice of my own. These thoughts threaten to suffocate me.

If only I could go back to Bangladesh, by whatever means necessary! Sometimes I feel like telling Mr B to make arrangements to send me home. I am sure he has wonderful connections with the government there. Anyway, relations between India and Bangladesh ought to be quite cordial now considering India's recent financial aid of 100 crore rupees to Bangladesh after the devastating floods there. If only

Mr B would take some sort of an initiative to convince Sheikh Hasina to withdraw the cases against me and provide me security! I could go back home, I could spend the rest of my life there! My mother dreamt that I would return home one day. I want to make that dream a reality, though I have never been able to fulfil any of her wishes while she was alive. Do I not dream of returning home? But I hide these unfulfilled dreams in the deepest, darkest recesses of my heart, not allowing them to come out and taunt me. As a result, the life I lead is perhaps not a real one.

7 January

Information and Broadcasting Minister Priya Ranjan Dasmunsi's angry comments against me were being telecast across TV channels all day yesterday. He is very angry with me, apparently because I have criticized Islam. This is India, transgressions like these are not allowed here! So he has asked me to apologize publicly, with folded hands, to all Muslims, for everything I have said till date against their religion. He has added that I should also remove everything I have written about religion from my book; in fact, he is of the opinion that the book itself should be banned. This is India. One must not speak about religion if one wishes to live here.

Mr Dasmunsi had publicly condemned the attacks on me in Hyderabad. In fact, he had even assured everyone after the incident that the Centre would seriously consider giving me citizenship. His words had made it seem that the decision had already been taken and that we were simply waiting for the formal announcement.

Does Mr Dasmunsi believe in Islam? If he truly did, he would probably have converted by now. He believes in

Hinduism probably, or he does not believe in any religion. I am sure he is aware that I have already deleted sections from *Dwikhandito*; that I have expressed my regret regarding any sentiments I may have hurt. So, what has brought on this new wave of ire? Rumour has it that he is reacting thus to secure Muslim votes. Is it so easy to give up on one's ethics and principles for the sake of electoral politics? If that leads to triumph, does such a victory bring joy? I mention ethics and principles simply because every democracy has a set of moral codes inherent in it. Everyone has a right to speak, and if one does not like what someone else has to say, one can always furnish a counterargument. Under no circumstances can violence be justified. Why bay for someone's blood? Why raise hell on the streets? Why set things ablaze and harm innocent people? Isn't that why he spoke out against the barbaric incident in Hyderabad on 9 August? That day, after his bold statement, he had seemed truly human, someone who was not afraid of speaking his mind. Anything he is saying now, regarding me getting down on my knees and apologizing, is because the politician has taken over from the human being. The two sides of Mr Dasmunsi are quite clearly different entities; the politician persona and the human persona seemingly mutually exclusive.

If I had been two decades younger, I would have expressed my regret for them. Now the regret is entirely for me, and my misfortunes. I was born in a simple family, was raised simply, and have lived simply too. How can someone like me become an object of political games? How can that happen in a country like India? No, I refuse to be such an object. Just like I do not deserve the excessive praise that is sometimes heaped on me, neither do I deserve the excessive censure.

Today, after Mr Dasmunsi's comments were aired, the channel Times Now declared that I have become an untouchable to all political parties ever since my ouster from Kolkata. That is perhaps true. Taslima Nasrin is now an untouchable in this country. I could have returned to Kolkata if there had been considerable public protest against how unjustly I had been treated. However, that is not possible in any country on my behalf. There can be no consensus with regard to me. I am a writer and I don't belong to a party or an organization. I have lived alone, written solely out of love, and that is how I have survived. As they say, one must care for the heart more than the body. I have always been a harmless and humble person. Some politicians and merchants of religion have used me for their own benefits. That is nothing new though, it is a tale as old as time. Writers have been jailed, they have been killed, but has anyone ever had to suffer such indignity? The fortunes of an exiled writer can turn with the rise and fall of governments. My exile is enduring; it has no end in sight.

Shankha Ghosh called and I got excited thinking there would be some good news. However, he had simply called to talk about 'Banished Without and Within', which someone wishes to translate and publish in an independent Bengali journal. There is no good news for me any more. M.A. Baby did not call and neither did Shyam Benegal. And Shankha Ghosh has nothing hopeful to tell me. If he so wishes, can he not speak to Buddhadeb Bhattacharya about me? Of course, he can. Maybe he feels it will amount to nothing! But how can one be so certain? It might just work!

I am growing more anxious as days pass by. Gradually, returning to Kolkata seems ever more impossible. With time, the political games around me are increasing.

8 January

An article criticizing Priya Ranjan Dasmunsi's demands, titled 'Writer Blocked', has been published in the editorial column of *Times of India*. The article ends thus:

> The problem with such a political strategy is that the more one appeases fundamentalists, thinking their point of view to be representative of a community, the more demands they'll raise. And the more powerful they'll become, once they are seen to be effective in translating their views into state policy.
>
> A secular state has to draw the line somewhere, otherwise it will give rise to a game of competitive fundamentalism that will damage the nation's multicultural fabric. Moreover, a democracy cannot stifle individual dissent. An individual, after all, is the smallest minority. It's on his defence that democracy rests. When calling on Taslima to bend and scrape before religious authorities, it's these democratic basics that the good information and broadcasting minister appears to have lost sight of.

I saw on the news today that the Congress has condoned Mr Dasmunsi's remarks. Their spokesperson has issued a statement to the effect that Priya Ranjan's demands are entirely justified and that I should definitely apologize to all Muslims.

Is there anything more horrific?

The BJP have now started demanding unconditional apologies from Sonia Gandhi and Manmohan Singh for their comments on the Ram-setu issue. Apparently, comments like

'Ram was not a real person' and 'Ram was a figment of the poet's imagination' have hurt the religious sentiments of the Hindus. Of course, why should apologies apply only in the case of one community and not for others! If one community can get offended by something, so can another.

I am astoundingly stupid, and an irredeemable ass. I have been driven from one nation to another in search of a home. I had tried settling in Bengal, tried building a small life of my own, and had spent most of it in solitude. Now I have been reduced to a pawn in their political games. I am so afraid that I cannot breathe. I sit and tremble, trying to fathom for how long I would have to endure this agony.

9 January

Such incredible things keep happening! Seven Muslim organizations, including the Jamaat-e-Islami and the Jamiat Ulema-e-Hind, have petitioned the government to throw me out of India and cancel my visa. Even Maulana Madani of Jamiat Ulema-e-Hind, who had declared peace after the removal of the offensive sections from *Dwikhandito*, has now applied himself with renewed vigour to the new movement against me. His colleague Maulana Nomani has gone a step ahead and alleged that I have written offensive things against Hinduism too, and representatives of all religions must form a unified front against the menace that I pose. They will soon approach the prime minister with their demand and on the 16th there is going to be a symposium of all religious communities on the issue.

In Kolkata, the Samajwadi Party has taken to the streets to protest against me. After the incidents of 21 November, Toha Siddiqui of Furfura Sharif had denied all ties with

Idris Ali in order to distance his party from any blame that might come their way. Siddiqui had put the entire responsibility of the bandh on Ali, explicitly denying that Furfura Sharif had had anything to do with it. The same Idris Ali has very recently been welcomed back by them. But that should not come as a surprise. The Congress had expelled Idris from their ranks after 21 November. If the leaders of Congress could visit such a crook in prison, if they could welcome him back into their clique, then why should one blame Toha Siddiqui for having reneged on his party's stance? Recently, Vijay Upadhyay of the Samajwadi Party has been heard viciously attacking me. They have written to the Publishers and Booksellers Guild demanding I be banned from the Kolkata International Book Fair; they have warned of dire consequences if even a single book of mine is sold at the book fair this year. Apparently the detective department is extremely worried about the situation. I had already told Prasanta Roy to make sure my books are not there at the book fair; I do not want to give them an excuse to throw me out again because of another untoward incident.

Sheela Reddy told me, 'You must be at the book fair! Whatever happens, you must! Will they set things ablaze? Let them! We must not back away. They have been given the licence to do whatever they wish to by these political parties. The time has come for the government to decide where to re-establish boundaries.'

With each passing day I have begun to feel a little more isolated. Things are increasingly not looking well. No one wishes to address the most crucial question: why have I been kept in confinement? The government has been asking me to keep quiet. *Anandabazar Patrika* could have effectively created public awareness about the issue, but they too have remained quiet. I was depending on Shankha Ghosh to speak on my behalf to the government, but he has asked me to stay quiet for some time. Sheela has told me that I should keep quiet because it's time other people speak for me instead. Quite obviously, no one else is speaking.

Shyam Benegal had promised to keep me updated but no news has arrived. M.A. Baby had promised to speak to someone within the Congress, but I am not sure where that has led. A close confidant of Mr B used to call quite frequently to know how I was, but those calls too have now stopped. Everything he did was on Mr B's orders. Does that mean he has been asked to cease all communication with me? Mr B has not informed me of any new developments either. Tapan Raychaudhuri had met him to talk about me and Mr B had assured him that arrangements would be made for my return to Kolkata. Tapan Raychaudhuri is, however, not entirely convinced. He has admitted to me that he does not trust politicians. Sambit Paul from Times Now called and regretfully confessed: 'I don't see any hope, didi. We are trying to keep the news alive. But no larger political movement has developed vis-à-vis this issue. We have tried, but we have not been able to consolidate public opinion.'

The only silver lining in all this gloominess has been a piece of news from afar. On the occasion of the birth centenary of Simone de Beauvoir in Paris, I have been awarded the Simone de Beauvoir Prize in recognition of my struggle for attainment of women's equality and gender justice. I had sent them my statement last night, and Christian Besse translated it into French and read it out to the assembly today, besides accepting the award on my behalf. Besse called me in the evening to tell me all about the thunderous applause I had apparently received, besides the numerous demands for my freedom and security from among those who had gathered.

I remain here, clinging to India because of my love for this land. People elsewhere are honouring me with awards, but their world holds no attraction for me. Who do I keep faith in—those people or this land?

10 January

1.

The book fair is back in Kolkata, like every other year. The only difference this year—I won't be there.

Since I have been in India, there has not been a single year that I have missed the book fair. At times, even when I have been busy abroad, I have chosen to fly down to Kolkata specifically for this. Besides, ever since I started living in Kolkata, the book fair had conveniently moved right next door. I believe, for a writer it is the most perfect space that exists—surrounded by books, interacting with readers or other writers, debating over a new work, exchanging new ideas, a haven of free thought.

This year, however, I doubt there is even a sliver of a chance that I will be able to attend the book fair, though I am not entirely sure why. In moments of great sorrow, sometimes there are no answers, only questions.

There are rumours doing the rounds that if I attend, the fundamentalists are going to raise hell. In all fairness, that is hardly a thing to get startled over these days. Raising hell has become such an easy thing to do, especially when it is implicitly supported by the authorities. When people are certain that violence will not cause them any harm, but will only add to their gains, why would they not choose violence?

My desires have never been extravagant. Born in Bengal, I had wanted to live in Bengal as well, and work in peace, on either side of the border. In the years I spent in Kolkata, I never harmed anyone, nor did I ever cause anyone any trouble. Instead, I generously gave as much as possible. I have always written about my beliefs and now nearly two decades and thirty-odd books on human rights and women's rights later, how could I be branded anti-Islamic? As if the sole objective for which I write is to contest Islam! The consequences of so many false allegations and lies are quite evident. What is also evident is what happens when an innocent person falls prey to political machinations.

This year the book fair has been organized very close to my poor old, abandoned house—in Park Circus. All my friends, well-wishers and acquaintances, everyone I know will go. Except me, of course. Instead, for as long as the fair is on, I will be sitting alone within the confines of a room in Delhi, reminiscing about the times when I used to spend hours strolling through the dusty lanes of the fair. I have lost my freedom because I have written about freedom. The shackles on my feet will not let me walk like before, nor would they allow me to take part in the festivities.

I do not wish to believe that the book fair is gone forever from my life. I do not wish to accept that my joys, my dreams, my desires and my choices have all been buried six feet under. So, I still dream. I still cross the seven seas in search of love. Even in moments of darkest despair, bent over with pain, bleeding from the lash of the merciless whip, and nursing my wounds, I can feel renewed life with just a fleeting touch of a loving hand. Even the smallest of such touches can instil in me a new sense of hope.

The Bengali reader has the same emotional relationship with the book fair as a writer has with words. They may have been successful in keeping me away this year, but from the next, let my unbroken link with Bengal remain steadfast. Let it be forever.

Some people have raised the issue of my security. All I know is that the love of the people is my strongest shield. I have lived in Kolkata for three years and I have never had to roam with guards or use bulletproof cars. So, what has changed? Do we stop doing things because of how someone else might react? If I know someone might whistle in a theatre, does that mean I will not go to watch a film? If I do that, then soon ten more people will join the fray just to see what else they can get out of it. Our problem is that we have gotten so used to remaining quiet that silence and inertia have become foundational to our culture.

2.

I kept smoking cigarettes in the morning. Perhaps I was deliberately trying to kill myself. Why else would I have cigarettes brought? Why else would I keep smoking? Not that I don't remember how cigarettes had ravaged me over the years, or how difficult it had been to finally quit. Despite knowing and remembering everything, I still could not help myself. The otherwise smiling female officer kept looking at me with pity:

Officer (O): Why cigarettes?
TN: That's easy!
O: How easy?

TN: Depression . . .

O: You will destroy your essence because of their politics? Why
do you wish to harm yourself? You are above all this, these
petty squabbles and the muck. Can you not ignore all of this?

TN: What is the use . . .

O: Use? How does it matter? You have done nothing wrong!
Just because they have kept you locked up does not mean
you should harm yourself and let them win. Stay alive!
Live with your convictions, your beliefs and your ethics.
We are proud of you. The politics of this place is not
something we can be proud of.

TN: When will this end?

O: Someday soon. It obviously cannot go on this way. The
government will find a solution for sure.

TN: I am so worried. That is why I am smoking. I am not
inhaling though. What if I get addicted again!

O: Quit cigarettes. Live! India is not everything.

'India is not everything'—these words gave me hope. I went
about my day as usual—wrote in the afternoon, took a shower,
and put on fresh clothes. In the evening, while watching the
birds returning to their nest, when I said, 'Even the birds are
returning to their nests, but I have nowhere to go,' she replied,
'Their nests get destroyed and they build new ones.'

TN: Yes! Like me! I have built so many in so many countries!

O: Have you never wished to have someone beside you?
Someone who would stand by you, and give you a sense
of support?

TN: Yes, I have. But I have usually chosen the wrong person
and suffered for it.

O: Don't you feel lonely?

TN: Sometimes. But I have been on my own for a very long time. I don't wish for anyone to come and disrupt my freedom. I don't mind love, though.

11 January

4.27 a.m.

Had a nightmare and woke up with a start. I was dreaming that they have taken the little blue book, my only permit for staying on in India, and torn it up. I could hear people arguing while I was on my hands and knees, trying to gather the torn pieces and put them back together again. The pieces were flying about in the wind. I cannot fully remember if I was running around after them or simply standing there flabbergasted.

4.30 a.m.

I lie staring at the ceiling; the white ceiling with the nearly - white fan hanging from it. It is not a very common sight in this country—a static fan. People are more used to the opposite. It feels as if I too have been hanging like the fan, for the longest time. Though, if the tether breaks, I don't know where I will fall, and how.

4.40 a.m.

It is all so absolute lonely. And so very cold.

4.42 a.m.

I keep remembering Ma whenever I close my eyes. I want to feel reassured by her touch, hug her tight, and whisper in her ear to take me away from this place. To take me home.

4.45 a.m.
The tears are rolling down on to the pillow.

4.46 a.m.
Except for the sound of my breathing, everything else is absolutely still. It is deathly quiet. Tears, as always, are reliably silent.

4.48 a.m.
I get up, reach out to my laptop and switch it on. The laptop had been the only thing I had taken with me from Kolkata for the two-day trip to the resort they had promised me. The thought sends ice running down my veins now! What a ruthless plan they had come up with to get me out of the way!

4.50 a.m.
Google it is, then. That piece in Merrynews.com was so upsetting! The writer has alleged that I have complained against the government by claiming to be under house arrest. How dare I demand comforts when so much money has already been spent on me? Did I know that there were nearly seven to ten thousand homeless women on the streets of Delhi itself?

I don't know how to react to such allegations. So, am I staying here of my own free will? Is it because I want to live off the government's money? I have always been self-sufficient and financially independent. I have never asked anyone for help. In fact, I have helped people when they have come to me in need. Why am I here? The only thing I crave for is freedom. Freedom and self-reliance—the only things I have fought for all my life.

5.00 a.m.

I check my emails. One of the mails is from Paris, about the award I got yesterday. The Simone de Beauvoir Prize. So many eminent academics and philosophers were present at the ceremony. Kate Millett was in the jury.

5.20 a.m.

A fleeting feeling of warmth has settled over me. I can imagine what a big auditorium in Paris will look like. I have spoken in such places before, in front of thousands of educated and socially aware intellectuals, artists, writers and philosophers. Nevertheless, this sort of an endorsement, from distant shores, seems like a fairy tale. Especially since it does not bring with it the freedom that I so desperately crave.

12 January

1.

Sometimes I wonder why this madness possesses me, this uncontrollable desire to be back in Kolkata. What has the city ever given me? It's not as if I had a sterling social life there! Rather, I spent most of my days alone. No engaging literary soirées I can recall or events and ceremonies where I had been invited—despite the countless ones that used to keep happening. Sometimes, Ranjan used to coax me to go somewhere, that too if he suddenly remembered me or someone reminded him of me. The few parties I attended, I did not like. Had I been a drinker, or very consciously fashionable, I might have been able to fit in better but those have never been things that have held any interest for me whatsoever. The only other attraction had been to meet a few interesting people, and to have some interesting conversations. However, there are not too many of those that I can recall! In Kolkata, I mostly met people running blindly after fame.

Anandabazar began ignoring me—perhaps simply out of a fanciful whim—about a year or so after I started living in Kolkata. I submitted the manuscript of *Narir Kono Desh Nei* (A Woman Has No Nation) to Ananda Publishers but they sent it back saying they did not wish to publish it. They do still print articles about me but perhaps that is simply because of its value as news. They have summarily written me off as a writer though, which is deeply ironic considering they have awarded me with the Ananda Puraskar twice. The only silver lining was the Wednesday column I used to write for *Dainik Statesman*— being able to write with some sort of regularity went a long way in assuaging hurt. Otherwise, there is no other example of a social life that I can recall. There were a few friends who used to visit regularly, none of them from the literary and cultural world. The people from this domain gradually severed their ties with me. After successfully appealing against *Dwikhandito* and managing to get it banned, Sunil Gangopadhyay and his friends and cohorts, along with the government's friends and acolytes, had deemed it perfectly acceptable to politically and socially reduce me to an enemy, a hostile alien needing to be kept at bay. A warm and lively person such as me had to spend months in solitary confinement in Kolkata as a result. Then why does the city fascinate me so? Is it the language? Is it because there I can speak to someone for a while in Bangla? Is it because I can go and watch plays in Bangla or read the Bengali newspaper early in the morning while sipping my morning tea?

I have no qualms in admitting that I have never been part of a truly literary or culturally vibrant social space. I cannot say if this was because I was taboo or because I was a celebrity—sometimes I am not able to differentiate between the two.

There were always people who used to come to me for their own nefarious reasons. An older man called Ranjan Sengupta turned up one day claiming to be a friend and well-wisher. His ulterior motive had been to extort money from me. Once he even borrowed nearly 82,000 rupees, promising to return it soon, which he never did of course.

I have had to face trouble over the smallest of issues in Kolkata—a household help, for instance. There was no one who was willing to help me find someone trustworthy who would be able to help me take care of my home. Whoever I have allowed in my life with trust has invariably turned out to be unworthy of it.

2.

Even though they have assured me time and again that they are not here to convince me to leave India, I do not believe that the two men posted here, to assist me, accompany me and keep an eye on me, have told me the truth. They know everything and they are here to find out all my secrets—what I am thinking, whether I am considering leaving India, and so on. In fact, sometimes they wonder aloud that it must indeed be better abroad, where there is freedom. That I should simply visit India during vacations. Why do they say these things? Is it because they are my friends and well-wishers? Or have their overlords taught them to say such things? I am inherently a suspicious person, or perhaps circumstances have made it necessary. Or it could simply be that there is a far more sinister game that is afoot. I am a colossal fool; what I am seeing is just the tip of the proverbial iceberg!

The whole day has been spent in trying to write— sometimes it has borne fruit, sometimes it hasn't. Other things have happened too. A group of young boys and girls have started a signature campaign to secure my safe passage back to Kolkata. Sunil Gangopadhyay signed but added a disclaimer to it: 'The way things have been publicized, that she is not being allowed to live a normal life in Delhi, is simply not true. She is well.' They went to Mrinal Sen too. Later, Sen called me up to talk to me and expressed deep shock and anger on hearing the accounts of my life here. However, he still did not sign. Instead, he told them, 'The letter is too harsh. Bring me a slightly "softer" version and I will sign.' When they requested him to write a softer letter, he instead passed the responsibility on to Manasij Majumder.[47]

Bijoya Mukhopadhyay has signed, but only after giving them an earful for not having taken an appointment before barging in. Sarat Kumar Mukhopadhyay[48] was, unfortunately, sleeping and could not sign. While honesty is not a crime one can accuse Bengali poets of, Sarat has always been an exception. Even now, he can startle his readers with a few quick poems about a prohibited figure like Taslima Nasrin! Dibyendu Palit[49] has signed, but with a carefully attached disclaimer: 'These are governmental issues. I don't think a signature makes any difference.'

How do signatures matter? I had read about two other boys previously, though I never met them. They had taken to the streets to gather signatures for a campaign to bring me back to Kolkata, eventually sending nearly 6000 signatures to Delhi. Where are those papers now? In the trash, most probably.

13 January

Enamul Kabir, as has become a regular habit, called in the morning to read out an article by Ghiyasuddin in the newspaper today. In the article the author has said that the biggest crime I have committed is to have been born to Muslim parents. He has gone on to boldly state that the people of West Bengal are not really concerned about their Hindu fundamentalists; instead, everyone is perpetually wary of their Islamic counterpart. This is true of everyone— renowned political leaders and social activists, artists, writers and the intelligentsia. Among the Muslims, those who are not orthodox remain quiet when something happens because they are afraid, while the non-Muslim population chooses to remain neutral lest their perfect secular images be tarnished. As a result, those persecuted by Hindu radicals find support among the intellectuals, while those wronged by Muslim radicals are almost always shunned.

Ghiyasuddin has made it clear that this critique has been composed keeping politicians out of its ambit; they are but slaves to power and will do anything to ensure their perpetuity is never jeopardized. He has primarily directed his questions at the intelligentsia who exhibit this duality without fail— to wilfully ignore the plight of those who have been prey to Muslim fundamentalism, especially if the survivors are Muslims. It is not difficult to ascertain why. So afraid they are of upsetting the Islamic radicals that they would rather treat such incidents as internal issues within the Muslim community, to be solved internally.

Ghiyasuddin has asked me a question too—he has asked me whether even I know why I have been punished. He has then gone on to answer this very question and reveal that all the other accusations levelled against me had been fabricated, imaginary and illogical, meant to hide another truly horrible crime: my Muslim parentage. How dare I, hailing from a Muslim family, assert myself as a rationalist, a feminist, a humanist and a dissident? Since I have been guilty of all of these crimes, neither the Quran nor the religious leaders will ever forgive me. With such powerful enemies, is there any wonder that the intellectuals are not on my side? The cultural elite pride themselves in being 'secular', and expressing solidarity with me would undoubtedly be too communal a thing to do.

Such things have been written before, usually by truly honest and daring proponents of secularism, most of them Hindus or associated with them. Muslim intellectuals rarely tread this territory unless they are someone as irredeemably atheist as Ghiyasuddin. There are not many people born to Muslim families in India who can claim to be atheists. Once upon a time, I had gathered a few such people around me to set up the Secular Humanist Collective to foster a scientific outlook and combat orthodoxy and superstitions among Muslims. Among other things, the collective demanded a society free of terror, education shorn of religious proselytizing, equal rights for women, and an adherence to basic human rights.

I thanked Ghiyasuddin over the phone and wished him luck for their press conference in Kolkata tomorrow.

There is another reason to be happy today. Karan Thapar has written an excellent article in the *Hindustan Times*, criticizing Priya Ranjan Dasmunsi who had asked me to get down on my knees and apologize to Muslims for having hurt their religious sentiments. Thapar has written:

> Who are they, whose sentiments cannot be hurt at all? Who are they in front of whom Taslima has to kneel and pray for forgiveness? Whoever they are, I am sure they are not like you or me, or anyone who is tolerant and kind and rationalist, aware, educated, well-informed and invested in the freedom of thought. Surely, they are of the fanatic kind, backward, narrow-minded, and blinded by religion and superstitions. Henceforth, will they demarcate the boundaries of our freedom? Have they been entrusted with deciding what can be believed or not?
>
> I have to assert that when Mr. Mukherjee says Taslima Nasreen must not say, do or write things that 'hurt the sentiments of our people', I do not recognise the pronoun 'our'. Am I part of it? Are you? Is he? Or does he only have in mind a small but vocal and violent minority—perhaps disowned by, or at least, embarrassing to the majority of their co-religionists—who, he believes, delivers votes?
>
> We don't expect very much of our politicians—if there is one lesson experience has taught us, it must be this—but, at the very least, they should stand up for their freedoms. Otherwise, they could soon be tolling the bell for themselves. Let them remember what they deny Taslima or us today; they could end up losing themselves tomorrow.

My captors arrived with yet another spell of freedom—a visit to the dentist. I usually get excited whenever I have to go anywhere, at the prospect of leaving the house at least for a while, irrespective of where we are going. So, we set off, a new road stretching out ahead. It was a bit like going somewhere in a prison van, the tinted windows separating me from the world outside, while I sat and stared at every passing thing with avid interest—the regular people going about their regular routines, from the middle or lower classes, who had no interest in knowing who I am, let alone demanding my head. Why should they have even cared! There are usually no security guards in the car, and as we were travelling, people saw me through the front glass. So what? It matters very little to people, for those who know me or those who don't. So, why keep me imprisoned? Apparently, if I am let loose, people will die; or so they keep trying to tell me. I will no longer believe their lies or their explanations.

I got excited at the sight of the new roads, at the prospect of a new place, even if it was the dentist's. Not that I asked my captors anything! However, very soon, a familiar lane came into view and out went all my optimism. We were headed to that other ghastly safe house, the one with the high walls and the big iron gates. The only person in the house who I have ever seen is the one who serves us tea and biscuits. I trust he is summoned for such special occasions.

The only bit of freedom I have managed to steal for myself thus far is to go for walks in the field nearby during these sudden excursions to visit doctors. When a person's world shrinks, even small spaces seem so vast!

The dentist came to see me at the safe house, with his tiny box of equipment. What harm would have befallen if we had indeed gone to his chamber? On our way back, my captors stopped the car to buy the medicines he had prescribed for me, before bringing me back to my cell again. The rest of the day passed like it always does; like the nights always pass.

14 January

A press conference was called in Kolkata today by a group of progressive Muslim activists. The group, also comprising ex-Muslims, and atheists within the Muslim community, gathered and gave a statement demanding Taslima Nasrin be allowed to come back to Kolkata. They argued that her presence in Kolkata will hugely benefit all undertakings for the development of the Muslim communities.

Nothing else of note happened the entire day. I had spoken to Supratik of PTI regarding the Simone de Beauvoir Prize; I saw a report on the same in *The Hindu* and *Hindustan Times* and a few other newspapers. The work that has earned me such an accolade in Paris is also the reason for the ignominy that has been heaped on me at home. What else is left to say after that?

Some phone calls I do still receive, and some I make, though the overall frequency of these exchanges is gradually decreasing. Shankha Ghosh called to congratulate me on the Beauvoir Prize. He had one complaint though. Why had I said that there was no one fighting on my behalf at home? I deflected the query by saying that it had been from a translation of an old piece of writing—*Le Monde* had translated it into French and published it—when in truth there had truly been no one beside me. Throughout the conversation I kept wishing I could tell him there aren't too many people now either. There are only a handful, and definitely none of the political parties or welfare groups. In fact, before Mahasweta Devi's protest meet and silent march, nothing had truly been done. Neither the political parties nor the numerous women's rights groups and the human rights organizations had issued a statement in solidarity. I further assured him that I had only thanked people in my subsequent article, the one he had even edited a few lines from.

Shankha Ghosh understood. He kept trying to convince me that there were many people fighting on my behalf. He reminded me of his promise that he would call Mr B and request his help in getting me back to Kolkata. He has not had the opportunity yet to make the promised call. Should I trust him any longer? Whenever accusations of being un-Islamic have been levelled against me, he has remained silent. He has never said a word, never revealed to anyone how I had given him 10,000 rupees a couple of years ago to donate to the welfare fund set up for the destitute Muslim survivors of the Gujarat riots. He had been in charge of the fundraising campaign on behalf of the intelligentsia of Bengal. Granted I had never wanted publicity from this, but when they were throwing me out of the country on false allegations, could he not have said something?

I owe Shankha Ghosh one debt of gratitude though. He edited my subsequent articles, be it for a seminar or for publication, to make sure there was not even a single utterance which would be perceived as hurtful to Islamic sentiments. Bengal's premier poet could painstakingly excise anything and everything communal from my writing, but nevertheless could not manage to attend the assembly held to demand for my return. He sent word instead that he was otherwise occupied.

I do not yet know when our leading poets and writers would finally stop pandering to censorship.

I was walking on the terrace in the evening under a clear sky flecked with a scattering of stars. My captors and their sentinels have seemingly given up office and spend nearly all their time here. I do not want to cause them inconvenience but it seems to be happening regardless. How long can they keep ignoring all their official duties in order to play nursemaid for me? I do not wish to live like this in India! All I wish for is love and acceptance.

Suddenly my captor asked:

C: Haven't you given up your house in Kolkata?
TN: No, I haven't.
C: Isn't it a waste of money? You aren't living there, after all.
TN: That it is.
C: How much is the rent again?
TN: Twenty thousand. Plus, another two and a half for maintenance.
C: You are paying that much extra every month?
TN: What can I do? I have asked my publishers to pay the rent and deduct it from the royalties.
C: Why don't you just give it up?
TN: I could have rented another flat, but who will do that on my behalf? I would have to go and do that myself. To try and find some place a little cheaper.

He kept quiet for a while before starting again: 'Won't you go to France to collect your prize?' I told him the ceremony had already happened, and my French publishers have accepted the prize on my behalf.

C: It has happened already?
TN: Yes, it's over.
C: When?
TN: On the ninth.
C: Won't you have to go to Paris to get the prize?
TN: Not really. It's a certificate and money. They will courier me the certificate and deposit the prize money in my account.

C: What does Svensson say?

TN: About what?

C: He doesn't call?

TN: Sometimes he does.

C: He doesn't say anything?

TN: What should he say?

C: He doesn't ask you to go back to Sweden?

TN: Where?

C: Sweden.

TN: Why should he do that?

C: He came. He saw how much mental pressure you were facing. That you aren't well. Does he not want to take you away from all this?

TN: No.

C: How is that possible?

TN: Why should he want that? He knows how much I love living here, that I want to keep doing so. He knows I don't want to go abroad, don't want to stay anywhere else any more. And what would I do there? I might not have freedom here right now, but all that is going to change, right? This cannot go on forever.

Through it all, there was one thing I picked up. That my captors had been instructed to learn everything they possibly could about me—what I was thinking, whether I was thinking of going away, if not, then what could they say or do that would make me consider it, and so on and so forth. My captors were supposed to make me feel convinced that I should leave India. One of the officers had once told me, rather randomly: 'Freedom is the most important thing. Unless we are independent, nothing else matters! Why are you not going away? What is the point in living as a prisoner?' His words had shocked me that day.

They are trying to break me. Have they been instructed to do this? Or are they just making polite conversation? What if I refuse to break? What will they do then, what new plans will they hatch? Will they use any means necessary? I should not be afraid, but try as I might, fear has begun to creep up on me like darkness.

15 January

I am not sure if the days are passing at all. I don't have a calendar, so the only way I can verify this is via the morning newspaper, which assures me that the days are indeed passing. My captors had called to ask about my teeth. In response, I had asked them if there was any news vis-à-vis my return to Kolkata. The voice had mechanically replied in the negative.

I just want news, be it good or bad. No one can go on living like this. I have been put in chains after having fought for freedom all my life. In this country of a billion people, a writer has been forcefully ousted from her home and shipped to a safe house in another state to be confined there for days on end. This is, as unbelievable as it is, happening in India. Those who used to call have stopped now, perhaps because I have been struck off the list of priorities. People generally prefer to keep a safe distance from irrelevant or blacklisted names.

Manas Ghosh's newspaper has printed a small article on yesterday's assembly of the Secular Humanist Collective. They have not mentioned that most of the members of the collective were progressive and rationalist Muslims. They had published the news of the first rally in a big way on the front page and had promised to write extensively about the meeting as well. Is this what they had meant? Is Ghosh too trying to distance himself from this controversy? *Anandabazar* had done it a while ago, and it is difficult to correctly assess the other newspapers. Only a relatively new entrant like *Dainik Statesman* had stood by me through all my ordeals.

I tried taking a nap in the afternoon; these days whenever I try it, I invariably have a nightmare and wake up. I have begun to feel very alone. I miss my parents and I feel even lonelier. I don't remember ever feeling this way. Fakrul mama called yesterday. It felt a little strange in the beginning since I had last seen him in Kolkata about seven or eight years back. When he asked me where I was, I could feel the pain twist in my gut. These are my family, my loved ones! They don't want to forget me, nor I them! I want to live in the same city as them, share their joys and their sorrows, and share love. I cannot because I am not allowed.

January 16

My morning call from Kolkata had a trove of information today. Shaoli Mitra[50] and Bhabaniprasad Chattopadhyay have written in support in *Dainik Statesman*. The Publishers and Booksellers Guild has also informed me that they have dutifully passed on to all my publishers the news of the embargo placed on my books at this year's Kolkata International Book Fair by the Milli-ittehad Parishad. Shibani Mukhopadhyay[51] has immediately declined to adhere to the draconian demand while Anima from Gangchil Publishers has countered saying none of their books are on religion. Subir Mitra from Ananda Publishers has issued a statement to the effect that it would be unnatural to keep the books off the shelves, and that there is enough time to further deliberate on the issue since the fair is still a few days away.

I called Manas Ghosh in the morning, but after a while I could no longer continue speaking through my choked throat and the tears streaming down my cheeks. I spoke to Prasanta Roy too about the Guild. Since the Guild had received the embargo they ought to have handled it themselves. However, they have passed on the responsibility to the publishers, as if they have a stake in this.

In her article, Shaoli Mitra has demanded to know if I am worse than a homicidal mass murderer, considering the way I have been kept locked up. Bhabaniprasad Chattopadhyay has advised that the way I have been going on, trying to effect change through writing, is no longer a feasible option against the rising tide of fundamentalist thought. The only option that apparently remains is to visit the uneducated and backward Muslims, from one door to the next, with explanation. To that effect, he has cited the example of Ishwar Chandra Vidyasagar who was much revered despite his critical and reformist attitude simply because he never said anything directly offensive to Hinduism.

I cannot help but doubt as to why it should be so. Why must we persist in thinking of these as the only means to effect social change? It has been years, isn't it time enough for change? What if I want to go about it differently? What if I don't wish to go from one house to the next? What if instead I continue writing, which is what I do best? Will that be such a crime?

Sudip Maitra writes a fantastic weekly column on Wednesdays, on social customs and common superstitions.

This week's entry is on faith and fanaticism where Maitra has tried to critique the old adage that I too have often countered with my writing—that faith is a good virtue while fanaticism is not. Despite how I have been made captive, how my thoughts have been made captive, to the threat of fanatic zeal, it gladdens my heart to hear someone speak the language that I have always spoken. I called *Dainik Statesman* to congratulate Sudip on his article and he seemed pleased. I have never met him previously and it saddens me to think how much time I spent in Kolkata in the absolutely wrong company while never crossing paths with the genuine people. I have decided to change my lifestyle entirely when I get back to Kolkata.

Nothing is happening. Something has to happen.

17 January

I had yet another nightmare last night. This time I dreamt that both my kidneys were malfunctioning. I spent the entire night suffering visions of disease and death, so much so that it was only after sunrise I could manage to convince myself that it had only been a bad dream. I have suffered the memories of the nightmare all day, though that is not saying much since things like dreams and nightmares, truths and lies have long become fuzzy and unclear. Not having seen anything in the newspapers and not having received any calls either, I called Tapan Raychaudhuri and found out that he has yet to write the letter he had promised he would write to Mr B requesting that the rules against my going out be relaxed. Besides, he also has not had the opportunity of discussing my predicament with someone influential within the Government of West Bengal. I feel so awkward calling someone up asking them for favours, especially for myself.

Everything seems a bit bizarre, this house, this state of being. I have to take deep breaths to calm myself down. So many people have promised so many things but everyone seems to have forgotten it all. No matter who calls from Kolkata, I keep asking them to call again—tomorrow, the day after or whenever. I can sense the terrible desperation that has me in its grips.

Finally, something happened in the afternoon. CNN-IBN had organized a small live chat with their readers, and a guy from the bureau sent me a bunch of questions and then called me to get the answers. Some time was spent on this for sure. But then? For me, it was back to the empty rooms, and the hours spent staring out of the window, and the intermittent long sighs. Besides, I have not been able to study or write. I have spent all my time in growing anxiety about when I would be allowed my freedom to lead an independent life.

Late in the afternoon, I was speaking to Shibani about our old book fair sojourns and the gatherings at Coffee House. We had always dreamt back then of having a decent place for the People's Book Society in College Street, somewhere we would go often to meet, talk and hang out. That space has finally been acquired and we were discussing when they were moving, when the room was going to be set up and the first meeting of friends to toast the occasion. Shibani confidently replied, 'Once you are back . . .'

I was having my tea while my captor was sitting and watching television, and laughing. Suddenly, a question out of the blue:

C: Have you sold your house in Kolkata?

TN: Why?

C: You were speaking on the phone. You said something about a new flat . . .

TN: No. That was not about my own flat. My publishers are moving to a new place.

They have never been nosy about anything to do with my personal life. I suspect these sudden questions are compulsions of the job. I have begun to be convinced that they have been told to keep an eye on me, to see how long I can endure before I break. These instructions have come from Mr B, the person who used to claim to have my best interests in his heart. Where did all his affection disappear? Does he not know that I have not done anything wrong? Is he not aware of how I have been? What have I done to not deserve mercy?

Christian Besse called from France with a proposal for a book about my strange exile in India. He has also informed me that they are making arrangements for my Beauvoir Prize to be handed over to me in India, though not by the visiting French President, but definitely by one of the accompanying ministers or high-ranking officials.

I took a few deep breaths, feeling some strength seep back into me from somewhere. I drew a plain sheet of paper towards me and wrote down everything I needed. I have handed the list over to my captor, a list of demands that I have previously been making verbally for the past few weeks.

I want to meet:

1.   Jabir Husain, a Sahitya Academy Award-winning poet and Rajya Sabha MP

2.   Sudhirnath, friend and cartoonist

3.   Arun Maheshwari, friend and publisher
4.   Sheela Reddy, friend
5.   A regular doctor who would examine my blood pressure, blood sugar, cholesterol, and treat me accordingly
6.   A therapist with whom I can talk about my depression, anxiety and apprehensions
7.   I want to go outside, walk, watch people and their lives unfolding. I want to see life again.

My captors have assured me they will pass on my requests to the relevant authorities.

18 January

The only newspaper in Kolkata to have stood by me was *Dainik Statesman*. The other newspapers have been studiously silent, while *Aajkaal*, a mouthpiece of the CPI(M), has been spouting venom against me since *Lajja* was published. I have known Manas Ghosh of *Dainik Statesman* for quite some time too, since his visit to Bangladesh all those years ago to interview me for the *Statesman*. It had not been a surprise that I would have his support when he decided to launch the Bengali version. I used to write regularly for them for a while and through all my trials and tribulations they were right beside me, boldly publishing news, articles and editorials in support of me when the other newspapers had turned their backs. Now it seems the *Statesman* has come to a resolution to gradually sever all ties with me.

Manas Ghosh does not call often any more; in fact, when I had suggested I begin writing the column again, he evaded my proposal with an indistinct 'Not now'. Two articles were published about me the day before, the more detailed one being the one by Bhabaniprasad where he had been critical about my choices. Yesterday, they published a letter complaining I have broken the laws of the nation. Today, the *Statesman* has published an article by Siddhartha Shankar Ray, where he has irrefutably declared that a foreign national has no right to say anything about any religion in this country, nor do they have the right to hurt the sentiments of 200 million Muslims. He has firmly called for a cancellation of visa for anyone unwilling to adhere to these laws.

Ever since I have read the article, I have begun to suspect that the Government of India is not planning to extend my visa. If the government had been sympathetic to my plight, I would probably have sensed it by now, and I would not have had to endure so much disgrace either. Even if the promised return to Kolkata could not be worked out, at least Mr B would have called me to tell me to stay in Delhi for some more time. I would have lived in Delhi on my own, moved about freely as I wished, asking for security only if required.

There is a month left before the visa expires. The foreign affairs minister, Pranab Mukherjee, has assured Parliament that there would be no issues vis-à-vis the renewal, but there is always the possibility that the government will cite some strange new development to go back on their word. My own country had disowned me. No matter how much I consider India my other home, at least on paper I am a foreign national here. Consequently, a foreign government has the right to cancel my residence permit any time they wish to. Of course, they will have to cite justifiable reasons for the same, but is the legitimacy of a claim something one can ever fully ascertain? They might as well say that the youth had taken to the streets to demand my ouster from India, so I will not be given another visa. Can that be something one can ever verify? I don't think dreams ever crash and burn like mine have. No big movements have come up to demand my rights. There have been a few articles in a few leading newspapers, and only some of my friends marched in protest and held meetings. I have even overheard pointed questions about the same: 'Where are custodians of human rights? Where are the Arundhati Roys, Romila Thapars, Teesta Setalvads, Shabana Azmis, Ram Puniyanis, Dinesh D'Souzas, Biju Mathews and John Dayals? Where is Sonia Gandhi or the *Tehelka* magazine? The salient features of development, human rights and secularism in India include the condemnation of Hindu fanatics while simultaneously endorsing any antisocial activities by Muslim and Christian fundamentalists.'

Try as I might, I cannot seem to push aside the heaviness that has settled over my heart.

I spoke to Abdul Gaffar Choudhury today to request him to try and approach the caretaker government to help me return to my home in Bangladesh. Gaffar Choudhury informed me that he has already had a word with Fakhruddin[52] regarding the same; the latter has apparently recoiled at the very mention of my name. None of them are willing to help me; no one wants me to go back. Gaffar Choudhury kept telling me, 'They will kill you here! They have already slaughtered the person who had started following your footsteps.' On asking who it was, he replied, 'You don't know? Humayun Azad! They killed him because they could not get their hands on you. If you come back here, they will do the same.'

I had a word with social theorist Ashis Nandy, who is famously called a political psychologist by the intelligentsia. He told me he feels the government will renew my visa, especially since Sonia Gandhi is quite fond of me.

TN: Even Mr B used to be fond of me. Is that still true?
    If so, why have I been kept captive? Why have I not
    been shown an iota of humanity? Why have I not been
    allowed a normal life like a free human being?
AN: Perhaps he is afraid!
TN: Afraid of what?
AN: Afraid of the consequences.
TN: If something were to happen, it would have happened
    already.

Although Ashis Nandy's words have managed to fill me with
renewed hope, some doubts still linger.

20 January

Arundhati Roy and Ritu Menon[53] had a talk with renowned
human rights lawyer Indira Jaising a while back. If anyone
can help at this point, it is Jaising. However, as usual, the
advice was to file a court case.

TN: Against who?
IJ: Against the government.
TN: That won't be possible for me.
IJ: Why not? You will win if you file a case!

Indira has called after that to see if I have changed my mind;
so have Arundhati and Ritu. The advice remains the same,
despite my repeated refusals. 'You have no other way out
except a court case.'
    I have tried explaining to them that I am not a citizen of
this country and that I have been allowed to live here by the
grace of the government. So, I will not file a case against them.

I am certain I will be released from this safe house if people who believe in human rights and the freedom of speech and expression come together to petition the authorities on my behalf.

Indira did not want to listen to a word I had to say. 'You just sign the paper allowing me to fight on your behalf. Leave the rest to me. The only way you can get out of this predicament is by filing a case. Otherwise, one of these days, they will just kick you out, and you won't ever be able to return. We have this way open till you have a valid visa, after which there's nothing much we can do. They forced you out of West Bengal and brought you to an unknown safe house because some fundamentalists protested against you. With the mental stress you have already gone through, there's nothing else left for you to lose any further. Now if they manage to drive you out of India too, there will be nothing else left for us to do, not even file a case. Take time and think about it.' She called a few days later and repeated the same thing but I still refused.

So it went on, them trying to convince me and me refusing again and again. One fine day, I finally said, 'No matter what happens, I will not file a case against the government. I will wait for the day their decision changes.'

Annoyed, Indira Jaising hung up on me.

23 January

After repeatedly asking my captors, they have sternly informed me that the list of demands I had submitted via them a few days ago have all been turned down by the Government of India.

27 January

'This is not to claim that for the first time the people who delve in this sort of divisive and fraudulent politics have been publicly unmasked. However, their complete failure in protecting human rights, freedom of speech and the integrity of the Constitution of India is indeed very painful to witness. There is nothing comparable to the heinous political experiments that have been done on Taslima both by the State and the Centre. Such shame even *Lajja* will not be able to mitigate.'—Anonymous

My captors have taken to constantly encouraging me to leave India. Besides, terrible things have been happening. The incident with the doctors has proved to me beyond a shadow of doubt how devastating mental coercion can be. I had been asking to see a doctor for my blood pressure for quite a while, but there had been no response from my captors. Since verbal requests were not effective, I even wrote an application stating that I wished to consult a cardiologist. There was no answer for nearly three weeks despite my earnest requests. Everything else I needed— clothes, shoes, toiletries—was brought in except for the doctor. That last request my captors summarily refused to grant.

TN: Why not?

C: Because of security.

TN: I can't see a doctor because of security?

C: No, madam.

TN: What security issues?

C: We can't take you to a doctor's chamber.

TN: Then bring a doctor here. My blood pressure now reads a 170 over a 120. And you guys are telling me I can't visit a doctor due to security reasons?

C: We can't get a doctor here either.

TN: Then take me to that other safe house where you bring
     people to meet me.
C: I will pass on your request, madam. I am sorry but I do
   what I am instructed. Please do not misunderstand me.
   You too must try and understand that everything we do
   is for the sake of your security. That is the only thing we
   are concerned about.
TN: My security will be disrupted if you bring a doctor here?
     But if I don't see a doctor, I will die!
C: Let me see what I can do.

After two months of repeated requests for a doctor, when
I began telling my captors that I was about to have a heart
attack, they did not seem too perturbed. In fact, it seemed to
me they were almost relieved. If I were to die of a heart attack,
it would have indeed solved a lot of problems for them. I told
them that people would think they have killed me, but even
that did not seem to be a cause for worry. Finally, when I gave
a statement to the media that I was not being allowed to see a
doctor, they were forced to arrange for one. I was taken to the
other safe house. There was no reason for me to be impressed
by the doctor I met there. He did not show me an ID, nor did
he tell me his name because my captors had asked him not to.
In fact, it did not seem to me he was a proper doctor, and it
soon became clear to every single person present there that I
knew more about blood pressure-related ailments than he did.
Besides, the moment he had recognized who I was, he had
begun to tremble and that was the end of his interventions.
The doctor left and I was brought back to the safe house.
   A few days later in the evening, I was taken back to the
other safe house. This time the doctor seemed like a proper
one and he examined me and prescribed a combination of

three drugs. However, my body began to react badly to the calcium channel blocker Amlodipine the moment I had it after returning to the safe house. I began to sweat profusely and I could feel my body give way. It was unlike anything I had ever felt. I was losing control of my senses, and slowly sinking into darkness. With the last bit of strength left in my body, I called Akash. He came and though I could not speak to him, he made arrangements for a stretcher to be summoned from the cantonment stores to take me to the hospital. My captors and the doctor were waiting for me there and I was admitted to the coronary care unit (CCU) immediately. I could not speak properly, each word taking me an inordinate amount of effort to articulate. A plethora of machines and monitors were attached to me to check my vitals, while the doctors set themselves to ascertain if I was having an allergic reaction. I managed to tell the doctor that it could be an adverse reaction to Amlodipine, or to the mix of medicines I had been prescribed. Around two at night, things took an even more serious turn, with the previous symptoms returning. I was feeling light as a feather and I could sense my blood pressure dropping rapidly. All I could do was to beg the doctor to save me. The saline channel was opened to full blast and steroids were pumped into my body to restore it in any way possible. I could feel life slipping away, images of Mymensingh, Bangladesh, West Bengal, all my friends, colleagues and admirers flashing before my eyes. It took nearly two hours for the steroids to be effective and for things to become a bit stable. Death had wanted to hold me in its cold, restful embrace but had had to content with only a few stolen whispers.

The doctor brought in by my captors examined me the next day and declared that I had had a poisonous reaction to the medicines. When asked which medicine had caused the reaction, he couldn't really say for sure, though he warned me that if it had been Amlodipine, I would not be able to have it ever again. I requested my captors to let me talk to Mr B and they told me that they have informed him of my request. I asked them by what logic I had been prescribed a combination of three drugs when everyone had known that I was taking 2.5 mg of medicine already. The doctor confessed that it should not have happened but now that it had, I should move on and not dwell on the past. He advised me to remain 'tension free' in order to recover faster.

The next Sunday, my captors came to visit me. When I inquired yet again about Mr B, they had nothing new to say except to assure me that he would speak to me soon enough. In the meanwhile, my blood pressure had not stopped being erratic. The doctors had recommended complete bed rest and absolutely no physical exertion. They had also been careful to remind me that stress and tension were the last things I needed because these were gradually pushing me towards death. Of course, that was easier said than done! For the next two days, I was kept in the CCU. The doctors had initially informed me that I would have to stay in the hospital till my blood pressure was normal again, but soon enough they changed their diagnosis. I knew that my captors had taken them aside and told them something, though I was not sure what that had been.

The government had decided that I had to leave the hospital, and the doctors accordingly complied and discharged me immediately. It was not until much later that I realized that the hasty decision had been a reaction to news reports in *Times of India* regarding my health. The report had perturbed my overlords; they were worried that it would make the news of my condition public knowledge, and consequently everyone would find out about the exact nature of my exile. It's a myth that the administration is never anxious of what the media might find out.

The other reason cited for the quick release from the hospital was that I had to meet Mr B. He could have called, of course, or come to meet me in the CCU, but apparently that was not possible. I remember how much my suggestion that Mr B come to the hospital had shocked my captors. Mr B was a minister in the government! How could he come to meet an ordinary person? So, I was taken out of the CCU to meet Mr B. Things were done so efficiently that we did not even waste the extra time we had before the scheduled meeting; I was brought back to my safe house instead of staying at the hospital. From there I was taken to meet Mr B in another empty house, yet another safe house in the endless chain that I had visited during the course of my exile in Delhi. This one seemed more like a government guest house, one in a row of similarly pretty single-floor houses, though I was never informed where exactly we were. This was not surprising, especially because my captors had successfully hidden even their names from me. Like everything else in this exile, this meeting too was held in utmost secrecy.

While we were waiting, tea was served. I kept trying to explain to my captors that in such a physical state, the best thing to do would be to pack me off to my home in Kolkata since I was somehow sure that this would not have happened had I been home in the first place. I was sure that all my health issues—the blood pressure, the gradually worsening heart—were due to my exile. Mr B arrived in about fifteen minutes. Meanwhile, I had noticed that my captors had fixed wide smiles on their faces; in fact, that had been the case this entire time. It was a little disconcerting and I could not help but begin to anticipate what was about to happen, hoping against hope that it would spell good news for me. Perhaps they knew Mr B would be sending me back to Kolkata! Or perhaps they were overjoyed at being considered close confidants of Mr B; such had been the dedication and efficiency with which they had done their duties! Nevertheless, tired and restless, the burgeoning hope of deliverance could not fully manage to animate me and I could still feel the ravages of my unpredictable blood pressure and the after-effects of drugs pumping through my veins. My captors had always been secretive. Perhaps that had been part of the instructions given to them. They had often seemed to me like wound-up dolls, and I could not fathom if their smiles too were part of the range of emotions they had been taught to display as and when required.

Mr B was in the other room with another unknown gentleman. As we greeted each other and sat down, I could not help but think that I knew nothing about what Mr B was thinking and what his plans were for me. The only thing I was sure of was the warmth and support I had always received from this man. Always a well-wisher, I had often visited his house besides speaking on the phone every so often. Despite all the pressure from the government, he had made sure to get my visa extended without a hitch. I was convinced that he was trying his best to get me back to Kolkata. Just like someone complains to a loved one, I complained to him about the delay in getting a doctor to check on me. In a rush, I told him about the entire debacle with the doctors, the first one a quack, and my near-death experience after that.

My captors were sitting nearby and I had hoped
Mr B would suitably chastise them immediately for their
negligence and for their part in endangering my life. So,
it was quite surprising when he said absolutely nothing to
them. Instead, skirting any mention of the things that had
happened thus far, he launched straight into his most urgent
query: 'I have come to assure you that you are an esteemed
guest of our nation; we give you our word that you would get
our visa without problems in the future and you are always
welcome to our hospitality. As promised, we will extend
your visa in February. However, it will be best if you go
to France soon to receive the award you have been given.
I have told the French President that regrettably a French
award cannot be given on Indian soil. The award can be
handed over only in the country from which the award has
originated or the country to which the recipient belongs.' My
attempt to intervene at this point was cut short by Mr B's
stern rejoinder: 'Please listen to me.' Satisfied that I would
be quiet, he continued, 'You are not a citizen of India, so the
award cannot be given to you here. Either you would have
to go to Bangladesh or to France. The French President
has already extended an invitation and we will make all the
necessary arrangements for your travel. Go and receive the
award.'

Sensing this was my opening, I looked at him with wide,
guileless eyes and replied, 'The award function has already
been held in Paris on 9 January. My French publishers have
accepted my award on my behalf. I have told them to mail
the certificate to my Kolkata address.'

Clearly dissatisfied with the reply, Mr B said, 'If you
go away to France for some time that would be the best for
everyone. I am assuring you as a minister, you don't have to

worry about a thing. We will make all the arrangements from here—your stay in France, if you wish to travel elsewhere, everything. Don't worry about money. The government will take care of everything.'

I was looking at Mr B. He was speaking to me but his eyes were trained elsewhere as he kept saying what he had come to say. Beside him, rather bizarrely, both the unknown gentleman and my captor were noting down our conversation in their respective notebooks. Mr B had come wearing a suit, with a woollen cap covering his head, quite unlike the usual dhoti I was used to. While I kept trying to find a smile on his suddenly unrecognizable face, or some remnant of his usual warmth, he was engrossed in his speech: 'We can't really say anything for certain about your return to Kolkata. They might create trouble again, that too right before the visa is up for renewal on the sixteenth. What if they do something the day before? At least if you are not here, we can tell them, "She is not here. We will think about it later if we are bringing her back." You can obviously come back as soon as everything calms down. If you are apprehensive that you won't be allowed to come back, then you are mistaken. I have already told Tapan Raychaudhuri. He is very fond of you. He has a daughter of your age and so has a soft spot for you. I had told him to let you stay at his house in Oxford if you wish to. Don't worry. You don't have to decide on dates right now. Take a couple of days and let me know.'

While Mr B was advising me to take a few days off and go away for a while, I could feel it in my gut that this parting would not be as temporary as he wanted me to believe. It would be for good, just like when I had left Bangladesh fourteen years ago. Like I had been coerced into leaving Kolkata only three months ago.

'Stay abroad for a while and it will be easier for us to get you back to Kolkata. You would be able to fly directly to Kolkata from France or anywhere else in Europe. Don't worry. We will make all the arrangements for the trip. You are a respected guest. We are not letting you lead a normal life or letting anyone meet you simply because of security reasons. Ninety-five per cent of the people are compassionate but the other 5 per cent might not be so. We don't want to take any risks.'

While he was speaking, my eyes were searching his face. The creases on his forehead betrayed his annoyance. I was finding it difficult to relate the person in front of me with the person I knew, the person whose house I used to visit so often, with books and flowers and sweets. He used to sit and recite poetry to me, and would often confess his love of poetry to me. I remember once I had gifted him all the best books of poetry by some of the greatest poets. He used to constantly tell me to visit him, even making his party members wait while we would be engrossed in conversation. He would remember the renewal dates of my visa more than me, even making arrangements with the home ministry on my behalf, and telling me only after the formalities were over. It was impossible to come to terms with the realization that such a person was now part of the enemy camp. I have always had problems with thinking the worst of someone, and yet there he was, issuing ultimatums, not a trace of love or compassion on his face. He was repeating the now familiar diatribe, the gist of which was one single line: 'Leave India!' The person I used to trust the most once upon a time, someone who had always been on my side, was now so far removed from his ethics and ideals, and so invested in political charades that he had cast aside all love and empathy to bribe me into leaving, all in the guise of a well-wisher.

It was my turn to speak as Mr B stopped. I must confess that I was immeasurably calm, perhaps because I had just escaped from the jaws of death. Death was still playing a macabre game of hide-and-seek with me, and I was almost light years away from dishonest politicians with their vested interests. Calmly I replied, 'I was abroad for ten long years. Not for a single day of those years did I feel that I belong to their society or culture. How can I live in a place like that, where I don't belong? I was well regarded abroad, had won many awards, but could never consider any of those countries as home. I am officially a foreigner in India, but I have never felt like one here. I speak in my own language here. I was raised a Bengali and our cultural heritage is similar. Not just in Bengal but anywhere in India that I go, I feel a connection with the land. It never struck me that I am not Indian, that I am a foreign national. Earlier, whenever I used to get my tourist visa, I would come to Kolkata. Then, after I was given a residence permit, I decided to settle down here. Whatever I had abroad I brought almost everything down to Kolkata, and I even asked my brothers to send all my books. You were the one who used to help me with my residence permit, remember? If you visit my house in Kolkata, I swear, it would seem like a three-decade-old household to you. Where will I go, leaving all this behind? I am a Bengali, I write in Bangla, and so I want to live there too. To live as I wish to, to write in peace, that is all I want. If it was possible, I would have gone back to Bangladesh. Trust me, I have tried. I spoke to my lawyer . . .'

'Sara Hossain, right?' he suddenly intervened.

Nodding in answer, I continued, 'Yes, daughter of Dr Kamal Hossain. I have tried contacting Dr Hossain but he does not want to address the issue of my return at all. I have written to his wife, Hameeda Hossain, too, but she didn't show any interest in the matter either. If I could have I would have returned, I would not have insisted on staying here. I stay here because of the language, because of the life I can have here, because of my roots, and because I have nowhere else to go. I can write freely here, and also have friends and family visit me from Bangladesh. I have not written anything against Islam. I had written *Dwikhandito* a long time ago while I was living abroad, much before I moved here. I have never written anything against Islam during my entire stay here. Besides, after Mr Pranab Mukherjee's speech in Parliament, I had even deleted the allegedly offensive sections from the book. Do you meet him? Ask him, he knows.'

Mr B nodded and I went on: 'If your government does not extend my residence permit, I would be forced to leave. I would know that there is no place for me in the subcontinent.' My voice heavy with tears, I continued speaking. A relentless stream of tears had begun to flow down my cheeks. Here was Mr B, a powerful member of the administration of a nation that was fast becoming a superpower, and such a nation was confessing to being unable to give me shelter among a billion citizens because the fundamentalists did not want them to! Though I was not unaware of how important fundamentalists were for votes and for the sustenance of power, I could scarcely believe such a blatant exercise of the same regardless of how it was affecting society.

Wiping my tears I went on. 'I might be able to survive abroad, but I won't be able to live there. If I have to truly live,

I have to stay here or in Bangladesh. I won't be able to live as a writer there either. I don't like living abroad, I am never happy when I am abroad, and I won't go. Rather, I will stay here where you have kept me thus far. The day you let me go back to Kolkata, I will do so happily. Till then, I will stay here. And so many people in India love me too.'

'Yes, they do,' replied Mr B.

'Those who don't want me here, they are far fewer in number. Why should my life be destroyed because of something they want? Their threats are nothing new. They keep threatening when they have an ulterior motive and stop soon enough too. I don't mind living in this safe house for a while longer. I simply wish to be allowed to meet a few friends.'

He listened to me, and then repeated what he had just said once again. I, too, repeated my earlier answer: 'I'm not going anywhere.' Suddenly, he looked at his watch and told me he had another important meeting to attend.

'I want to call you but I feel awkward about bothering you. You are such a busy man.'

'Call after 10 p.m. Meanwhile, let me have a word with the Bengal government,' he answered with a smile.

I had assumed that his stance towards me had softened after our long conversation. The assumption was short-lived—I received a call from him on the way back to my personal jail. He had two things to tell me: that I should try and understand that he was genuinely trying to help me, and that I should not talk to the media about our conversation.

On the way, I tried coaxing my captor to take a longer route via a restaurant or at least a café. These days, I sometimes forget that I am a captive and I should not demand such things. My captors are made of sterner stuff though. And so we head back to the safe house.

Strolling on the roof, my mysterious captor by my side, my train of thoughts was suddenly broken by his voice.

C: Your presentation was great. I was amazed.
TN: I did not go there to put up a performance. I was speaking about my life.

While walking, I had forgotten about my senseless blood pressure, about the CCU. On measuring, it read 220/120.

TN: You have to take me to the hospital right now!
C: They won't admit you. There's no use going.
TN: Why won't they admit me? Hadn't they initially refused to let me go until my blood pressure became normal? It's not stabilized yet. I have to go to a hospital. Yesterday the reading had fallen from 200 to 50. I can't trust this instability.

I could tell that my captors did not want to go, but I was adamant. While packing some clothes for the hospital, I kept thinking back to when the doctors in the hospital had insisted that I stay there for some time only to change their stance at my captors' behest. I kept thinking that though Mr B had been constantly pressurizing me to leave the country, what was far more inhuman of all the things they had done was the cavalier attitude they had shown with a patient of irregular blood pressure. What if my heart had stopped in shock?

All pretences have been abandoned. The gloves are off. It's clear as day that they want me to go away. A person is depressed when they are unwell. These people have chosen their time very carefully, using my weakened spirit against me. I may have refused to leave but I don't think they will rest easily. They are obviously fuming, angry at my stubborn stance. But I doubt they have given up. I'm sure they are biding their time, hoping that a lonely, unwell woman will crack sooner or later.

I had to come back from the hospital. They refused to admit me.

This exile, it has torn me up, like a rabid animal digging its talons deep into its prey. My house, my cat, my books, my friends, and my life—I have had to trade all of this and more in exchange for months spent in uncertainty in an unknown dark, musty, old house. The heart, torn and broken, eventually gave way and brought me face-to-face with death. But who cares? Did that stop them from delivering yet another killing blow? Go away! Leave! But where do I go? This is my land. This is where I wish to be buried.

Dig into the earth, pull out my roots and see for yourself whether I belong here or not! No one cares enough to find out, to feel empathy for someone whose entire world has been snatched away from her!

Having cast me aside into the darkness yet again, the big, important men have gone home. I wish them all the very best.

5 February

Do I live only for myself? Do I make these demands only for myself? If that had been so, wouldn't I have compromised or apologized long back for the sake of safety? My fight for my freedom of speech and expression is also how I fight for the same rights on behalf of others. I want this freedom to be recognized in the state or the country I had been driven out of. I want this freedom to be recognized the world over. All I wish is that henceforth, no one will be barred from expressing their views and opinions, that society will no longer have to stay in the dark, that it will be able to walk towards the future. I wish that the country, its people and their precious society will no longer have to suffer the ills of misogyny, intolerance, superstitions, dogma, stupidity and prejudice. I know I will not be able to see even a fragment of this change while I am alive. My only hope is that humanity will last for generations, learning to live in peace, harmony, security and tolerance. Let the future of humanity be free of religion and false customs. Let it be free of the snares of greed. Let it thrive and let it learn to love.

7 February

French television channels have managed to accomplish what the home media and television channels have thus far been unable to do—to show how my life has been in the safe house. The French journalists came down to India for it and went to Kolkata to meet my friends and well-wishers. They also took photographs of the meetings and protest marches besides interviewing me over Skype.

9 February

The days seem to have fallen into a rut and no matter how much I huff and puff, I cannot seem to propel them even an inch further. They sit sulking, refusing to budge, waiting for the critical 17 February to see if I am allowed to live on in India. If I am not allowed, I do not know what I will do or where I will go. All along I had assumed my visa would be renewed. Now, however, I am not so sure, despite all the reassuring things they have declared in Parliament regarding my visa renewal.

21 February

I have not written anything for quite some time. I simply did not feel like writing, what with so much that has happened over the past month. The only thing I have accomplished—I have managed to write a few poems during this time.

It's the 21st today, the International Mother Language Day. It used to be celebrated so grandly in Bangladesh! Now I cannot for a moment believe it was my home. Was it ever truly my country? Had I not thought of India, especially West Bengal, as my country too? Now that too is a lie. My dreams, at the cruel mercy of both these nations, have crashed and burnt.

A hunger strike has been called by some activists demanding my return to Kolkata. The activists, mainly comprising a group of sixty-five to eighty-five-year-old veterans, have set up a makeshift platform at Behala. It warms my heart to see people like Sunando Sanyal and Amlan Dutta there. With talks and speeches lined up throughout the day, the strike will continue till the 23rd.

I had a very surprising conversation with Enamul Kabir in the morning where he advised me to leave India. Kabir— the convener of the Secular Humanist Collective who has always been by my side and has always supported my decision! When did he change so much? From what he told me, he had sent a letter to Buddhadeb Bhattacharya, along with a copy of his journal *Nabamanab* (The New Man). Buddhadeb answered both the letters, adding his phone

number in the second one. Their ensuing conversation
on the telephone had begun with Buddhadeb confessing
that things were not looking good. Even without Enamul
telling me how the rest of the conversation had gone, it
was not difficult to catch the drift of what Enamul was
being unable to articulate. Why was I insisting on staying
in a place where I had faced only insults? Why had I not
already left?

For a while, I could not come to terms with the fact that
it was Enamul who was telling me to leave India. Of course,
his reason was that the chief minister of Bengal would never
allow me to go back to Kolkata. Bhattacharya had often
publicly expressed his wish that I leave. Perhaps I truly
should consider it!

I told Enamul that if one were to observe closely enough,
every nation had its flaws. That did not mean the solution was
to walk away. Then one would not be able to live anywhere!
Tapan Raychaudhuri had given up all his ideals and ethics
in the face of power. Enamul has done the same. The
former had been in collusion with Mr B while Buddhadeb
Bhattacharya has employed the latter.

Despite such devastating news, the hunger strike in
Kolkata has managed to restore some life in me. The State,
its politicians, the religious fanatics, the uneducated, the
backward, the thief and the rogue—such forces have always
spoken against the freedom of expression and they will
continue to do so. Similarly, writers, artists and intellectuals
have always sided with truth and freedom. When the
opinions of intellectuals begin to resemble the opinions of
the government and the fanatics, there is only one thing
one can be certain of—that our society has begun to rot.

I am anxious about the decay that has set in Bengal's sociopolitical milieu. The hunger strike has managed to allay some of that anxiety.

22 February

I was not allowed to meet the French prime minister, but the moment I asked to meet the Swedish ambassador, the request was promptly approved. The ambassador had invited me for lunch, but I did not want to go to the consulate. Once inside the consulate, I would have been under Swedish jurisdiction. What if my captors had refused to bring me back? The ambassador, Lars-Olof Lindgren, made arrangements instead at the Chambers' Room of the Taj Hotel, much to the delight of my captors. They took an entire suite and laid out an extravagant lunch for us. The reason behind this spectacular display of hospitality was simply to cajole me into leaving India. It was yet another of a series of attempts that my captors have been constantly employing to make me change my decision. Had the ambassador too been coaxed into an arrangement to convince me to go back to Sweden? Otherwise, why should my captors feel the need to make such a festivity out of a simple lunch where other officers and employees of the consulate had also been invited? Thankfully, Lars Lindgren did not attempt to give me any advice whatsoever on my moving back to Sweden. On our way back to the safe house, I could feel my captors, who were hoping for some good news from my side, buzzing with excitement. Realizing that I would not share any information on my own, they simply gave up the pretence and asked:

C: What did you talk about?

TN: He asked me how I was. And how things were.

C: What did you say?

TN: Exactly how I have been and how things have been.

C: Everything?

TN: Yes, I don't hide things.

C: You told him you aren't well?

TN: I told him I had everything except my freedom.

C: What did he say?

TN: He listened. He did not say anything.

C: He seemed like an excellent man.

TN: Yes, a completely modern man. Have you had lunch?

C: Yes. What else did he say?

TN: About what?

C: About you?

TN: He seemed to know well about me. He seemed to be
    quite aware—about what happened in Kolkata and
    why, about what happened in Bangladesh and why.

C: And about what is happening in Delhi?

TN: We spoke about it. What can he say? He is not a citizen
    of this country.

C: Obviously. But you are a citizen of his.

TN: On paper. Tell me, do I look Swedish to you, or do I
    look Indian?

C: You are trapped here in this safe house without any
    independence to speak of. You cannot go back to Kolkata.
    You have been a victim of political hypocrisy in India.
    Didn't you talk about all that?

TN: He knows everything.

C: Didn't he give you any advice?

TN: Why should he? Am I a child? I know what I have
    to do.

C: Of course, but an expert's advice is always helpful.

TN: He didn't feel I needed advice.

My captors were quiet for a long while. As we were approaching the safe house, the silence broke again.

C: The ambassador did not say anything about going back to Sweden?

TN: Where?

C: Sweden.

TN: No, he did not.

C: He didn't say anything? He didn't ask you anything about your lack of freedom? You have not been able to work due to increasing stress, and it's also causing immense strain on your physical and mental health. Didn't he say anything about that either? He didn't ask you to go back to Sweden?

TN: No, he didn't say anything like that at all.

C: Nothing?

TN: No.

C: Why didn't he?

TN: He didn't because he knows very well that I can go back to Sweden whenever I want. But I don't want to. I want to live in India.

23 February

My captors have told me that I am allowed to go about as I wish, wherever I wish. They have added a *clausula salvatoria* though: I would have to make arrangements for my own security. My blood pressure has risen and I don't feel too well. I can feel that I am slowly and inexorably

walking towards death. Should I try to save myself? Or
should I just give in?

24 February

I don't think I will be able to live in this country any more.

26 February

I received news in the morning of Shibnarayan Ray's passing.
He had wished to write about my book *Narir Kono Desh Nei*
(A Woman Has No Nation) but *Anandabazar* had shown no
interest. Did he manage to finish the article or did he leave
it half-written?

Annada Shankar Roy is no more. Neither is Nikhil
Sarkar. Now Shibnarayan Ray too has passed away. All
my friends are gone. There is almost no one left for me in
Kolkata Apart from Anil Dutta, I would not have any other
true friend in Bengal. I would be completely alone.

Shibnarayan Ray was an extraordinary man. He was
always by my side, especially through some of my most
difficult times, no matter which part of the world I was in.
A fearless fighter, he cared very little that I did not have the
support of the administration. Such was his stature that he
could stand by his convictions and no one dared say anything
to the contrary. Just a few days ago, unfazed by my obvious
despair at my slowly crumbling dreams, he had told me:
'Keep writing. No matter how you are, where you are, never
stop writing. Remember, your pen is your life.' His fiery
presence had helped me grip my pen tighter; it had helped
me keep fighting. When the entire world had abandoned me
to fate, he had been steadfast in his support, alone like me.

Great men like him are slowly disappearing; the world's store of the brave and the selfless is gradually depleting, with the weak and the selfish taking their place. Their loud boasts and ugly threats have become the norm of the day. A bitterly icy darkness has begun to consume my world.

28 February

My poems are being published in *Dainik Statesman* every day. Every day I am getting excited congratulatory calls, with people telling me how they wait for my poems. Renowned literary scholar Samik Bandyopadhyay has already translated a poem, and he has even told me of his wish to bring out an entire collection of my poems in English. I have been writing about my life in the 'safe house' in my poems, a life where I do not know if I am a captive or not.

They will say I have a better life than I would in jail. Or that there are people with worse misfortunes! Does that mean that the injustices I have been subjected to are acceptable? Does that mean I have to silently bear it all? No, I will fight for every last right. I will not rest thinking I have been given more freedom than the next person, and so I should be grateful. I will not allow anyone to take away any of my rights. My independence has come under fire because someone else has a problem with something I have said or written. Do they not know what freedom means, these men who want my head? If someone does not understand what freedom means, or if they do not wish to understand, why must I change my ways for them? Let the government or the education system or the media teach them the definition of freedom. Let them also teach the people about democracy, about the meaning of rights and about the right to free speech.

2 March

It still amazes me how much people believe in religion. My captors don't touch non-vegetarian food on Tuesdays because it's the day they worship Hanuman, the Monkey God. Each and every one of them is unwaveringly devout. They regularly perform the puja rituals, and sport a sacred red string around their wrists as proof. Not simply religion, their faith is resolute vis-à-vis all forms of superstitions. In fact, till date I have not found a doctor who has not spoken to me about God. How God has made my body, how He is the one who has given me illness and how He will also provide the cure—these days all I can do is sit and listen to this drivel in stunned silence. Almost every person in this country, irrespective of gender, wealth or educational background, is religious.

Such a profusion of beliefs, rituals, fasts and various other customs and benedictions is something that is truly unique to India. Even in Bangladesh I have not witnessed something of this nature. Earlier, whenever in a debate a western scholar would call India a country of religions, I used to take great umbrage. I used to immediately launch into a litany of India's glorious ancient tradition of atheists and *lokayat* philosophers. There is no sign of all that any longer though and atheists are a rarity now. Instead, it's a nation of narrow-minded, superstitious fanatics and astrologers. The cantonment has a temple within its premises where recorded hymns are played throughout the day. Every single soul in the cantonment, civilian or military, except me, is devoutly religious. Now isn't that a scary thought!

There is a small hut, more like a single room, near the main entrance of the cantonment. Outside, there is a board which reads: 'If you have it once you're a wise man, twice a glutton, thrice greedy, and then you are dead!' What sort of nonsense is this that passes off as truisms? Is there no way left to reform this faith-obsessed nation?

Every day I am forced to interact with people who wear their patriarchy, their religion and their superstitions with pride. I have to speak to such people every day. They are my sole companions since I don't have the liberty to choose my own.

3 March

I have lost a lot of friends along the way. Some have chosen to cut ties because a friendship with me would undoubtedly be politically risky. I have gained a few friends along the way too, but in the sort of life that I am allowed, one can never be sure how long such fragile friendships last. A girl from Patna, Keya, calls every night and we chat for a long time. She is a voracious reader and an ardent admirer. Sumit Chakraborty calls regularly to ask after me. Many others, some of the names a little fuzzy, keep in touch. Yet another such person is Diptesh, a journalist. In fact, I had asked him to put me in touch with a Bengali cardiologist and he did. I spoke to Dr Tarun Bagchi on quite a few occasions until he abruptly stopped taking my calls. I told my captors that I wanted to meet Dr Bagchi but they sternly rejected it saying I would have to keep seeing the doctor who had been chosen for me. Suddenly, Diptesh too stopped taking my calls. One day, after managing to get through to him, I asked him directly if he was trying to avoid me. He stayed silent for a moment and then exclaimed, 'It has been terrible. The police came to my office asking for me, trying to gather information on me.'

TN: Why?

Diptesh (D): Because I gave you that doctor's reference.

TN: Dr Bagchi?

D: Yes.

TN: But he is not taking my calls. I have been trying for quite some time.

D: He won't either. He is very scared. The police went to his chamber and threatened him too.

TN: He won't speak to me any more? How strange! You are not making this up, are you? I can't believe the police will go and threaten an innocent doctor because he has spoken to me over the phone!

D: I have had to change all my bank accounts.

TN: Why?

D: I am being constantly watched. It's been terrible.

TN: Don't be so scared, Diptesh.

Quite by chance, I found out that the doctor from AIIMS who has been treating me, Dr Bahl, is Diptesh's doctor too. I asked Diptesh for Dr Bahl's phone number so that I could speak to him directly regarding my fluctuating blood pressure. Since he had not gotten me admitted to a hospital to take care of the problem, it was imperative I have his number for emergency purposes. I had never managed to acquire the phone number from my captors who used to maintain a strict chain of command. Whatever health issues I had, I had to tell them, for it to be passed on to the doctor. The good doctor's diagnosis and prescription used to similarly trickle back down to me. My captors never let me speak to even the junior doctors of Dr Bahl's department, following the same chain of command in such cases too. If I had not been a doctor myself, this perhaps would not have bothered me so much. But this transaction of medical information via multiple channels was especially tiresome and annoying, given that all I wanted to do was to talk to another doctor in medical terms. Diptesh was unable to give me the doctor's phone number because the latter had asked him not to. Apparently, Dr Bahl did not want to lose his job. It was strange that he was willing to forgo his responsibilities towards his patient to that end.

Diptesh's account seems too implausible. The police visit to his office, their questions, is he making all this up? But to what end? Does he not wish to keep in touch with me any longer? Why would a journalist who loves my writing not want to stay in touch? So, has someone else instructed him to sever all communication with me? Is it the government? But what would they gain? Sometimes, these things don't make any sense to me at all.

10 March

Tapan Raychaudhuri had come down from Kolkata for the second time in these months, ostensibly to meet me. The first time he had not said too many things in support of Mr B. This time, however, he had come for all intents and purposes to convince me to leave. The conversation started off with praise dedicated to Mr B and what a great man he was, and how he deserves much bigger accolades like the Bharat Ratna rather than the small recognitions he has gotten thus far. Eventually, the mood shifted and when it came to me, Raychaudhuri's ire was evident.

TR: You should leave. Why are you still in this country? At least in Europe and America, you would be able to sit and write in peace. Besides—
TN: Besides what?

TR: There are threats here.

TN: What threats?

TR: The Governor has said there are threats.

TN: Of course, there are threats. I have lived with threats
     for the past two decades or so. And which place is
     safe? Where in the world will you not find Muslim
     fundamentalists? Won't they simply follow me
     everywhere if I'm on their radar?

It did not matter where I went as long as I consented to
leaving India—that was the gist of this entire charade. My
fate, whether I lived or died, meant very little to these people.
Raychaudhuri continued, 'CPI(M) will simply make sure
you vanish if they have a problem with you.' When I asked
what that meant, he informed me that they would murder
me. The implications were clear—not just the zealots, but
the political cadres too I had to be wary of.

After our conversation had gone on for a few hours, and
on realizing he would not be able to change my mind about
leaving India, he became quite angry and unrecognizable.
Gone was the person I had known for years, and who
had admittedly always been quite fond of me. These days
whenever I meet someone I keep wondering where the face
ends and the mask begins.

There was a car waiting to take him to the airport in the
afternoon. However, he lied to me saying he would meet Mr
B on his way when I knew he had no such plans. Besides,
he had already lied to me about having reached Delhi two
days before. He had no luggage with him, and he had also
admitted by mistake to having read a magazine from Kolkata
on the flight that morning. It clearly meant he had flown
down to Delhi that very morning after having received

urgent missives from Mr B for help in convincing a stubborn woman to follow the orders given to her.

The people around me are progressively becoming unrecognizable.

11 March

The senior bureaucrat Sanatan Sengupta had once behaved horribly with me regarding a letter I had written to Madanjeet Singh. Trembling with righteous fury about the alleged rumours I had been spreading around the globe, and about the fact that I had dared to speak out against the government that was keeping me safe, he had warned me of dire consequences. Chastising me about my heinous crimes, he had asked me to desist, despite my earnest attempts to explain to him that I had written nothing against the government. I had simply written about my dire conditions. Sengupta had refused to listen though, and had kept on screaming the same things over and over again, so much so that I had thought at one point that he must be a machine with a switch behind his head that someone had accidentally left on.

After the renewal of my residence permit in February, I had written to the ministry requesting them to give me some degree of independence to live and move around in Delhi on my own. There could be guards like in Kolkata, but all decisions regarding my life would be my own. In response, Sengupta had refused my request gravely citing the status quo.

TN: What do you mean?
Sanatan Sengupta (SS): I mean things must go on as they are.
TN: No change?

SS: No, none.
TN: For how long?
SS: Indefinitely.

I have always felt that bureaucrats don't always approve of a minister's actions or decisions even if they have to follow their orders. If that had not been true, Sanatan Sengupta would not have admitted to me that despite all that he had said and all that had come to pass, as a human being he was proud of me and respected me deeply. Neither would he have confessed that I was a remarkable individual and that he would like to salute me for my honesty and determination.

12 March

They have tried all available means to make me understand that the only life I can hope for in India is that of a captive. This is how I would have to survive, I would not be allowed to go out, nor would anyone be allowed to meet me. I would not have a social life. Instead, I would have to stay within the house, only getting some reprieve if I am unwell and need to visit the doctor. If I do not approve of the arrangements, they have told me to make my own.

I have been told that I am going to be moved from this safe house. Where would I be taken? To a cave or to some distant mountains? Would all sources of communication with the outside world be cut off? The telephone, the Internet, everything? I am under the government's protection, rather I am in their custody, and they can do whatever they wish with me. But how long can I endure this? How long can anyone endure this? Perhaps politicians can, but I am not a politician; I have no stake in their struggle for power. I have fought for freedom all my life, but today I have no freedom to make my own decisions. For the past seven months, the government has been taking all the decisions. I am beginning to comprehend that it will progressively get more difficult for me to live here. Why am I waiting for the powerful to have a change of heart? There is no sign of something like that ever happening. In fact, most of them are quite happy with my condition, while I am bearing the brunt of their insensitivity. People will believe whatever they see. Perhaps they have been made to believe that whatever has been done to me has been for my security. Not many will pause to consider, let alone ask questions! Those who wish to will refrain from doing so out of fear.

I am alone. The protests have stopped and people have gone back to their lives. I am a child of this world, but I don't have the right to go back to a life I desire, to a place I desire, to spend my life in the service of humanity. I am being constantly called from abroad, but I have been refusing all the generous offers. I do not wish to live elsewhere! Democracy, freedom of speech, free thought, human rights, health, equality, peace, security, reason, and life—they are ready to welcome me with all this and more! Here I have only poverty, pollution, corruption, terrorism, insecurity, captivity, torture, dogma and bigotry to look forward to. The only gifts certain here are discrimination, terror, uncertainty and, perhaps, death.

Where should I go? The world is telling me to leave and survive. It is telling me to choose compassion and accolades instead of wallowing in insults and contempt.

I had chosen a life here but my dreams have lost to their politics.

13 March

It has nearly been seven months—four months of house arrest in Kolkata and three in Delhi. I was driven out of Kolkata and sent to Jaipur on 22 November and was driven out of Rajasthan the very next day to be brought to Delhi. I had initially thought the capital had taken me in out of compassion. When Mr B had told me about buying me clothes, books and other essentials, it had almost been like my father making the promises. What I had failed to understand then was why he was taking so much trouble on my account, especially since I had assumed I would be packed off to Kolkata immediately. Now I understand why he had gone through all that trouble. It has taken me nearly three months to understand his political games, though that is surely less time than anyone would have expected me to take. Besides, it's not that I have understood it all by myself! Far more astute minds, used to seeing through political skulduggery, had recognized it long before I did. They had even warned me that everything was being orchestrated to coerce me into leaving.

They did not let Svensson stay with me, nor did they let us meet. The few meetings they did allow, it was with an ulterior motive. They had assumed that we were lovers, and Svensson, on seeing my condition, would surely convince me to go away with him. They could scarcely have expected that Svensson would do just the opposite. The second friend they allowed was Asesh Ghosh from Kolkata, that too because he had come with some things for me packed in a suitcase. Without the suitcase, I doubt he would have been allowed either; besides, I had already had to put in a request for the visit. I had to put in a request for Svensson too, both to the home ministry and Mr B, only for it to be rejected. Except these two men, the only other people I have been allowed to meet thus far have been their cronies. M.A. Baby had come on behalf of CPI(M), and Tapan Raychaudhuri had been sent twice by Mr B to convince me to leave India. It was not until the second time that I realized he was working for Mr B and not because of his love and concern for me. A man who I had always respected and looked up to, who had always been a vocal advocate of the freedom of speech besides regularly writing on the plight of oppressed artists, was working as an agent of the administration! Even an old friend like Enamul Kabir could seemingly turn over a new leaf overnight and advise me to leave at Buddhadeb Bhattacharya's behest. Some of these instances would have once been inconceivable, and yet they have come to pass and those closest to me have turned away without a second glance.

Why have I been kept in this house for three months? Why have I been stopped every time I have expressed a wish to go anywhere? Why have I not been allowed to meet anyone? All this has been done to punish me, to make me feel so unwelcome that one day, tired of the shackles, tired of having been barred from society, I would just give up. Even if my captivity has not really inconvenienced anyone else, why should I keep suffering this unjust punishment! They can obviously afford to keep me locked up like this indefinitely. Save a few of my friends here, no one would raise a hue and cry. As it is I am hardly 'news' any more, and the newspaper articles too are few and far between. No one cares where I am, so certain they are that the government has seen to my safety.

It is impossible to describe how secure one feels when one has to live in a government safe house. It's a feeling you will not be able to make sense of unless you have been through it. When the State keeps you enveloped in a security bubble simply to force you to leave, such safety can be anything but conducive to one's sanity. It's a focused effort by the caring state to crush your spirit.

It is only now that I have begun to realize the true extent of these efforts, the repeated attempts to keep me in a sustained state of terror. Initially, the efforts had been directed at making me leave before the residence permit could come up for renewal. When the French president, Nicolas Sarkozy, had been on an official visit, his contingent had put in a proposal to hand over the Simone de Beauvoir Prize to me in India. The proposal had been immediately turned down with the official reason that the ceremony could not be held in India since I am not a citizen. It would either have to be held in Bangladesh or France. The French government had immediately complied and extended an invitation for me to travel to Paris, without ever realizing that the reason cited had been patently fabricated. Or perhaps they had understood, but their diplomatic relationship with India had been too important to jeopardize. Anyway, I had to publish a statement declaring that the prize distribution ceremony had already been held in Paris on 9 January, where my French publishers had accepted the award on my behalf and read out my speech. There was no need for me to go to Paris for the certificate of the award as it could easily be couriered to my Kolkata address. Could the government have been any more desperate?

14 March

Where am I? Honestly, if someone asks me where I have been, I would not be able to say. It would be the same answer if they ask how I have been. Sometimes I am even unsure of my very existence, unsure whether I am alive or dead, unable to touch or feel the person I am, the part of me that is hiding in some corner of my soul. Instead, I just lie there, like an inanimate object, or a corpse, in the same room, day in and day out. Death creeps in sometimes to come and sit with me, putting its arm around my shoulder. This did not start just the other day when I was driven out of Kolkata; this goes back to a decade-old conspiracy to slowly poison my life, to destroy the brave, resolute, dynamic, unyielding part of me that makes me who I am. I have also begun to realize that I cannot fight against the forces that be and expect to win. I am nothing but a lone voice and those who claim to stand beside me are never visible once the darkness descends.

So, I am left asking myself what I may have done to deserve this, to have been saddled with this life, where none of the decisions are my own. What have I done to deserve this life away from all human contact? What sins have I committed that society has punished me so? I had confessed only the truth, written what my convictions had told me to write. Have I not written on plain paper? Have I pelted a stone at someone or cut off someone's head to write with their blood? Then why is what I have written a crime? Why am I being punished because I have different opinions from the others? There was a time when a person could be hanged for speaking against the king, and everyone else would come and watch the spectacle. Have I not been persecuted too for having spoken out of turn, have the people not seen my pain and humiliation too? Do they not realize how much hurt and loss of faith can make a person retract their own words? I have been cut, I have been crushed and I have bled, so much that I have cried out to them to remove whatever they wish to from my books. Would this save me from their politics, or from their faith and their cruelty? Perhaps not. Perhaps they will keep feeding on me till not even a single droplet of blood remains in my veins. I have been forced to disavow the truth and renounce the forbidden words. Words are harmless and the truth is incapable of defending itself. This explains why power reigns supreme everywhere and why the pen has always lost to the sword. How can I match up to them? I don't even know how to lie!

The only thing I have is my love for humanity, my desire to see people evolve and thrive. Let there be love among everyone, let there be no sign of hate, this is what I have always desired. The way they wish to erase my words with hate, I wish to use love just like that to expunge hate. Probably, the world will come to a standstill if there is no hate, no oppression, no cruelty and no torture. Even if I must cease to be, the world cannot be allowed to stop. If something happens to me, it will hardly cause even a ripple in the great fabric of things. I had only hoped it would cause a ripple in my beloved West Bengal at least. Even that was not to be.

For a long time after leaving Bangladesh, I had felt like an orphan. After years of wandering down lonely roads, when I settled in Kolkata, I had but one desire—to live out the rest of my days surrounded by the sense of belonging that I feel in

West Bengal. It is unthinkable that there is no place for me there, no place for a woman for whom the Bengali language and culture has been an intrinsic part of her soul.

I am a guest in this nation and so I have to hold my tongue. I have not come here to hurt anyone. Instead, I have come here to be hurt, repeatedly, just like I have always been hurt everywhere else. Even at the risk of offending you, I must tell you all that I have learnt here! I have learnt the definition of electoral politics. I have learnt that secularism in this country means siding with Muslim fundamentalists. I never wanted to believe any of this, so much so that I have tried shutting every new revelation out. Instead, I have often felt like talking my heart out to the creeping spectre of death that has cast its shadow over my exile. Right now, there is no one closer I can talk to.

Taking Bengal away from me is akin to snatching a baby from a mother's embrace. This excruciating pain is no less than the feeling of devastation when I had lost my own mother. She had always hoped that one day I would return home. The day I moved to Kolkata, I thought I had at least managed to fulfil her dream partially. I can never tell her that I am still a refugee, that the people I had been banking on to be on my side have turned their backs on me. She would be devastated. So, I tell myself that I must have committed a grievous crime to have been punished with such an exile. Isn't telling the truth a huge crime in itself in this day and age? The other people speaking the truth, are they being persecuted too? Or am I special because I am a woman? After all, is there anything easier than attacking women!

I know the people have not exiled me. Left to their own devices, I would never have been forced to leave Kolkata. Democracy, however, hardly runs on the will of the people.

It is the rulers who decide whatever will be. I am an ordinary woman, who lives on her own terms and writes what her convictions dictate. I don't lie, cheat or intend anyone any harm. I have never been consciously dishonest, nor have I ever been able to participate in political games. What I have been through, I don't know who it has benefited but for me it has ushered in nothing but misfortune—my exile has only strengthened the fanatics.

Despite having spoken at length about humanism, human rights and women's right in India, no political party, no human rights organization or women's rights groups, nor any no social justice collective had spoken on my behalf after I was attacked. I don't know this India. There have been a few dissenters who have stood by me—writers, journalists, intellectuals. Whether they have read my work or not, some have stood by me simply to provide aid in the struggle for the freedom of speech. However, the new face of India that has terrorized me is the inability to organize collective action for seeking justice and rights. At such instances, I have encountered only a deafening silence. Is this the new India or is this how India has always been? Since my girlhood, I have thought India to be a great nation. I wish to survive even more now simply because I hope to be able to see that great nation again. I pray my assailants wait. The day I realize India has again learnt to stand up for itself, learnt to stand up to dogma and blindness, I will summon them of my own accord. Even if I don't live long, I know India will survive for thousands of years.

15 March

The ophthalmologist examined my eyes and confirmed retinopathy. It is apparently a result of unstable blood pressure, though right now there is no danger of losing an eye if the pressure can be kept under control. In this exile, how am I supposed to do that? I have not been allowed to speak directly to a doctor. The Bengali doctor I had found has been threatened so much that he no longer takes my calls. Everything around me seems strangely ghostly, as if I have been transported to a planet far away from earth. I have been kept a prisoner in the alien planet and I am so vastly different from the other inhabitants that I have been deemed highly dangerous. I do not believe my blood pressure will ever be under control considering the mental stress that is my life in this safe house.

I have come to a decision. Immediately, I have pulled out a sheet of paper and started jotting down the reasons why. I have written whatever has come to my mind so that even in the event of my death, the few people in the world who respect my writing will get to know why I have taken this decision.

I have to disentangle myself from this deathtrap. I used to call this a torture chamber but now I know that this is nothing but a slaughterhouse. The doctors had advised me a long stay in the hospital, for at least a fortnight, till my blood pressure became normal. But I had not been allowed to stay there. Instead of the doctors, the decision to move a sick patient from the CCU to the safe house had been taken by my captors. The day after the doctors proclaimed their advice, the news of my visit to the hospital came out in the newspapers and I was immediately forced to return to the safe house. Even my mobile phone was taken away from me.

No doctors were allowed to visit me, nor was I allowed to visit or speak to one. I asked for the doctor's phone number countless times, but in vain. When, on visiting the hospital, I asked some of the doctors for their phone numbers, they confessed that they had been forbidden to share them with me. Whatever I wished to discuss regarding my health, I had to first tell my captors, who would pass the questions on to the doctor and bring the answers back accordingly. The doctors had identified stress as the primary reason for my irregular blood pressure and had advised me to try and not let stress affect me. Is it possible to live a stress-free life in this exile?

Besides affecting my eyesight, irregular blood pressure is causing the walls of my heart to harden. One fine day, all my primary organs will stop and I will die in this safe house. I have never had such health concerns before this exile! Before this ordeal began, never in a million years has my blood pressure been a cause for alarm.

On returning from the ophthalmologist, I let them know my decision—that at long last, I would be leaving India. I requested my captors to let me go back to Kolkata if not for an entire day then at least for a few hours, to get some of the important things that I had left behind. I also had to come to a decision about the empty house. As usual, my captors refused. What else could they have done? They had orders from above.

17 March

I am a tiny, insignificant being. How can I hope to compete with a behemoth like the State? Despite that, didn't I keep them at bay for so long? Didn't I try fighting valiantly for seven months? I am leaving because I don't wish to die.

My darling India, if I am alive, we will meet again for sure. We will meet no matter how much you try to suppress or silence me. No matter what you do to end me, I will always love you.

No, Not Here! Elsewhere! In Another Land!

In the end, I had to leave India. It was my decision entirely, though it's not as if I had a choice at the end of the day. My blood pressure, constantly fluctuating, had taken to this macabre dance which was wreaking havoc on my system. It was not even dependent any longer on stress or anything like that. Blood pressure medicines were no longer working for me, and the doctors advised me to get my kidneys and eyes checked.

Whenever I got my blood pressure checked, it showed me startlingly odd things, so much so that it was becoming increasingly difficult to trust any of the reports. Someone else would probably have succumbed long ago to its ravages. Eventually, after about a year of trying to quash it, doctors from New York gave me frightening news—my blood pressure had reached such a state that no medicines would be effective on me any longer. It would fluctuate constantly, rise and fall at its own convenience, and I would have to live with that. There is this thing about blood; once it starts dancing, it hardly wishes to stop. My blood had learnt to dance because of the safe house and a potent alloy of wrong medication.

There were only two places in the world I could think of as home—my native house in Shantinagar, Dhaka, and my long-abandoned house in Kolkata. The Kolkata house had been a rented one but it was also something I had paid for myself, and all my important things were there. Ironically, I was not allowed to enter either house. Not just that, I would not be allowed entry into the respective cities either because I was a prohibited element. So, yet again, I recommenced my exile abroad. Whether this exile was for a short while or for good, I wasn't sure. As always, I set sail despite being uncertain of how far I would manage to reach.

The Government of India bought me a one-way business class ticket to Sweden, from Delhi to Stockholm. Once upon a time, the Government of West Bengal too had bought me one-way tickets to Rajasthan, from Kolkata to Jaipur. The second farewell happened with much more pomp and show, somewhat like how a guest is plied with lots of good food or a man on death row is allowed one final wish before being taken to the gallows. On the day of my departure, having heard that friends would be allowed to visit, many of mine had flown in from Kolkata. Arrangements were made in a five-star hotel for their reception. The flight was scheduled for late at night, so a dinner was organized with everyone in attendance. A suite was book at the Taj Hotel for a couple of hours on the night I was scheduled to leave, with an open room service for us to order in anything we wished. Besides, the government even took care of the accommodation and other expenses of my guests. Were these gifts being showered on us because I had finally consented to leave? My captors had made all the arrangements despite my repeated protests that too much money was being spent unnecessarily and that my friends would take care of themselves. Of course, nobody listened to me, so immersed they were in celebrating a mission successfully accomplished!

I wasn't sure what the government was assuming about my departure but I knew I was leaving for health reasons. If there had been no immediate health concerns, I would probably have never left India in a thousand years, even if I would have had to stay as a political prisoner. I would have stayed to protest against the punishment I had endured without having committed any crime; I would have stayed to fight for the freedom of speech. I am aware of how archaic I sound, how my ideals don't seem to fit in this new world, appearing to be ghostly whispers from the '40s or the '50s. So, whenever I make these claims, people stare at me astonished, as if I am hiding some nefarious plans up my sleeve, or other ulterior motives to serve my own ends.

A crippling weariness had settled over me that day. I had lost. I was doing something I had never believed I would do—I was leaving India. Things had come to such a state that survival had finally taken precedence over which country I wished to live in. Except India and Bangladesh, every other nation had always been foreign for me. I had chosen Sweden simply for medical reasons. Swedish nationals, or anyone living there for that matter, are entitled to the national healthcare scheme; any medical expenses incurred anywhere else in Europe or America are only available to the rich.

On reaching Sweden, I was met at the airport by Maria and Maj-Britt of the Swedish Pen Club and Cecilia Wikström, a member of the Swedish Parliament. They had already made all the arrangements for my stay, including a grant or scholarship from the department of culture, and an apartment in the city of Uppsala. Svensson was also there to receive me. There was no way I could have stayed with him though, especially when everything between us was beginning to appear flaky and superficial.

Cecilia drove me to Uppsala. Her behaviour towards me, very cordial and excessively emotional, had begun to grate on my nerves. It was as if she had known me for years already! I was put up at a hotel in the city, and Maj-Britt stayed back with me. I must confess that after living in India, my mental state had been decidedly odd too. There was no security deployed specifically for me but I knew that they were closely monitoring everything. Despite this, I was feeling uneasy without being surrounded by a horde of policemen, although I knew that I was in Uppsala and not in Delhi or Kolkata any more. I have had to stay confined and terrified all the time in India, always having to watch my back. Besides, fundamentalism is now a global concern and there is hardly a nation that can boast of having completely withstood its onslaught! In fact, in Sweden too, an artist had been attacked and eventually forced into hiding because he had superimposed the face of Prophet Muhammad on the photo of a dog.

Maj-Britt and I went out for dinner that evening, quite reluctantly on my part. I could feel that I was walking awkwardly too, constantly looking around to see if someone had recognized me. Not that I could avoid anything despite my anxiety. The Swedish were evidently happy about me being there. There were people greeting me warmly and someone even came up to me on the road and presented me with flowers. As for me, my sole concern was how they knew who I was.

Cecilia made arrangements at a hospital in Uppsala for a complete health check-up—eyes, heart, blood pressure, and other possible pressure points. Dutifully, the doctor checked me for everything and finally reassured me that there was nothing wrong. He also decreased the dosage of my blood pressure medicine.

I had a lot of stuff lying around in Svensson's house—clothes, computer, etc. Despite moving to Kolkata, I had never managed to clear out all my things from my life in Sweden. I had left the country, and had also left a tonne of things behind. After all, how much can one carry within the twenty-three kilos stipulated by the airline authorities! Everything was still in Svensson's house and it was quite clear to me that staying at a hotel, while almost a chunk of my life was simply lying around nearby, was simply not feasible. Svensson brought me the router to the hotel room on my second night there, and by the third we set out for his house in Upplands Väsby. My study in Svensson's house was exactly how I had left it, the popcorn I had spilled still strewn all over the floor. The teacups I had left on the table had been left untouched, except for the tea which had long since dried and left a stain at the bottom. I had known Svensson would never clean my room, even if he was cleaning the rest of the house. He would simply let the room be, abandoned, for a thousand years. Back in the day, whenever I used to clean, I used to clean his study too. Male nature is defined by an inherent affinity towards selfishness.

I found in the house a sense of familiarity, having lived there before for a long time. I could easily slip into the comfort of belonging. As before, I began spending the larger part of the day in the study. Meanwhile, the scholarship

being awarded to me had been formally announced and
the news was being widely shared. Svensson's behaviour
was erratic at best and I had increasingly begun spending
much of my free time with Maj-Britt. One day, she dragged
me to Uppsala to show me the house being given with the
scholarship. A pretty house, but it was evident it was not
for long-term accommodation. I had no desire to continue
living as a stranger's guest any more. All I wanted, what I had
wandered in search of all these years, was a home from where
I would never have to move again.

The house was very near Uppsala University. A very
pretty place, there was even a forest-like grove a few yards
away. I could not decide what I wanted. Something was
keening within me. No, not here! Elsewhere! In another
land! Cecilia was trying her best to coax me into accepting the
scholarship they were offering me from Uppsala University.
Yet, I could not shake off the longing for another land,
not there, but elsewhere. Besides, even if I had to stay in
Sweden, there was no point in staying in that house. I knew
I could stay at Svensson's and if that did not work out, I
could simply rent a place I would not have to leave after six
months or a year.

Cecilia had latched on like a leech by then. She called
me over to her place one day, extending the invitation to
my friends too. I confess that she had initially come across
as a nice girl, intelligent, hard-working and sincere. That is
how the impression would have remained had Cecilia not
tried to corner me into attending a press conference. I had
told them in advance that I would not speak to the press. I
did not want to announce to the entire world where I was.
A press conference to publicize the scholarship would have
been akin to posting my whereabouts for the public. I knew

it would not take too long for someone to find the house and I could not afford to take the risk. Cecilia, however, was not to be convinced. She tried explaining to me how no one would get to know that the inaugural scholarship of Uppsala University was being awarded to me, that the city of Uppsala would henceforth always side with oppressed artists and writers, and fight for the freedom of speech. One day in her apartment, having yet again failed to convince me about the press conference, she left in a huff telling me she had to get to a meeting. I found out the truth about the meeting the next day only when, on opening the morning newspaper, I read the news of the press conference where Cecilia Wikström had announced the scholarship, being awarded to me by Uppsala University, to the world. Such a curious thing is the lure of fame! Such is the lust for power that one can stoop to any depths to be able to rise in the eyes of the world! That very moment, I bid goodbye to Cecilia from my life.

I went instead to the south of France, to visit Madanjeet Singh. Singh's house was right by the sea, with the mountains behind and the Mediterranean spread out in front. In between, on a hillock, Singh's palatial home was situated. The vast blue sea was visible from the bedroom windows, and one could hear the song of the breakers on the coast. White sailboats could be seen on the surface of the sea, birds flying over them under a vast blue sky. However, much more impressive than the beauty of the surroundings was the man himself, Madanjeet Singh, an octogenarian and an atheist through and through. At eighty, he had acquired 200 million dollars which he had unhesitatingly donated to the cause of South Asia. The amount was to be distributed as scholarships to South Asian students studying in various universities abroad, to ensure that students from diverse linguistic, social and cultural backgrounds have a chance of pursuing higher education and to foster interpersonal bonds among them. Madanjeet Singh is a dreamer, much like I am. A sincere and humane individual, the world would be a far better place if there were a few more like him. He had written to every important person of his acquaintance, including the prime minister of India, demanding I be freed from house arrest and allowed to go back to Kolkata. He had urged them not to give in to the demands of fanatics, although I am not certain how many had paid heed to his advice. Once a diplomat for India, Singh is a painter and has also written many books, and continues to write. I have always listened to him with rapt attention, and not a single thing I have ever heard him say has been meaningless.

Meanwhile, a lot of other things were happening one after another. I was to be awarded the Simone de Beauvoir Prize and the award was going to be handed over in Paris by the human rights minister of the ministry of external affairs. There were a series of interviews scheduled with French journalists. This is usually a common feature in Europe. For instance, whenever a book is about to be launched, the publishers usually organize interviews with the writer on TV, radio, newspapers and weeklies. Not that it happens with everyone since the media shows interest only in someone of renown. The publishers there had hurriedly put together a book whose title, roughly translated from French, meant *From My Prison*. While under house arrest in Delhi, the publishers had requested me to write something or send them something already written. I had tried explaining to them that I had only a few poems, and some small pieces here and there. The publishers, however, had been adamant that they would be happy with whatever I wanted to send. I had countered that I was already writing my autobiography and would send that across once I was done. Yet, they had kept insisting that they would like to put together a short collection at the very least. Two poems and a few personal reflections did not a book make! It was a sort of fraud one often committed with the reader which I have always had a problem with. Back in the day, *Lajja* had been published amidst swirling rumours of an impending prohibition. The readers had surely read the book and been unable to fathom what all the fuss had been about! The books which actually had fatwas hanging over them were either never published, or no one bothered with the fatwa once they were.

Everyone had a copy of the new book and I was attending one interview after another the entire day. A full-page article was published in *Le Monde*. Mark Johnston, a film-maker from Canada, had arrived to film a documentary on freedom of speech—*Empire of the Word* was going to be narrated by Alberto Manguel, the author of *A History of Reading*. The radio interviews would begin early in the morning, followed by journalists who would start coming in at ten. By the time I returned from the TV interviews, it was late in the night. The inaugural Simone de Beauvoir Prize was awarded to me at a gala event in the ministry of external affairs. I was not the only recipient of the first edition, with the other winner, the Dutch feminist writer and politician Ayaan Hirsi Ali, having already received her prize.

I was then invited to Paris to receive an honorary citizenship conferred on me by the Paris City Council. At the town hall, or as they say *hôtel de ville*, the mayor, amidst expensive gifts and earnest words, tried to assure me that the citizenship was not in name alone but they sincerely wished I would choose to stay in Paris. After he had finished tabulating the reasons why I ought to be made a citizen of Paris, each of the 180 representatives of various political parties had stood up in unison to applaud and endorse his comments.

Irene arrived from Belgium to see me. I could clearly gauge how much she had changed after Steve's[54] passing, both her obsessiveness and her dependence on psychiatric drugs having increased manifold. From the moment she arrived, the complaints began—about her financial troubles, about age, how she had been unable to sell Steve's records, and mostly against the person in Ghent whose house she was living in. The relentless onslaught of her misery soon began to grow tiresome. I could not help but remember how horribly she had behaved with Steve's friends and even me, how she had not allowed anyone to visit the dying man, treating him as property. She had found Steve's illness intolerable and used to misbehave with him in retaliation. Such an indomitable woman was now a mere husk of her old self.

Behaving almost like a petulant child, she insisted she accompany me to the dinner being hosted by the mayor in my honour. I did not refuse her, and her joy at having witnessed the conferring of the citizenship was palpable that evening. I have always had a soft spot for her, and I could not help feeling sorry for her. I have forgiven Irene far too many times; she has been well aware of it and she has often apologized too, and I have been with her through many difficulties. It pains me a great deal to see her having to take medication in order to function in society, to keep calm, and to steer clear of thoughts of suicide.

Soon after, I received another invitation from Paris—for a gala event in honour of every recipient of human rights awards from the Government of France. At one such dinner, I was left star-struck by the legendary French celluloid icon Catherine Deneuve who I have always admired and considered the most beautiful leading lady in the history of cinema. Her films from the '70s and '80s have, in particular, always held immense fascination for me. I was invited to become a board member for the PPR Corporate Foundation for Women's Dignity and Rights, a foundation established by Pinault-Printemps-Redoute (PPR) to aid women in securing social justice and safeguarding their rights. With renowned personalities like Stella McCartney, Waris Dirie and many others involved, we were all committed to working for the betterment of oppressed and battered women, especially from Asian, African and Latin American countries.

It was around this time that something happened to remind me that my circumstances continued to remain dire. I had gone back to Delhi before the expiry of my Indian residence permit and they had allowed me to stay at a friend's empty house, surrounded by hundreds of police officers. However, soon after, my permit was renewed for six months and I was packed off to Europe again. It was as if the only way I was going to be formally allowed to stay in India was if I promised that I would not actually stay for long. I was asked to give my acquiescence in writing, which I did; I had no other choice. This became a pattern. Six months later, I went back again and the same thing was repeated. The permit was extended and I was forced to leave within three days. I had one primary concern— where was I to live if they were not going to let me go back to India, to Kolkata? It was not possible to spend my life

moving from Svensson's house in Sweden to Yasmin's in
New York and to someone else's after that! I could have
lived at Svensson's but I knew it could not be for long. The
French had made me an honorary citizen of Paris and the
mayor too had requested me to live there. My friends had
told me the French government had a lot of property to
spare, though judging by the number of homeless people I
had seen in Paris, I could not help but remain sceptical of
my prospects. Not just *Le Monde* but other journals too had
featured articles about my homelessness after I had been
forced to leave India. Eventually, I was offered a six-month
scholarship by Bertrand Delanoë, the mayor of Paris, along
with a small apartment in the artists' quarter and a monthly
stipend. The house, beside the Seine and almost in the heart
of Paris, excited my friends much more than me. We even
had a housewarming party where some of my littérateur
friends came over for dinner and we ended up spending a
fantastic evening. I never managed to stay in the house for
too long though; I was soon given a fellowship from New
York University and I left for New York.

Although I was based in New York, I was spending
much more time travelling to various countries for various
events—the International Literary Festival in Sweden,
a seminar against censorship held at Bilbao in Spain, or a
poetry festival in San Francisco where the Beat poets used
to read their poems, especially in iconic locations like North
Beach, the legendary City Lights Bookstore and Vesuvio
Café. Besides, there were other poetry festivals in Italy and
Luxembourg, a symposium in Amsterdam on free thought,
and a seminar on social justice held in Vienna. Something
or the other was always there to demand my attention—be
it the twenty-fifth anniversary of the Sakharov Prize given

by the European Parliament, or an honorary doctorate from
Louvain Université, Belgium. There was no way left for me
to quietly sit by myself for a while and simply write. At the
same time, the hectic schedule was helping me evade the
tedium of being confined to a room.

I was nevertheless not invited to the seminar on freedom
of expression being held in New York. Instead of a writer
who had been treated viciously for her stance on the same,
who had been forced to leave a democratic country like India
on account of her beliefs, they invited numerous unknown
authors with absolutely no stake in the issue. Did the
American Pen Club, the organizers of the event, not know
about me? Were they not aware that I was in New York? I
was sure they were perfectly aware, like the rest of the world,
of the ordeal I had been through—the fatwas, the house
arrest, the humiliating send-off from Kolkata, the months
spent in Delhi and the eventual departure from India. How
could they have not been aware of all this with a chairperson
like Salman Rushdie at the helm? So, was it because of him
that I had not been invited to speak at the seminar? Was it
because of my article for the German journal *Der Spiegel* so
many years ago where I had argued that Rushdie should not
have given in to the demands of extremists? I knew Rushdie
had been angered by my comments, but I could never have
guessed that he would hold such a grudge!

In New York, I was staying at Yasmin's place, though her
daughter Bhalobasa was not too happy with the arrangement.
She had become a strange and stubborn person over the years,
devoid of any common sense whatsoever. She was doing
bizarre things such as slitting her wrists, complaining about
her looks, and grumbling and ranting about why she did not
have a boyfriend. Like I had done before, I suggested taking

her to a psychiatrist, but Yasmin was deeply offended by my suggestions. She argued that her daughter was not mentally unstable; hence, she did not need psychiatric help. Just like she had been obsessed with anal fissures after having suffered from it for years, her daughter was her latest obsession. The daughter was thus the queen of the house, her parents waiting on her hand and foot, and so went on the role play in their house. Unable to tolerate the noxious atmosphere, I began searching for a place of my own. Not that finding an apartment in New York was an easy task! A credit history was one of the primary requirements, which I did not have, along with proof of annual income, with the stipulation being that I would not be able to rent a house unless the annual figure was 100,000 dollars. Despite all these conditions, I still managed to find a place near the absent twin towers, by the Hudson, thanks to a maverick guarantor who assured me that he would take care of the stipulations should I fail to fulfil them. To be able to find a person like that in New York was in itself a huge achievement. Strange are the ways of the world! The person I had initially approached to be my guarantor, someone who had known me for years and who could have vouched for my reliability, had backed out while the person who finally agreed was a complete stranger.

The arrangement put in place by the Government of India was running unhindered. My residence permit was being renewed every six months, but with the implicit condition that I would not actually stay in India. Of course, no one else really knew about the arrangement, and I was forbidden from revealing it to anyone. Consequently, I kept paying the rent of the abandoned house in Kolkata for quite some time. Eventually, forced to confront the realization that I would not be able to return to Kolkata, I wrote to my friends asking them to send me the things I had left behind. The government had already offered to pack everything on my behalf and bring the lot to Delhi to be put in a storage locker. I had refused, as I didn't like the idea of all my things being dumped in a room. Wishing to relieve the government of yet another responsibility pertaining to me, I instructed my friends to pack it all up and post it to me, and paid for the entire transaction myself. A few extra pieces of furniture had already been stored in Delhi; I got those back too after nearly two years and the government did not even charge me for it.

My brother visited me in Delhi during one such visit for visa renewal, and I asked him to get Minu from Kolkata. She was flown to Delhi to meet me, and before leaving, I made sure my brother took her back home with him to Shantinagar in Dhaka. Truth be told, it's not that I had a choice in the matter. I had tried my best to have her kept in Delhi, had spoken to cat lovers and animal rights organizations alike, but in vain. Someone had even told me they could keep her caged for the six months I would be away! So, Minu had to fly again, this time leaving India. Being a cat, she had to endure the entire journey in a cage! People have grown so used to the invisible cages they inhabit that their presence makes no difference to them after a while. Animals, however, never wish to be caged. Yet again, I had to leave everything behind, bid my farewell to India, and set off for the unknown.

The prime minister of India had once replied to the letter Madanjeet Singh had written to him. It had been a wonderful letter, and I am not sure if any other prime minister of any other nation of the subcontinent could have ever written something like that:

Dear Shri Madanjeet Singh,

I read your letter with great interest. Let me share with you that many of us here share the sense of anguish you feel at Taslima Nasreen's plight. It is most unfortunate that someone like her should be the target of extremist elements. Actions of this kind, though by a small minority, tend to undermine our secular credentials and damage our image as an inclusive society.

You may rest assured, however, that we shall never deviate from our age-old traditions and principles. Right through the ages we have offered sanctuary and a home to anyone who has sought our help. We have always shown compassion to those who have been persecuted. His holiness the Dalai Lama is one shining example. We are unhappy at the turn of events in the case of Ms. Taslima Nasreen, but in her case also we have honoured our ancient pledge. I can't say how pleased I am that you have offered her a place to stay in Paris, till such time as she finds it convenient to return to India.

Taslima has been a victim of the politics of hate that a small section of extremists within our country are now pursuing. Her preference was to stay in Kolkata, but the West Bengal Government apprehended that this might lead to a law and order situation in the State. I cannot say whether this apprehension is valid, but we nevertheless welcomed her here in Delhi. Taslima misses being in Kolkata, however.

It is not correct to say that while in Delhi she was kept in solitary confinement in a small room. Certain restrictions on her movements had to be imposed based on perceptions of the threat to her personal security. Otherwise she had relative freedom of movement. The restrictions that were imposed, no doubt, weighed heavily on her mind, and I can understand her predicament. External Affairs Minister Mr. Pranab Mukherjee, and senior officials did meet her from time to time to assuage many of her concerns.

She left for Sweden on her own volition, and not because we asked her. She will always be welcome in India as our guest. Her personal security, however, remains a matter of concern and we will need to take precautions to ensure her protection as long as she is our guest. We can try and see whether she could go back to Kolkata where she feels comfortable, but for this we would need the cooperation of the West Bengal Government.

India's glorious traditions of welcoming people irrespective of caste and creed, community and religion will continue, whatever be the odds. The atmosphere of hate being perpetrated by a small segment within the country will not prevent us from persisting with this tradition. We recognize Taslima Nasreen's right to remain in a country of her choice, viz., India in this case. She should also have the option to choose whichever city of the state she chooses.

I hope you would try to make her understand this. You should also try to persuade her to realize that whatever was done while she was in India was dictated by the necessity to ensure her safety and security.

With regards,
Yours sincerely
Manmohan Singh

It had been a proud moment, receiving the letter. It had instantly revived in me the enduring dream of being able to live permanently in India, if not in Bangladesh. Despite the letter, I was still not allowed to stay in Delhi for two more years.

In February 2010, the French-German television channel *Arte* started filming a television documentary based on me. I had to fly to Delhi to renew my residence permit yet again. I found the crew already waiting there ahead of me; they were apparently spending a million euros for a sixty-minute film. For quite some time, they were to become my shadows, trailing me across the globe—from Lyon, to Delhi, to New York. Simultaneously, they were to visit Kolkata, Dhaka and Mymensingh, places I could no longer go to, to look for my lost memories. They were perhaps waiting till the decision on my residence permit was made official, hoping that my request would be denied and they would get the prime opportunity of capturing on film the historic moment of my final departure from India. A part of this feeling may also have fed on my ever-present anxieties regarding the same every time I visited Delhi.

The residence permit was extended, but this time the order came along with a letter. It stated unequivocally that since five years had passed, this was the last extension of my visa. I would get no further visas from the Government of India, and henceforth should I wish to visit, I would have to apply for a visa in the Indian consulates abroad. I don't believe I have ever read anything more quietly devastating than that. For the first time in two years, there had been no imperious instructions along with the order, I had not been asked to go away immediately either. Unable to react, unable to think of what could be done, or where I would go, I turned to every Indian I knew for help, only to be met with blank faces of incomprehension. Apparently, not too many people except me were familiar with residence permits, extensions and immigration law.

In March, an article of mine sparked off a riot in Karnataka. The English weekly *Outlook* had published my article on the burqa, written in 2006, that too without my permission. Some people alleged that this riot too had been politically motivated, particularly by the Congress which was trying to use the communal tension to cause trouble for the ruling BJP. As it is, I have always been a convenient target for such controversies; it has been easy to put fatwas on my head as there would be no one to raise a hue and cry, or organize protest marches and vigils. In the article I had written that women should not have to wear the burqa even if the Quran told them to do so. The proponents of the burqa took to the streets in anger, with the TV channels airing footage of a mob of nearly 15,000 people marching in protest, with the madness soon spreading from one city to the next. Shops, truck and buses were set ablaze. The images were terrifying, shooting my already erratic blood pressure up, and freezing my limbs in abject horror. I was nearly certain that soon another fundamentalist group would come in search of me to murder me. At the very least, I would not be allowed to stay in India ever again. Switching all the lights and the television off, I simply went to bed unable to bear the anxiety any longer and certain that my heart would give in any moment. I also informed Pallav Bhattacharya of PTI that I had not given my consent to the magazine to publish anything.

The home minister's statement, however, managed to make everything better. In an address to the media he declared: 'Taslima bears no responsibility for this riot. The editors of the journal had published the article without her consent. This whole thing has been set up by them.' The office of the weekly was vandalized by an angry mob. Though a part of me was relieved that I had been absolved of all blame, I could not help but be anxious about the direction the debate on freedom of expression was taking in this country. The editors had not been guilty of anything except an infringement of copyright. Why would there be no freedom to express a different opinion? Wasn't the blame to be squarely laid on the intolerant rogues who were rioting on the streets and burning buses?

I flew off to Melbourne to attend the Global Atheist Convention. There, amidst a crowd of fellow agnostics and apostates, in a space where I was comfortable after a long time, I spoke about the Karnataka riots. The convention had nearly 2500 delegates attending from various places in Europe, America and Australia. Renowned people like Richard Dawkins, P.Z. Myers and A.C. Grayling were scheduled to speak. Among all the delegates, my speech was the only one to receive a standing ovation, an honour that ought to have lightened my mood. Yet, I refused all requests for interviews, and did not answer any of the emails I received. Instead, I simply strolled around on my own in Melbourne, watching people, or running off to see racing penguins. An old friend from school, Mamata, flew down from Sydney but we never managed to meet, lost as I was in my own world.

I refused all subsequent invitations for conventions and such. I cancelled a trip to Denmark even after the tickets had been bought. Instead, I stayed mostly at home, playing with my cat. I could feel that there was no more drive left in me to live out of a suitcase. All I wanted was a home, and that had been impossible to find.

At the end of the day, I returned to New York, to my apartment on the twenty-third floor with its 'million-dollar view'. One entire wall of the apartment was made of glass, opening out to a panoramic view of the sky and the Hudson beneath it, all the shades of the sky and each and every current of the river visible. It was a truly safe house, symbolizing a range of future possibilities when the fellowship would have run its course—a possible teaching job at Connecticut, teaching in various universities as a Woodrow Wilson Fellow, being involved in a Broadway musical or an event at the Lincoln Center, or getting acquainted with the feminist circles of the city. Despite all these possibilities and so much more, I finally made the decision to leave everything behind and move back to India. I knew I would have to abandon my makeshift family in New York, Robert Quinn of New York University, old friend Allen Smith, Meredith Tax and so many others, besides this beautiful city itself. Yet, I was firm in my resolve that I would not bow down to the draconian diktats of the Government of India. If the government was admittedly all-powerful, then why would I have to apply for a visa at a consulate in another country? I was tired of this back and forth, this constant indecision regarding where I truly belonged. That is how I had already spent a large chunk of my life, drifting from here to there, searching for one fixed address.

My visa was to expire in August and I resolved that I would get it renewed in India. I knew if my visa expired, I would never get another one again. I was especially wary because this had happened twice before—once in Bangladesh and then again in Bengal—when I had believed the assurances that I would be able to come back 'after a few months when everything had calmed down'. Some farewells are meant to be permanent.

A few authors from abroad had issued a statement regarding my right to live in India, requesting the government to seriously consider my appeal. Due to my travels, I had run out of pages on my passport and had gone to the Swedish Embassy for a fresh one. There I heard that a group of representatives from a number of embassies were about to be sent as an envoy to the home ministry with an appeal to allow me to live in Delhi. The news warmed my heart. Later, when people remarked how it had all been God's grace that had come to my aid, I had corrected them and stated that it had been the grace of good people still left in this world that had helped me in my hour of need. There were still some people left in the world who believed in the freedom of expression, or so I came to believe that day. What else could explain the incredible outcome of the entire episode? Thanks to the kindness of some unknown individuals who had decided to rebel against the unfairness of the treatment being meted out to me, I was given a visa for an entire year, to be renewed annually. I must confess to having been overwhelmed that day by my gratitude for such progressive and humanist individuals. I had been aware that since I had no rights as a citizen of India, if they did not renew my visa, I would have to silently accept the cruel decision. I was not special, not by any stretch of the imagination. The only strength I could boast of was my writing, although combating patriarchy through that had always been considered an archaic approach. As it is, most men and women have a less-than-kind reaction to feminism, having been socialized to naturally assume that equality between men and women is an accomplished project, and that usually only uneducated barbarians misbehave with women.

By the time I received an unconditional approval to stay in India, near the end of 2010, I had already become a prohibited name in the literary circles of the subcontinent. Bangladesh had stopped publishing my work nearly seventeen years earlier. West Bengal had caught on only recently, and no journals were publishing my writings any more. *Dainik Statesman* had long since stopped my weekly column, despite it being very popular. Other newspapers and journals—*Anandabazar*, *Desh*, *Pratidin*, and its Sunday supplement *Robbar*—too had fallen in line. Rituparno Ghosh, the editor of *Robbar*, had started a weekly column of mine with a lot of ceremony, but that too stopped after only one week. I had later been informed that the instructions to cancel it had come from 'above'. For a while, I had started writing in a Hindi journal from Delhi, *Jansatta*, but the riots in Karnataka pulled the curtains down on that. Clearly, everyone was receiving orders from 'above' to make sure my books did not sell and that my voice was no longer heard. Not that this was because no one was interested in reading my writing any more, or because my books were no longer selling! In fact, newspaper sales would increase when there was an article by me and my books would consistently be on bestseller lists!

BAG Films from Mumbai stopped production of their adaptation of *French Lover*, despite having acquired the rights. Renowned film director Mahesh Bhatt announced with a lot of fanfare that he would be writing my biopic, but he too fell silent subsequently. Even a company like UTV had to stop production on a film about me for unknown reasons. In Kolkata, the telecast of the Bengali TV serial based on my story was stopped despite having finished shooting nearly 100 episodes. Similarly, three directors from Kolkata had to shelve their upcoming productions based on my life and my novels, in spite of having signed the contract. It was clear that there was a shadow that had been cast over me. A sinister darkness was slowly creeping towards me and it sent a chill down my spine; I began to fear that after it was done devouring everything else, it would come for me.

Most of my friends too cut off their ties with me, leaving me completely alone in this vast country. I could not help but wonder if any author had ever been so summarily excommunicated by their own people. Perhaps Galileo had been, 400 years ago. It was difficult to come to terms with the fact that this was happening to me in twenty-first-century India.

Besides, I was not entirely happy about settling down in Delhi either. I was sure that unless I managed to return to my language and my cultural roots, I would not find peace. It was no longer a question of being able to live there, since I was not sure if I would live in Bengal again. It was a matter of principle. It was a matter of being entitled to certain rights, to my right to speak and express my opinions. If I could not win back the right to go back to the places the fundamentalists had succeeded in driving me out of, then it was as if we had conceded victory to the forces of intolerance. This was far bigger than me, for the greater good, even though I was the only one to have waged war. There was but one goal—no

other person in the world should have to face prohibition
and exile for having exercised their freedom of expression.

Delhi was desolate. I had only Minu for company, the
one creature that had always been dependent on me her
entire life. I often had to leave her in Delhi for my trips
abroad. Though the only ones I attended were the ones
I could not refuse—honorary doctorates from Belgium
and the University of Paris, honorary citizenships from a
number of cities in the West, a seminar on human rights
at the European Parliament, or the Humanist Congress in
Norway. Even with these, I tried spending as little time as
possible, always eager to fly back to my cat. I hated leaving
her alone; we had become so fond of each other. People who
say cats are selfish creatures that cannot love haven't met
Minu. Minu has always loved me, quite ardently, in her own
way. We used to spend days with each other, talking about
our love. Rich people in India always have dogs in their
homes, never cats. Cats they fear; cats are inauspicious. So,
there was no one in Delhi to take care of Minu, just as there
had not been anyone in Kolkata either. I used to train people
before leaving Minu with them, but in Delhi I did not even
have that luxury. Jaiprakash Agarwal from Burdwan used to
take care of Minu in my absence, but his relationship with
her had become progressively hostile. One reason for that
could have been the fact that he used to believe nearly all
the extant superstitions in India regarding cats. There was
no way I could have asked anyone else, though it is not as
if I did not know anyone. It is just that the acquaintances
had never really deepened into friendship; perhaps we
had both been lazy, though that laziness had never been
an impediment in Kolkata. Whether I wished to or not, I
had been surreptitiously excommunicated; or perhaps I

was simply being a loner, preferring my own tiny world far removed from everyone else.

I may have been born in the Indian subcontinent, but I was not allowed any freedom here. It was only in Europe or the West that I could speak freely, where I could talk about my convictions, and engage in debates and conversations. Not that one could discuss religion freely everywhere in Europe either. There would always be a lot of security, either on the stage itself or within the auditorium for sure. The world was increasingly becoming an unsafe place, with the intolerant ascendant almost everywhere. The only time I attended an event that was seemingly outside mainstream western society, I had to walk off the stage midway. This happened at Banga Sammelan, an annual cultural conference of Bengalis, organized by the NRI Bengali communities of America. I had not been too keen on attending the conference, but had been forced to accede to the repeated requests of the organizers. A section of the audience, a crowd of devoted war-loving patriots, took offence to some of the poems which were about America's intrusive foreign policy and warmongering. I was booed off the stage.

Such incidents happen whenever people expect only that part of my story which is about Islam; they always expect the anti-Islamic Taslima Nasrin. Whenever I wish to speak about the other half, about my concerns for the Muslims who are dying like cattle in this false war, they wish to hush me up. I have always faced such petty conflicts when I have tried to critique the myriad other wrongs being committed against humanity. Attempting to distance myself from such pettiness has gradually pushed me far away from people. There are people who are different, but I hardly ever bump into any of them.

A series of messages about me, interchanged between the US consulate and Washington DC, were made public by Wikileaks. Here are two pieces from one such conversation, titled 'Author Taslima Nasreen: Pawn in Political Web'[55] from 28 November 2007:

11. (SBU) After Nandigram, Nasreen represented a convenient foil for both the CPM and fundamentalist Muslim leaders in Kolkata. From their actions (or lack thereof), it is clear
    NEW DELHI 00005119 003 OF 003
India's main political parties could not care less about Nasreen or her writing beyond how their parties' reactions to events play to voters. Not wanting to offend the Muslim vote bank, neither Congress nor CPM has officially supported an extension of Nasreen's visa. Both parties want the situation to go away. The BJP will ensure that will not happen by raising the issue in Parliament to batter both the CPM and Congress and to burnish their own tarnished secular credentials. The BJP has seized the high ground and will milk the controversy for all its worth. For Taslima, the last week has been chaotic, but will no doubt provide ample material for her next book. As for the CPM, the public are increasingly aware that their lofty rhetoric about looking out for the little guy rings hollow, since they have stooped recently not only to kill peasants at Nandigram but to abandon a female author in order to pander to vote banks. Surely they could have found space for one woman in a teeming city of 16 million? MULFORD

12. (SBU) Comment: Even though few in the Indian Muslim community are familiar with Nasreen's work,

there is a general sense among the Indian Muslims community that her writings have somehow insulted or disparaged Islam. The Muslim groups' public opposition is a reflection of this unhappiness with Nasreen. There are also politics at play. The Communist Party of India Marxist (CPM) had originally driven Nasreen out of Kolkata to divert attention from the CPM's central role in the Nandigram violence, as well as to win favor from Muslims who were main victims of the Nandigram brutality (ref E). The Muslim groups have put pressure once again on the UPA government to act more decisively on Nasreen. Vote bank politics has been an important factor in the Nasreen controversy. India's political parties are ready to use any target of opportunity available to pander to voting groups in preparation for the next national election, due before May 2009. The UPA's hot-cold response in the Nasreen affair illustrates that the Congress Party, the original and still most prolific practitioner of vote bank pandering, is attempting to juggle its national image and the Muslim vote. End comment. MULFORD

Around the same time, Joy Goswami, one of Bengal's leading poets, was in the midst of dedicating his book of poetry, *Amar Shyamshri Ichhe, Swagata Ichheguli (To All My Desires, Welcome and Unwelcome)* to me. In fact, one of the poems, dedicated to 'Taslima Nasrin, Beacon of Our Times', had been about me:

> What if we had to fight your battles?
> We stood apart, in our safe corners
> To try and find all the faults we could,
> Never taking another step forward,

Never touching the flames.
The rope was hanging from the window,
But you chose to remain in the burning house,
Because your fight had more life than my life did.
Now I am spent.
I sit and wait for them,
To grab me by the scruff of my neck,
Drag me to the field and leave me there to rot.
I won't fight back,
Nor will I stand my ground.
If you have been a friend, o brave one,
Simply wish me this,
That I may die peacefully,
With my head still in the sand.

Many poets wrote poems for me in 2007–2008. Many books and journals were published, compiling essays, short stories and poems, written by people demanding my return to Kolkata. People marched on the streets with posters and banners, and protested with hunger strikes. 22 November was commemorated for some time as a mark of protest against the injustices committed by the State. Gradually, everything began to fade from public memory. The elections came around again, and Mamata Banerjee's historic victory effectively ended thirty-four years of Left rule in West Bengal. Except for a couple of very close people, everyone forgot about me. It was almost as if I had died, and it was no longer important to talk about my return. A Bengali writer's enforced exile from Bengal could very simply be wiped away from the pages of history.

The earth is but a fragment, the birth and demise of its people insignificant, in the face of the sheer vastness of our ancient universe. The entire expanse of human history is a fleeting instant, a footnote in the history of time. Not a soul in the universe will ever flip through its pages. Is it not enough that even amidst this infinite insignificance, I am still swimming against the surge?

Notes

1. The phonetic sound 'K' is also the sound of the first Bengali consonant.
2. Syed Shamsul Haque is a celebrated Bangladeshi poet, dramatist and novelist.
3. Sunil Gangopadhyay (1967–2012) was one of the most versatile Bengali writers of his generation. Twice winner of the Ananda Puraskar, one of the most coveted literary prizes for any writer of Bengali, he moved from writing poetry to novels, short stories and plays, even dabbling in journalism, with amazing agility.
4. Humayun Azad (1947–2004) was one of the most influential Bangladeshi writers of his generation. On 12 August 2004, he was found dead in his apartment in Munich, Germany, where he had arrived a week earlier for some research work.
5. Nima Haque is a theatre actress from Bangladesh.
6. Asad Chowdhury (born 11 February 1943) is a poet, writer, translator, radio and TV personality, and cultural activist in Bangladesh. He is a former director of the Bangla Academy, Dhaka.

7. Quoted by Mirza Ahmed Afzal Farooq in 'Pornography in Literature: The Taslima Nasrin Context', in the *Literary Herald*, vol. 1, no. 2 (September 2015), p. 4.

8. Samaresh Majumdar (born 10 March 1942) is a renowned writer from West Bengal who has consistently written for both children and mature readers. He created the character of Arjun for a series of young-adult thrillers featuring the eponymous sleuth, while his novel *Kalbela* is considered a modern classic.

9. Sonagachi, located near north Kolkata, is reputedly India's largest red-light area.

10. Subodh Sarkar (born 1958) is a Bengali poet, writer and editor, and a recipient of the prestigious Sahitya Akademi Award. His wife, Mallika Sengupta, was also a poet.

11. Shirshendu Mukhopadhyay (born 2 November 1935) is a celebrated Bengali author who has dabbled in a wide variety of genres. He is especially regarded for his contributions to children's literature.

12. Nabanita Dev Sen (born 13 January 1938) is an award-winning Indian poet, novelist and academic. Both her parents, Narendranath Dev and Radharani Devi, were renowned poets.

13. Bani Basu (born 11 March 1939) is a Bengali author, essayist, critic and poet. She received the prestigious Ananda Puraskar for her famed novel, *Maitreya Jataka*.

14. Mallika Sengupta (1960–2011) was a Bengali poet and feminist activist, and wife of poet Subodh Sarkar. She passed away due to breast cancer-related complications on 28 May 2011.

15. Gautam Ghosh Dastidar is a Bengali poet.

16. Azizul Haque is a former Naxal leader and a contemporary of Kanu Sanyal, one of the founders of the Naxalite uprising in India. Haque was detained and tortured for a long time during the height of the Naxalbari Movement.

17. Shankha Ghosh (born 6 February 1932) is a Bengali littérateur and critic, and one of the foremost poets in Bengal today.

18. Shibnarayan Ray (1921–2008) was a Bengali thinker, educationist, essayist and literary critic. A radical humanist, Ray is widely known for his writings on the Marxist revolutionary and political theorist Manabendra Nath Roy.

19. Siddhartha Shankar Ray was a prominent barrister and a leading politician of the Indian National Congress. He served as chief minister of West Bengal during the tumultuous Naxal uprising from 1972 to 1977.

20. Begum Rokeya (1880–1932) was a Bengali writer, essayist, philosopher, educationist and social activist. A renowned social activist of her time and an advocate for women's rights, she is considered a pioneer of the feminist movement in Bengal.

21. Sujato Bhadra is an eminent human rights activist who has also played the role of an interlocutor with the Maoists in West Bengal.

22. Nikhil Sarkar (1932–2004) was a Bengali author, social historian and journalist who was an associate editor with *Anandabazar Patrika* for which he ran a column called *Kalkatar Karcha* (The Kolkata Notebook). Under the pseudonym 'Sripantha', he wrote numerous books and was awarded the Ananda Puraskar in 1978.

23. Rudraprasad Sengupta (born 31 January 1935) is a Bengali actor, director and cultural critic who has been the driving force behind the celebrated theatre group Nandikar, and one of the leading personalities in Indian theatre.

24. Amlan Dutta (1924–2010) was a Bengali author, radical humanist, economist and educationist. During his long career as a teacher, he served as the pro-vice chancellor of the University of Calcutta, and vice chancellor of the University of North Bengal and Visva-Bharati University, Santiniketan.

25. Prasanta Roy has been a long-time associate of Nasrin and the publisher behind People's Book Society which has thus far published Nasrin's work in Bangla and was at the forefront of the *Dwikhandito* controversy.

26. Manas Ghosh was then a senior journalist with the *Statesman*.

27. Buddhadeb Basu (1908–74) was one of the most significant literary figures in Bengal of the twentieth century and a major figure in the post-Tagore literary landscape. Also an eminent critic and editor of his time, he is considered a major modernist in Bengali poetry. He won numerous awards, including the Sahitya Akademi Award, the Rabindra Puraskar and the Padma Bhushan.

28. Annada Shankar Roy (1904–2002) was an eminent Bengali essayist and a poet.

29. Sitabhog and mihidana are iconic Bengali sweets famously originating from Burdwan, West Bengal, originally made by Bhairav Chandra Nag, a local sweet-maker, to mark the occasion when Viceroy Lord Curzon

visited Burdwan to confer the title of maharaja on then
king of Burdwan, Vijaychanda.

30. 'Don't let them silence Taslima Nasrin—Stand up for
the Sake of Freedom of Expression in India: An SACW
compilation of statements and opinions (27 November–6
December 2007)', www.sacw.net>defendtaslimaDec07

31. http://www.sify.com/youth/fullstory.php?id=14568036

32. 'Competitive Intolerance', *The Hindu*, 5 December 2007.

33. Srotoshini Bhalobasa is Nasrin's niece, her sister Yasmin's
daughter. Bhalobasa was born on 6 December 1992. In
Bangla, *bhalobasa* is the common noun for love.

34. Tapan Raychaudhuri (1926–2014) was an eminent
historian who taught at Oxford University from 1973
to 1992. He was also deputy director of the National
Archives of India, a former director of the Delhi School
of Economics, and a Padma Bhushan winner.

35. Joy Goswami (born 10 November 1954) is a Sahitya
Akademi Award–winning Bengali poet and columnist,
widely considered one of the most important poets of his
generation.

36. 'Politics and Play', Ramachandra Guha, the *Telegraph*,
8 December 2007.

37. http://www.mainstreamweekly.net/article505.html

38. Aparna Sen (born 25 October 1945) is a renowned
Bengali actress and film-maker. A leading lady in the
1960s to the 1980s, she has acted in many iconic films
such as *Aranyer Din Ratri*, *Jana Aranya* and *Basanta
Bilap*. She later moved on to making several critically
acclaimed and awarded films like *36 Chowringhee Lane*,
Parama and *Mr & Mrs Iyer*, among others.

39. Hameeda Hossain (born 1936) is a prominent academic
and human rights activist in Bangladesh, a founding

member of the Ain o Salish Kendra and the wife of jurist, statesman and freedom fighter Kamal Hossain.

40. The Ain o Salish Kendra, or Centre for Law and Mediation, is a non-governmental, civil rights and legal aid organization in Bangladesh which regularly consults with Amnesty International.

41. A cleric, usually the imam, who delivers the sermon and leads the prayer.

42. Baitul Mukarram, located in Dhaka, is the national mosque of Bangladesh.

43. 'Let Her Be', 22 December 2007, timesofindia.com/edit-page/TODAYS-EDITORIAL-Let-Her-Be/articleshow/2641964.cms

44. 'Counterpoint' by Vir Sanghvi in *Hindustan Times*, 2 December 2007, blogs.hindustantimes.com/counterpoint/2007/12/

45. Abdul Gaffar Choudhury (born 12 December 1934) is a British writer, journalist, columnist, political analyst and poet of Bangladeshi origin. He is the celebrated writer of '*Amar Bhai'er Rokte Rangano*', the anthem for the Bhasha Andolon.

46. Mahasweta Devi (14 January 1926–28 July 2016) was a social activist and a leading writer. She won numerous awards, including the Sahitya Akademi Award, Padma Vibhushan, Padma Shri and the Ramon Magsaysay Award.

47. Manasij Majumder is a well-known writer and teacher, renowned for a number of books on artists like Sakti Burman, Sunil Das and Bikash Bhattacharjee.

48. Sarat Kumar Mukhopadhyay is a Sahitya Akademi Award–winning Bengali poet who was closely associated, along with his wife Bijoya Mukhopadhyay, with the influential Bengali poetry magazine *Krittibas*.

49. Dibyendu Palit (born 5 March 1939) is a Sahitya Akademi Award–winning Bengali poet and novelist.

50. Shaoli Mitra is a renowned Bengali theatre personality, and daughter of iconic actors Sombhu Mitra and Tripti Mitra. Bhabaniprasad Chattopadhyay is a Bengali writer and columnist.

51. Shibani Mukhopadhyay is Prasanta Roy's partner at People's Book Society.

52. Fakhruddin Ahmed (born 1 May 1940) is a Bangladeshi economist and civil servant who served as the chief adviser to the non-party caretaker government of Bangladesh amidst the political crisis in 2006.

53. Ritu Menon is an Indian feminist activist, writer and publisher. She was co-founder of Kali for Women in 1984 and founder of Women Unlimited thereafter.

54. Steve Lacy (1934–2004) was an American jazz saxophonist recognized as one of the foremost players of the soprano saxophone. In 1999, Steve Lacy composed 'The Cry' based on Taslima Nasrin's poetry. Irene Aebi, a Swiss singer, was Lacy's wife.

55. 'Author Taslima Nasreen: Pawn In Political Web', 28 November 2007, http://wikileaks.org/plusd/cables/07NEWDELHI5119_a.html

Scan QR code to access the
Penguin Random House India website